*A Peasant's Guide to*

# CANADA

## LYN MARSH

ISBN 10: 099274170X
ISBN 13: 9780992741709

*For amos christ*

*Best of the yard*

*Much Love*

For Claire and Caitlin

# Let Us Repair to the Annealing Wild

It is expected that people feel attached to their homes; but often, in dramatic landscape our characters seem to spring from the very geography that we inhabit. In spite of coming from a long line of Scandinavian fishers I fell deeply in love with a ramshackle Ontario farm and was profoundly changed by that experience. My genes probably adapted to being land-locked, but I suppose hunter-gatherers can be as content on the land as on the water.

I have floating memories that promised where and how survival, and some measure of happiness, were possible and I pasted them together at that farm. My not-too-stable mother told me, an isolated child, that a flying saucer might come and take my brother and me away to a better place. I think she was quite used to unexpected travel arrangements. My immigrant father, dragged from a civil war zone in Finland as a child, was certain we would all soon be blown to Kingdom Come by a nuclear bomb (how he loved the grainy footage mushrooming over and over again on television in 1953, promising an end to all his problems). And some fundamentalist preacher in a warehouse on Vancouver's waterfront described The Kingdom as the greatest piece of real estate imaginable. I had no idea who I was, where I had come from or where I was going. I wasn't even sure if the world would last. I was surprisingly hopeful, malleable and open to suggestion. Sweetfield Farm provided some of the answers to my questions.

Encouraged by my grandmother to spend lunch time in the warm Charles Dickens Elementary School library when it was cold and raining, I found a *National Geographic* magazine, with pictures of astrophysicists gazing at stars and planets and I thought they might find my family a good place to live if things got out of hand down here on Earth. I squirreled the magazine away in my room in our bookless house, and in the evenings I gazed skyward from my window in utter confusion. When I learned that wonderful word "astrophysicist" my mother told me "there must be some very high falutin' people at that magazine if they know how to make up words like that." No one in my family had ever made it past grade eight and higher education was for those who were without real skills or were too lazy to look for a job. Fragmented memories forged in family, shaped by a mapless and shifting geography, driven by ideas from an incomprehensible world, conspired to set me dreaming about a safe and simple happiness.

We were a family of hard-working women and rough-hewn men. I have an image of my paternal grandmother sitting stoutly on the grass in our East End back yard nattering in Finnish, March tulips bursting bright red around her. She is braiding my hair like bread dough, as I sit twisting and rolling torn rags into skeins for her methodical rug weaving. She and grandpa lived downstairs in what was a constantly shifting, crowded household of immigrant boarders and distant relatives. My older brother, Martin, seemed to be always off at school or cross-country skiing or just out. My mother, Laura, and her elder sisters Elizabeth and Mary—arthritic, diseased women speaking quickly in two languages—lived on a mountain of despair built on endless chores, children and hard marriages. Forged by their deracination, they had to be willful, stern and highly skilled. I seemed to be the family tag-along as these women tried to teach me sewing, cooking, cleaning, and food preserving, but my feeble mind was constantly distracted by the world they had no time to worry about.

I remember gazing, for what seemed like hours, at the enticing vortices of the surging Fraser River as my mother picked berries on the banks of the Delta one morning. "Great berries! And only six cents a pound!" my mother said. "Hurry up, eat lots, fill up the buckets and pick harder before we have to go home and get them into jars. Keep your mind on your job or we'll all starve to death next winter!"

I remember my father, Lenni, and his brothers, Levi and Leo, loud and brutish men, fishing for salmon off the west coast of Vancouver Island. I was hopelessly slow at washing gutted fish; instead, I watched for albatross buffeted on wind, the turbulent Pacific fierce in my head. For some reason I was all emotion, without consciousness and unable to reflect or talk or plan or follow orders. I felt like an annoyance, along for the ride, an expensive burden. "We earn our bread by the sweat of our brow," my parents used to say. "Now work!"

At seventeen, right after high school, I left the frantic atmosphere of our newly-built suburban home in Coquitlam, unable to concentrate under the critical gaze of my demanding mother and unable to speak against the arrogance of my father who shouted at me, "Get busy! Girls are to be seen and not heard! Peel potatoes, little Fatso!"

I started to emerge from my shell about a year later as a student at the University of British Columbia (my incredibly kind high school English teacher helped me fill the application form) and went searching for friends and ideas in the greasy bars near Stanley Park, the Cecil Hotel pub downtown, and the head shops run by hippy entrepreneurs springing up along Fourth Avenue near Kitsilano Beach. One day, as a student, listening to faintly misogynist poetry in the U.B.C. music building where women (and especially mothers) came off rather poorly, I realized I reacted differently to the world from my family, differently from the string of roommates and differently from the melancholy gay poet I had chosen to live with. I was not in step with the rants in the *Georgia Straight* gobbled up by the hoards of young people streaming into Vancouver. I didn't believe most of what people said to me. There was a voice in my head that questioned everything.

I took to odd silences, to singing Leonard Cohen songs, to loving the scent of rainy Japanese gardens that offered calm, sentimental satisfactions. I rejected my family culture, or my perceived lack of it, indulged my defiance, felt myself naïvely free and unencumbered in true 1967 narcissistic fashion. I don't regret a moment of it. Vancouver was in the thrall of peace and love and hippy nonsense but I managed to keep reading, stay in school and even graduate, much to the shock of my entire family.

"Lyn reads lots of books," my mother would brag to the relatives who would ask where I was working. Privately, in moments when she was really distraught, she would sneer at me. "You're a real free thinker, you are," which was the best attempt she could make to disguise her true feeling—a distrust of time and money wasted reading dead people. My mother hated being criticized by outsiders and when she tired of justifying my lack of money and career accomplishments to others she could make a regular BA in English sound like the Nobel Prize for Literature. She was constantly conflicted and anxious during my four undergraduate years and so my visits home became rarer and rarer. She wanted me to become a real estate agent or to study law. My father, a peasant with no such pretensions, was always warning me "Boys don't make passes at girls who wear glasses." He was always threatening me, by raising his fist above my head, ordering me not to get too "women's libby" and would pointedly ask, "What will you do for a living? What will you do for real money? What if no one marries you?" Canada provided great social mobility and my father qualified to become a garage mechanic and then a real easte agent but worried that I would never get a real job. The criticisms ended when we stopped speaking entirely after he left my mother for his secretary and found himself no longer interested in talking to his daughter.

At a graduate English department lunch, a milieu I loved as people chatted endlessly about E.E. Cummings or Emily Brontë or other such "meaningless and financially unrewarding" things, I met TH, blond and handsome and oddly foreign. After ten tumultuously passionate days we decided we wanted to live together. He was teaching sessional courses in Canadian Literature at UBC while completing a degree from McMaster in Hamilton, Ontario, and trying to pay off his student loans. Enamoured with walks in Stanley Park, books, ideas, and sex, we fell in love with each other. He was born in England but lived in Toronto, a city all westerners love to hate, and we argued constantly over Vancouver—a sunny LaLaLand—versus cold big business Toronto. After graduating, thanks to having wasted months of time in art galleries, I won a summer internship at the press office of the National Gallery in Ottawa. TH stayed in Vancouver winding up his contract there and we decided, over the phone, to quit both our jobs and move to England so that we could be together and see and do everything we wanted. Nothing else mattered and being separated was not that much fun. A good partner can save one from all sorts of ills. Or so I wanted to believe.

London in 1972 was a sweet place to live for the rebellious and irresponsible. We wanted to escape what we then perceived as the nice, utilitarian, intellectual blandness of all of Canada, our complicated families, and the wet or cold winters, to experience something that would shake us out of our received histories, out of our youth and into adulthood. Our bohemian natures had the best of us and the time was rich with delights. For ninety pence we could sit in the back row of the Old Vic and watch Diana Rigg as Lady Macbeth. For three pounds we could get out to Kew Gardens, spend the day prowling through greenhouses smelling exotic plants, have lunch in the pub and be back in time for Tina Turner and Mick Jagger at Wembley Stadium. On Fridays we would leave our dingy sublet in Battersea, take the train to Dover, the hovercraft to Calais and another train to Paris. In England we escaped the nagging bank reminders of our student debts and the horrors of family gatherings neither of us wanted to attend. Instead, we could swap digs with a like-minded academic couple from Quebec for their cold-water walk-up in Les Halles and spend the weekends in the Louvre or wander aimlessly from one major cultural oasis to another.

The thirty pounds a week the London Council was paying sessional lecturers at the time didn't go very far for us. I held down two teaching jobs: days in an English department teaching journalism students literature and odd nights at Hackney Technical College teaching plumbers O levels. TH took a day shift teaching at the Southbank and night shift with a dodgy estate security firm. It gave us over a hundred pounds a week, which at that time was enough to feed our *wanderlust* and culture habit. We did this for several years, getting away every weekend to France, Wales or Cornwall, Brighton, Oxford or Exeter—renting cars, eating in restaurants and buying books. There were three-movie Sundays and cases of cheap wine from the off-license. Every show we wanted to see, from the Neoclassical to the Impressionists at the Royal Academy or the Wallace Collection or Munch at the Tate, we saw. We had weekly walks on Hampstead Heath and boozy lunches in Soho. It was a time of boundless energy and we didn't worry a whit about leaving jobs and moving around as long as we had a few bob in our pockets. In three years we tried five different boroughs in London. Nothing seemed difficult nor was anything written in stone.

Then, one day, we discussed the possibility of having children. The next week we sent our résumés to every tenure-track job posting we could find, and at the end of August—crossing off the list job offers in Hue, Vietnam, and Jeddah, where I would have to observe *purdah*—we were on a plane back to Canada with full-time positions in Toronto colleges, the only big-enough city where we could land two academic paychecks with pensions and medical plans. What a tyranny human chemistry is and how quickly we compromise our desires when reproduction takes over the number one slot.

*1974.*

*The fishing boats.*

# The Backwoods of Canada

We bought a run-down row house in Riverdale on a borrowed deposit and began tearing down walls, ripping out plumbing and painting drywall. After marking freshman papers we would prowl hardware stores, lumber yards and junk shops. TH, rather like his father, hated the idea of doing anything that involved tools and would quizzically look at which end of one plug fitted another. However, we mastered the trial and error method and grew accustomed to the late night smell of plaster and paint stripper. With no cash to call in professionals I skimmed the municipal building code and developed passable building skills by watching videos in hardware depots and trying to remember what my manually skilled family had taught me. Borrowing from the bank and running credit cards to keep eating, we were rarely able to find much relaxation time or sift common sense through our desire to get the house finished.

The house, like most in that Toronto district, had been lived in by a Greek immigrant family who tended a vegetable patch and kept chickens in the backyard. They slaughtered the birds in the basement and I ended up cleaning feathers and feet from between bloodied floorboards and under steps. This had moments of quasi-Lutheran satisfaction but in 1978, as the project was nearing completion—the William Morris wallpaper hung and hardwood floors gleaming—other ideas began to push aside the carpentry gene and I waffled about finishing my graduate degree before having children.

I registered at university to do an M.A. in English and recipe cards with bibliographical entries started replacing the pots of paint. Books tumbled down from the top of the fridge and late nights in libraries left me thinking about how life should be lived. Doing research into the lives of 19th century women writers who struggled with an environment more hostile than my own, made anything seem possible. It could not be harder for me, could it? Juggling renovations, teaching, evening lectures and a relationship had its challenges but, like a dumb moth to a flame, I kept going.

The idea of a having a child had moved from our heads to between the sheets and, thinking it would take a long time to get pregnant, I stopped taking birth control pills.

We bought a grand standard poodle, a hunting dog we named Max, (practice for parenthood, we foolishly thought) and dutifully walked him every day around Riverdale, which was full of young families with dogs, and wondered what our lives would be like in ten years.

Toronto was clean, orderly, workable for families in all senses: there were exotic restaurants, first-run movies, inviting parks, small bookstores, lots of theatre, jazz and the St Lawrence market but our European experience, especially the memory of long country weekends when we were not time's prisoners, had ruined us for city life. We oddly felt we didn't belong here. We had been contented expats in Britain but here, in our own country, we seemed to be outsiders.

We tried to fit in but we felt like actors, and not very good ones at that. Perversely, as we walked, we decided we couldn't raise children in a place so easily accommodating, so relentlessly normal. Everyone seemed so happy, collecting their dog shit in neat little bags and placing it in the receptacles the city provides. Everyone had the right baby strollers and running shoes and I was innately suspicious of the studiously picture-perfect neighbourhood with its almost theme-park Greek restaurants and the tyranny of so much responsibly manufactured civic goodness. This was a club I didn't want to belong to.

My husband missed the irony of the East End, the cruel ease of the British papers, the cosmopolitan chaos. We wanted to create our own world, live in a wilderness as I once did in northern British Columbia, have the papers mailed in—the best of North America, the best of Europe. Caution we would save for our old age; risk excited us. That night we went for dinner, drank too much wine and contemplated the possiblities. The next day my stomach began to heave and I vowed to stay away from even one glass of Greek wine but that was not the cause of my morning sickness.

I was pregnant.

After coming to terms with the shock we decided Toronto was not the place we wanted to raise children and the only thing to do was relocate by the end of the school year. We listed the house that evening. Toronto was in the midst of a housing boom and in one week the agent sold it and we ended up with a thirty-thousand-dollar profit. We bought a map and, as we began looking for the perfect piece of land (within our modest price range—or whatever the bank would lend us) the circles we drew around the city kept getting larger. A devastating winter had descended into southern Ontario but we persevered in driving further afield every weekend.

TH particularly wanted a place where we could keep horses—something we could ill-afford and really knew nothing about—but the memory of his English grandfather who had once raised and trained thoroughbreds in Newmarket kept coming back. I feared, because we could not restrain ourselves from following our impulses, we were destined to buy at least one old nag. One of TH's uncles had run a pub on Old Compton Street in Soho where he trained boxers in the back room and his father, a salesman of sorts, had managed to make his first bit of money reselling goods that tipped from lorries during the war. Another uncle was a developer in South Africa and a bit of a thug. With such progenitors what could go wrong? After travelling in Africa, a childhood in Cape Town and finally emigrating to Canada TH had enough survival skills to take a chance anywhere. His history prepared him, he claimed, for a life in the country. Anyway, it was a bizarre tenacity that kept him driving through blizzard after blizzard that winter, and a hungry desperation for something I couldn't name that kept me navigating.

In spite of our eagerness, what we were looking for didn't seem to exist. The suburbs were expanding forever, covering the once bucolic hillsides, and we felt trapped by some image of meandering fence lines, barns and galloping horses we had imported from some indolent visit to the Cotswolds; but, in Canada, such tutored hills seemed not to be found close to the city. We had combed through Peterborough, Uxbridge and Halton; chocolate box Caledon horse farms were priced out of our reach. Day after day we zigged and zagged across sideroads and up concessions. Finally, one freezing late January day, a terrifying hour and a half from my college office, high in the Niagara Escarpment, we found the rolling hills of Mono Township, close to the small town of Shelburne, the old Home District of Scots and Irish immigrants, a cattle and pig farming area.

We were mesmerized driving through silent waves of land, intermittent snowdrifts plowed high on the shoulders of the roads. Crystal oceanic moraines and jagged cliffs lay stilled under a burnished sky. Slowly, following the agent's cryptic directions, we came upon a farm: ragged fencing, cattle manure staining the snow, a barn barely holding on to its eaves, a lopsided Victorian house.

My heart sank. A heavy blizzard was developing but we had our eyes on the farm. TH plowed into the ditch, precariously dropping the car's front end into we didn't know what. A good omen, we hoped.

A farmer, on his way to drop hay for his cattle, started hovering like the evil guy in *Deliverance*; he surmised we were city folk and for a quick thirty bucks pulled us out with his tractor. "Keep in the ruts," he toothlessly hissed between the yellow icicles on his beard. He didn't mind helping but he couldn't resist giving advice: "Drive straighter. It's a wee bit icy. If this was summer you'd have rolled and destroyed your perfectly good car." He was shaking his head in contempt as we pulled up the driveway.

"Shall we take him home in the back seat?" asked TH. "Maybe he has some insights we can share." Advice, like route direction, was not embraced by my husband who believed that following his nose was the best compass a man could find. My *Darling Buds of May* vision of my future country neighbours was shattered.

We waited for our agent, freezing in our city coats and silly London boots. What folly! Six feet of snow! We couldn't see anything of the land, only the rolling horizon, some hearty pines and naked maples pointing their foreboding fingers. Susanna Moodie and Catherine Parr Traill had been better prepared a hundred and fifty years earlier. One side of the house was invisible behind a nine-foot ice wall thrown up by the snow blower; a trickle of smoke snaked out of a collapsing chimney. We were dumbstruck as we waited, wondering if any realtor would show up for such an improbable sale.

When she did and we got into the house it was even worse than we'd imagined: wallpaper torn from wallboard, old greasy linoleum floors, six small rooms, cracked windows, a ceiling just above eye level (the house had been modernized in the 50s). Down a rickety flight of stairs we found old maple beams in the basement, fallen in. Ten feet from the house the plumbing pipe ended in the window of a rusty old truck half dug into the ground, serving as a septic tank. The smell of warm raw sewage wafted through the frozen air.

"I'm afraid it's a bulldozer special," the chirpy agent said. "There's nothing here to recommend other than the land and you can't see that under the snow. The owner moved to Florida when his parents died and the renters haven't made a payment in months." The price was lower than the current 1979 value as it was a desperate year for country real estate. "No one will buy it in winter. The house is absolutely worthless."

Now I was feeling more than just morning sick but TH insisted on looking at the barn. We trudged through waist deep snow to where a few skinny heifers were mulling over a pathetic bale of hay. The manure was three feet over the foundation and.e as the agent spun her flashlight from hand-hewn beam to hand-hewn beam she noted the only positive thing she could find. "Good solid beams here."

I felt like weeping. No one had cared for this place in generations. No doors, straw bales stuffed into the broken windows, no electricity, no water, leaky roof. But it was large, probably built before the house, 40 by 70 feet. I watched in silence as TH mentally counted out six brood mare stalls as he paced through the frozen manure.

"It's an easy convert into horse stalls," he smiled.

"Hah! Convert what? There's nothing here!" I was astonished.

"Build them, I mean. Don't you think we could build them? I'm sure we could build them. You know about carpentry. Remember your father. Just look."

Silently, and mysteriously, breathing that mythic air, I began to relent. Maybe it was the hormones, maybe my mind was numb with cold. Maybe the fact that I didn't know what I was looking for kept me from seeing what I didn't want to see. The fieldstone foundation was beautiful and, as the afternoon light began fading, a glassy blueness hung over the drifts. The cows seemed contented.

That night, in sheer madness, we made the ridiculously low offer of a thousand dollars an acre and told the agent to see what would happen. As we drove back to Toronto, the black sky was shimmering with northern lights and a million distant stars, flickering a grammar all their own. Maybe it was the thought of children, maybe my husband's oft repeated horse fantasy, maybe my peasant grandmother's peasant soul wafting through the air, reminding me so much of Sibelius and the glacial buzz of Finland in winter. Maybe it was the plunge into the ditch, but whatever it was, we wanted that farm, a dream within our grasp.

13

The roll of the hills played over and over again in my mind like a musical refrain and there was an intriguingly elegant line to the Victorian Gothic cottage roof, the little dormer (a perfect child's room), and the certain maples. There was a tantalizing hint of what might be.

The joke, as we waited the next day for the agent to call, was that perhaps under all that snow the land had been paved over for parking. When the call came we knew nothing of the ponds, the nesting Canada geese, the wolves, foxes, rabbits and weather. Nothing about the community, or about horse farming for that matter. I couldn't even find the road again on my map. A few hand-hewn beams and turbulent snow was all I could recall for our banker as we signed the mortgage papers. Not a lot to go on but there we were. Like thousands of people before us, we had come upon a farm that promised sustenance and seclusion, love and labour, family and friends. Next to mating and motherhood, land is the most powerful bond I know. In a burst of romantic faith we named our seventy-five acres Sweetfield Farm.

*Sweetfield in the summer.*

## Running in the Family

Like most Canadians my family had a very recent historical relationship with this land. Italian friends, who trace their lineage back to some general in Caesar's legions, mock my second generation Scandinavian heritage. However, on the level of courage and bizarre idiosyncrasies I think I could match them relative for relative.

My paternal grandparents were skilled, hard-working Finns who emigrated to Canada with four children in tow in 1922 when the Civil War and postwar revenge killings got dangerously close to their villages. Both had lost siblings in the 1918 conflict. The northern Finnish Reds were regularly persecuted and they were used to moving on when things got tough. When fish were few, the reindeer waning, the hunting sparse or the harvests failed they just moved to where they thought they could survive. All Finns, by virtue of the geography, were suspicious of their neighbours with good reason. The history of relationships with the Russians, Swedes and the Germans was of constant conflict. They were squeezed from all sides and the Canadian government was looking for hearty peasants to open up sections of the country and work in the forests, lakes and rivers. In Ontario they were wanted, valued and safe.

The first wave of Finns, 350,000 strong, migrated mainly to the States before the Great War, and later, in the 1920s, 4,500 Finns a year came to Canada until they were barred from entry as enemy aliens during World War Two. My grandfather began fishing on Lake Superior and my grandmother started salting fish, mending nets and digging potatoes for sale. She was constantly carding wool, spinning and knitting, as well as making rugs, and they made a home in a geography and climate very similar to the one they had left. When the Depression hit and the economy collapsed and the waters did not provide enough to keep body and soul together they moved further north.

From the age of sixteen my father worked in the bush as a lumberjack, felling trees and clearing log jams on the rivers, one of the most dangerous jobs in logging. In his twenties he learned machine and vehicle repair and joined the union of the Employees of the Marathon Paper Mills of Canada. My mother cooked the food in the men's bunkhouse. They met, at some Finnish Community Hall social, and were quickly married. My brother was born in that logging town in 1947 and a couple of years later I was born. We lived in a two-room shack at the mouth of the Pic River. My grandparents and Uncle Leo went to Vancouver which offered a milder climate, another Finnish community and more income from salmon than from whitefish. Hoping for a less brutal life my parents followed.

Emil Isa (meaning father), my grandfather, worked on a salmon boat; Hilma Aiti (mother) mended nets and made more rugs. Their children had children and, as the number of mouths increased, they just produced more food. They planted their own onions and picked their own fruit and made their own bread. Aiti knitted socks and dresses for us and sewed shirts for grandpa. Carding wool and counting balls of twine became my favourite childhood game. The Finnish word *sisu* translates as strength or guts or fortitude, and my family had more than the usual serving of courage.

In fifty years of living on the west coast, neither Aiti nor Isa learned to speak more than a few words of English; their entire lives were lived as Finns—no hyphens, no accommodations, until the day they died. They learned a few words of hybrid Finliska that no English speaker could understand and they weren't interested in talking to strangers anyway. They read the Finnish papers and kept track of where all of their friends had moved via the obituaries.

Aiti was a tough bird; tenacious in the extreme, she spoke her mind bluntly, entertained no reproaches and rarely regretted even her bad decisions. I spent most of my childhood in her kitchen while my parents worked and she taught me more than how to make pancakes. What others found intolerable in her bossy personality, I found encouraging. I spent a lot of time with her and came to love the smell of her sweat, the way she placed her hand on my head when she wanted me to listen to her. She showed me nothing but concern and kindness and made up for the absence of my parents. It wasn't that they were neglectful, it was that they had to work constantly—my father at a garage fixing cars until he got his own service station; my mother as an aide at the hospital. This was the fifties and people didn't consider family conferences, talking things out and "quality" time. But as I grew up in Aiti's extended household in the East End, she taught me that doing things together was more important than anything else. Rugs got woven, potatoes got peeled, cardamon seeds got crushed, apple rings got made and eaten, and that was very satisfying.

I walked to school, trailing behind my older brother, Martin, who was not interested in my company. He and his friends seem to inhabit a more exotic domain, and his activities did not include a kid sister so I stayed home with grandma and our mongrel hound, Boy. It was also the culture of the times—girls stayed home and cooked, boys went out.

Aiti was a bickerer, constantly snapping at my mother and anyone else within range, but she never raised her voice at me. In 1953 when Elizabeth II was crowned, she unofficially changed my name to Elizabette, never popular with my mother, and they remained at odds about this and every other issue until death. She often spoke about how I should marry Prince Charles and go live in Buckingham Palace. She was prepared to yell at anyone who stood in my path to becoming the next Queen of Canada. She swore constantly in Finnish, cursing at those who got in her way to "go smell your own shit." When I was five and six we would go on the Knight Street bus to shop at Woodward's Food Hall, a trip that would take an hour each way, and return with only a few peppercorns for the fish soup or some new needles for her knitting.

My job was to ask directions, translate the cost of things and inquire about what other colours of yarn were available. If the bright reds of her tulips and the blues of the Finnish flag she coveted for stockings were not available, Aiti would tell the polite Chinese attendant to go smell her own shit and I would translate that as "OK, I'll try again later. Thank you very much." I loved the subterfuge and she was delighted that people in Canada took to her cantankerous ways so respectfully.

Aiti died in 1979, the year we bought Sweetfield and the year Claire was born. I spent the last few days in the Vancouver General Hospital, holding her hand, pressing my bulging belly to the railing, as another stroke took her away. When my father and I went back to tell Isa she had died, he simply answered, "I want to go now." And, a few lonely months later, after daily recalling passages of their lifetime together, he too was dead. I was deeply affected by their loss and thinking about her still brings tears to my eyes. My parents never spoke about her death. I hoped some of Aiti's tenacity would get transferred to my child through me.

More than anything in this difficult world we all need *sisu*. She would have approved of the farm: the pioneer labour, the circadian rhythms, the waxy potatoes in the garden. She would have treated the locals to her usual reprimand if anything went awry in her world and I would have translated it as "Have a good day." I wanted my children to have that survival instinct.

My mother, not always an easy person to get along with, could not understand my fascination with country life in eastern Canada. For her, the best place to live in the world was Stockholm, like her aunt, or Helsinki, like her other aunt. (My mother identified completely with her educated, middle-class, Swedish relatives not with the peasant side.) Third best was Vancouver. On her first visit to the farm, soon after we got the well working, she was clearly appalled.

"So far from your college! So isolated! So bleak! So bitter cold!" Laura would shake her head. "I wouldn't live here on a bet!" Her own immigrant childhood on a Depression homestead on Lake Superior had led her to hate "field work" and "stump farming" and blinded her to the delights of our present situation. "This is a god-awful place," were her parting words after her first visit. "I don't think I'll ever come back again."

Over the next few years she took perverse pleasure in repeating the stories she had heard from her mother about the wonderful middle class life available to professionals in cities and the thousands of failures that occurred on farms. When she couldn't remember a story of dejection to discourage me she made one up and such stories often featured teachers who failed to pay their bills, women who lived too far from their jobs, and women who married lazy men who loved horses. They always rode off on their horses to another town and another younger woman; betrayal was a theme my mother loved to expand upon when talking about any man. She became slightly less harsh in her judgments about our farm life ten years later as stock brokers and lawyers and bankers moved into Mono and she became more desirous of visits to her family but, in the beginning, she was nothing if not outright hostile.

It annoyed her enormously to see me living in a "desolate" place, picking wild berries, as she had done, to feed us all. She wanted more for me. More wealth. She saw nothing but a sink-hole for our paychecks and bad weather to lead us into depression and, finally, death. When it was clear there was little she could say that would change our minds, and I had developed a selective deafness to her remarks, she tried another tack. My mother didn't like losing.

As the renovations continued she tried to see it less as a squatters' homestead and more as an estate. Prestige was important to her; it reflected, she said, on a lost part of her Swedish grand-mother's heritage. "Water seeks its own level," the aspiring soci-ologist in her would note. As real estate prices rose, her heart warmed to the landscape. "Soon you'll be able to sell it at a profit, then it won't have all been an absolute waste of time and energy. If you can make money on it, I suppose that makes it worthwhile. Perhaps some Swedes will move here when the drunk Irish and all those cheap Scots leave."

The original Irish peasants had died long ago and only their very Canadian descendants still had names on mailboxes which annoyed and discouraged her as we drove along the sideroads. "Imagine living next to the Irish!" she lamented. "The Scots are such a moody people. Too much rain." It always takes someone who suffered discrimination to find a nationality they feel is lower on the totem pole. The Swedes could look down on the Finns and the Finns, she felt, could certainly look down on the Irish and, sometimes, the Scots. It was a constant source of argument as to which country consumed more alcohol per capita and whose descendants were more worthless—my father's or the Irish. She wasn't about to forget or forgive anything.

Neither was she willing to reveal too much. She believed in the great Swedish virtue of secrecy. When Gustav III ascended the Swedish throne in 1771, as an ambitious 25-year-old and an avid reader of Machiavelli, he displayed great skill in conceal-ing his real thoughts and feelings. This is a source of tremendous national pride, much respected, my mother told me, by my mater-nal grandparents (of whom I remember very little, so well did they conceal their emotions). An enlightened despotism was vaguely hidden behind the veneer of social democracy. No one dared step out of line in that household.

Always praising the homeland, some 1.2 million out of 3.5 mil-lion Swedes left anyway, emigrating at the turn of the century. They are littered across the length of the Canadian border as well as in the northern States, a community joined by labour unions, suffrage workers and pension reformers. My mother applauded

Swedish political goals and their neutrality during the war but she also approved of shipping ore to armament factories. "During the war everybody had to make money somehow," she said, when I read her the story from the paper. "Sometimes we have to compromise our principles and the less said about that, the better." Gustav set a fine example.

Late into her life she still remained uncomfortable revealing too much. When she was asked a personal question, her answer was certain to be a lie. My mother categorized family deception as white lies, necessary lies and "it's none of their damned business" lies. When pressed, my mother spoke very little about her parents, Bertha and Richard Tuomi. They were simply always right and behaved properly. Her mother was Jewish, a Winburg, with family still alive in Sweden. Her father, a Finnish Lutheran who looked like Abraham Lincoln, had changed his name to Tuomi (translated as either a type of tree or *tuomio*—a life sentence) when they were forced to leave Helsinki and then Stockholm, children in tow, for Port Arthur on Lake Superior in the 1920s. The scandal of their marriage may have been more than antisemitism but we'll never know. She may have been pregnant out of wedlock (*de rigeur* in our family), or too well bred for my grandfather's working-class prospects. Whatever the reason, Canada welcomed the unacceptable and they made their home here.

One of the surviving family albums shows Bertha and Richard, with their children Mary, Rae, Elizabeth and baby Laura, smiling in front of their wooden homestead, a stack of firewood behind them. Richard and his workhorse, Clydesdale Billy, pulled lumber on a flat sled from the rocky Canadian Shield around Suomi, Lappe, and Finmark and sold it to the mill. There were no synagogues in this new Finland and so Bertha became a Lutheran, but her photos still reveal tiny Stars of David over the heads of the deceased. She became who she had to become, like many people who emigrated here.

One winter evening when my mother was visiting us at the farm, at least fifty years after my grandmother's wounding emigration,

I suggested we watch a few Ingmar Bergman movies. "If they're Swedish they are sure to be good," she stated. But, to her utter dismay, after a controlled beginning the stories started to unravel, and she flipped from one to the other until she could watch no further. Bergman, my mother said, had the proper clothes and attitudes and settings in his films but showed great disrespect. No Swedes would let themselves go like that. It was simply unheard of. All emotions are best bottled and aged, for centuries if need be. There were standards to be maintained, codes to be followed even when things were not as they should be. "Who paid for these movies?" was her final condemnation. "It was your husband, wasn't it? What a waste of money!" This solidified her notion that men were not only rogues and philanderers but spendthrifts as well.

At the time of our farm purchase my mother was certain that teachers must be receiving pitiful salaries if they had to live in such reduced circumstances; she took to sending me care parcels whenever she found something that she thought would be useful to the rural poor of the eastern provinces. Her elder sister, Elizabeth, had recently died and, as we shared the same genes for large feet (ten and a half) my mother cleaned out the closet and sent me a dozen pairs of shoes worn out by years of deformed arthritic walking: torn cloth slippers, white fake leather sandals with broken straps, pumps with heels removed. Not one pair was suitable for Sally Anne. The next parcel contained old single sheets, torn and stained, thrown out by a nursing home in New Westminster she had some investment in, and some empty cottage cheese containers, chipped single pieces of china, an old lampshade not sold at her neighbour's garage sale. Many boxes of old clothes "Far too good to throw out!" arrived with her in taped suitcases at each visit. "No one else wants them but you can use them on the farm." She was perpetually stuck in her bleak childhood of 1936 and I had to work hard not to feel offended by the castoffs she sent my way. She never bought anything new so presents were out of the question and I later taught my children to fake gratitude when used school binders retrieved from the trash came wrapped up in newspaper for birthdays.

One dark evening she risked her life on the 401, traffic swerving all around her, to pick up a trunkload of onions that had spilled from a tipped truck that failed to negotiate the rain-slicked off ramp. "Enough onions for a lifetime!" The topper was a salmon she had picked up from a fisherman on the shores of the Fraser River, wrapped in newspaper and frozen. "Half the price, less than half the price!" When thawed it had to be buried in the compost, rotting as it was after spawning. "Waste not, want not," she would wag her finger. "To everything there is a season and then some."

Laura came to visit us on the farm every year, when she wasn't living with or visiting my brother and his family in Ottawa, and spent the last few months before she died banging her squeaking wheelchair into the "damned tiny" doorframes of our home. Her arthritis, diabetes, osteoporosis and congestive heart disease never stopped her from flinging flour over the counter tops to make coffee bread and rolls everyday. That image sticks with me, along with some residual pain and a few family pictures.

My mother often mocked my notions of "choice" in this world. There was no such thing as free will and we do not *choose* to do certain things. "Rubbish and garbage!" she would tell me. "If I had a choice I would live in Stockholm with my aunt. I wouldn't have married your father and I wouldn't have to work this hard. There's no such thing as choice in this lifetime and maybe not even after."

If modeled behaviour has the impact on us that psychologists claim, as well as being in some deep trouble I had inherited her notions of endurance. I liked to work hard on the farm even though it was physically challenging. It was a source of enormous satisfaction to tear down and rebuild with my own hands; an expanse of garden in full bloom is heaven on earth; a fresh coat of paint and a clean house still thrill me no end. In a few years we would be thinning our back forest and it would be fun to have Richard and Billy, my grandfather and his horse, to show me how it should really be done, my Jewish grandmother celebrating one of her thirteen annual holidays, my mother baking bread and cursing poverty for our return; but time indulges no one except in imagination and in my mind I like to recall only the good things that she taught me. Much of her personality sticks with me and I can now laugh at some of her idiosyncrasies. A little bit of madness is good for the soul.

When my brother, Martin, and I cleaned out her house after she died, the pathological depth of her parsimoniousness astonished even me. There, on a shelf, littered with bottles of colour sorted buttons, old zippers, bread twist ties and canning jars was a box neatly labeled PIECES OF STRING TOO SMALL TO USE. Most of the garbage we threw out in a dumpster but some of it I could not throw away. The buttons I glued onto a piece of painted plywood to create a landscape and the string turned out to be good fire starter. I never imagined myself a button artist but the save-it side of the Tuomi-Winburgs is hard to expunge and I just couldn't throw away buttons that she had neatly clipped and sorted and saved for decades.

My mother was also a kleptomaniac as the hospital bedpans stacked in her bathroom attested. There were bandages, rolls of gauze and even green hospital gowns folded and ready for wear. Her ancestors had never been without comforts in Scandinavia and she would never be caught short-handed in Canada, no matter what. It was a question of family pride. No one recycles as we do; no one is tidier, no one upholds standards so meticulously. And no one claimed to be more virtuous about it than my mother. I now put some of her habits down to an obsessive-compulsive disorder brought on by too many episodes of childhood deprivation and insulin shock. It is a mild madness not so uncommon amongst women of her generation. But this parsimony made her a great saver and when she died every penny of her pension was still in the bank. From farmer's daughter, scrubbing floors for her room and board at thirteen, she entered the middle class by the time she was forty. An astute businesswoman, she had managed to accumulate three rental properties in Vancouver and left an inheritance of over a million dollars to her grandchildren.

But on most counts her side of the family had it hands down over my father's Finnish relatives. She had married my father, Lenni, because she found herself pregnant in the bush in northern Ontario at the age of twenty. She claimed she was never certain how it all happened, how she came to be involved with him, but once they were married and had two children that was no longer an issue. Certainly there was the war shortage of eligible men but, whatever the reason, she ended up married below her station and it took another twenty years to crawl out. My father's siblings, "to the man" she often stated, were womanizers, drunks, gamblers, loudmouths and boors and although sometimes I agreed with her I often found myself secretly enjoying their company.

My father's brother, Uncle Leo, came to visit the first August we were on the farm. I got to know him best during the several summers I'd spent hanging out on Long Beach on Vancouver Island between undergraduate semesters at the University of British Columbia. He was a salmon fisherman then, like his father, and, with his wife Mary, fell into the category of my favorite relatives (something I had to hide from my mother). His boat, the Hilma S (named after Aiti), was a salmon trawler cast from cement and he often took me and my friends out fishing off Vancouver Island, or for a run up the coast to Tofino. He was a natural joker, an old sexist, and an alcoholic who would have been a horror to live with but he was a great sea captain and loved to provoke his hapless passengers.

"So what they teach you down at that university? They teach you how to fish? How to earn a living? How to keep seals out of the nets?" he once mocked my softly bearded then-boyfriend. Leo picked up his 22 rifle and began to load it, lifting his foot on the gunnel to steady his aim. "Bang!" The gun went off. "Bang" again. Then another "Bang" and "Damn! I've shot myself in the foot!" and, to the horror of my boyfriend, he exposed a large hole in his rubber Wellingtons.

"God! Get back to shore. Lyn, do something!" My friend was distraught.

"Leo, stop it!" I shouted. Then, to my traumatized mate, "He has a wooden leg. He does this all the time."

"See!" he would intone. "They don't teach 'em nothing down at that university. What fisherman would blow a hole in his own foot?" After which, the rum or vodka would come out and he would sit and ponder the waste of education, the stupidity of youth. My poet boyfriend lost his taste for fishing—and many of my relations—after that. If there was a natural with the boorish turn in our family, it was Uncle Leo and he was always the centre of attention.

Although always offensive, he made me love him for his madness, his zest for life. He had lost his leg under a train when he was a boy, jumping from car to car. He gambled, like my father, and lost much of his season's pay packet at the roulette tables in Las Vegas. They had both learned to play cards and shoot craps in the logging camps as young men and it was a lifelong habit that neither could shake. He would bet on anything: the chances of rain, the cost of bananas, even my living room window breaking. When he came to visit, Leo liked to open a window and chip golf balls through it onto the lawn outside. He thought it funny that people would get on edge, waiting for the window to crack. He wanted, again like my father, to be the centre of the universe, and if that meant discomfiting those around him, so much the better. The hard life they had learned in the bush stuck with them and, from the outside, it was amusing. Close up was another story.

The week Leo arrived to see our new farm the pig breeder across the road put up his FOR SALE sign and began to sell off hogs. The bank was foreclosing and he had three weeks left. Leo, out putting his golf balls over the hills, met him and offered him a hundred and fifty thousand for his farm and the remaining pigs.

"Could take up pig farming," he said when he returned and opened up the vodka bottle. "No seals out here."

"But lots of wolves," responded TH, too quickly. "And terrible winters and no casinos." We convinced him that it was impossible and my husband rushed out to apologize to our neighbour. "He doesn't have the money; he's a bit mad." He was one you always had to pull out of the quicksand, keep on the straight and narrow until he fell to his bottle and musings about pigs. My father, Lenni, was not so easy.

When the bank foreclosed on his house in Vancouver, he drove across the country with a truckload of old appliances and no insurance; he was bankrupt again and decided that our farm had to be sold and he was going to buy a house in Toronto and find himself another wife (his third) and we could all live together happily ever after. He had already found a house, a "fixer-upper" duplex, close to his sister's place in Etobicoke, and could see no reason why TH and I weren't willing to move. He was tired, he said, of having to put on his own socks and needed someone to cook for him and scratch his back. He borrowed money from us and took to buying wads of lottery tickets. He had once won a small amount and, like all compulsive gamblers, felt the next big win was just around the corner. He had moved into real estate after his garage business failed but lacked the stick-to-itiveness necessary to be competitive. He never opened a book but always read the funny papers, his lips moving between bouts of demented laughter, and the horoscope page. He would nod sagely as he read out loud from the tabloids, giving preposterous advice to the rest of us according to his reading of the stars. Like my mother, he was a lifelong believer in numerology and was perpetually blending birth dates and street addresses to come up with the string of lucky numbers that would take him off to Bora Bora. It took weeks to get him to understand the farm was not his to sell, nor our money his to gamble away and he finally left in a huff, vowing to find a rich widow who already had a house of her own and could appreciate a man with a gift for numbers.

These visits always left me with a blinding headache and took about two weeks to work their way out of my system; without the real work in the garden and the house rebuilding I could not have dealt, even metaphorically, with reconstructing my own world. My mother's notion of "dealing with daughter" veered between soul-murdering criticism and benign neglect: my father, narcissist that he was, demanded constant adoration. "Do as I say, not as I do!" and "It's my way or the highway, Little Fatso. Just don't forget that." Neither of them was an easy guest to accommodate and I repeatedly failed in both their estimations. My mother's "What an idiot thing to spend your money on—horses!" was matched by my father's "You think too much. More work on your hair and less thought in your head." No one in my family has ever respected the three-day/dead fish rule for visitors and with such loose boundaries crises were sure to occur. But these, in the early days, I kept mostly to myself. Public feuding, my mother would remind me, was reserved for my father's side of the family.

There was a lifelong rivalry between my father and uncle Leo. They were superficially civil but every now and again my father would rib his brother about his drinking and what a loser he was and Leo would remind my father that he had served during the war in the Merchant Marine while my father was stuck in the bush. Finns were considered Enemy Aliens during the war and, to my father's eternal shame, his passport had been stamped and he was denied service in the Canadian forces. Leo, given his flair for "baffling them with bullshit" as he always bragged, had managed to convince the military medical board that he was Canadian and fit for service. Despite one leg too few (as Peter Cook observed in the Tarzan sketch) Leo was fortunately only required to strip to the waist and spent the final war years travelling around the Pacific. I'm sure their low-grade sibling hostility had more to do with just this bit of fraud but nothing was ever said when I was around. Death ends all disputes.

Most of that generation of my family is now buried in the cemetery on 33rd and Knight Street in Vancouver where many immigrants ended up. A few went to the now near-dead coastal community of Sointulla (socialist Finns still hoped to live a Utopian life based on mining, fishing and music; the name of the town means Harmony) and some moved to the Okanagan interior of British Columbia. They were longshoremen, loggers, fishermen, builders, cooks, mechanics, net menders, fruit pickers and real estate agents. My dozen cousins in the next generation ended up as teachers, lawyers, and business people, following the typical pattern of Canadian immigrants everywhere. The black sheep in my family (one died of a gunshot wound after a failed bank robbery, one ended up in prison for trafficking in heroin) were never spoken of again.

Most of us have inherited Aiti's *sisu*—we take risks and carry on. Without that, I suppose I would not have been able to throw myself so totally into building the farm and having a family. The farm became an escape from madness, a sanctuary from the cacophony of family feuds, a place where I was beyond most criticism, beyond bullying. A place where few demanded anything from me but what I was willing to give. (Except, of course, from time to time, my genetically lazy husband.) To my as yet unborn children I was willing to give everything I had, including things I had not known myself—foremost of which was a childhood of creative play and space.

*My two grandmothers, Hilma and Bertha.*

*Me and my mother, Laura Tuomi, 1949.*

*My father fishing.*

*Home sweet home: my mother, father, brother Martin and me, 1949.*

*The first Tuomi homestead near Surprise Lake, Ontario, 1930.*

*Grandpa Richard and Billy.*

## Roughing it in the Bush

We took possession of Sweetfield that promising April, 1979. My morning sickness had somewhat subsided and I anticipated breathing fresh air out of doors. But, at 45 degrees north, 1,650 feet above sea level, sometimes all seasons can occur on one day. The temperature ranged from a northerly January minus 20 Celsius to a southerly plus 20 July day. This means snowstorms followed by flooding thaw and my moods seemed to swing with the winds. Ice storms drove me underground and then, just as swiftly, the summer heat forced the flowers through green shoots like Dylan Thomas never imagined.

The ground released five months of ice in one day; a thick smell, like rotting clover and sulphurous eggs, assaulted the nose. The driveway, a ridged sinkhole, was impassable and, as the truck arrived with my piano, washing machine, dryer, and seventy-five boxes of deadweight books, we knew there were going to be difficulties. The driver took one look at the roadway and began unpacking, 300 meters from the house.

"No further than this, don't have chains, gotta get back to the city, don't take cheques, that's your problem."

Two days later, hauling with mud-runner sleds and dollies, our earthly possessions were crammed into the confusion of the front room. Knowing the supporting beams were rotten we went to bed fearing the whole floor might fall through to the basement. We slept on a mattress surrounded by the remains of Chinese takeout and pizza boxes; fine cuisine, or even garlic, had not yet reached Shelburne and I had no idea when or how we could arrange a makeshift kitchen in the disorder of all those tiny rooms. There was a pantry with an old sink that drained into a sump in the yard and a counter top no self-respecting cook would use to chop an onion. I looked at my boxes of cookbooks, wondering if I would ever get to poaching pears and grilling sea bass again, and put the cases to hibernate under a wooden box I used as a cupboard. The place had to be gutted, everything had to be burned and there was clearly no time for spinach and anchovy tarts.

We began that first weekend taking down walls to a fire pile outside in an effort to create some space. Our school prep we did around the kitchen table jammed between our mattress and the door. Max, constantly mud-caked, was going mad with the new olfactory world and kept bringing home unrecognizable dead things to decompose on the porch. Not since mud-hut settlers had people lived in such cruel chaos. It was a drunken Kreighoff nightmare, but we were blithely happy, sleeping deep ten-hour nights, certain our work would bear fruit at some vaguely distant time.

Finally, at the end of April college exams were marked and our grades were loaded on the computer. With the daily commuting over, our farm labour began in earnest. Given that my husband had always been content with no more than an hour of physical exertion a day we had a problematic start. He was, at best, a klutzy carpenter who always blamed the poor quality of his tools for the time it took to complete a project. I was somewhat more skilled but I preferred to potter as my belly swelled. We weren't sure our citified spirits were capable of the indefatigable demands of rebuilding. But if necessity is the mother of invention then pregnancy is the riding crop. In my family there was no such thing as impossible and my grandmother always clothed and fed her children. First concerns, first.

"Sisyphean," my husband muttered. "I'm thirty-five and as lazy-ignorant as a sloth."

"Three-toed? Utter madness," I agreed. "But I love you."

"I think we can do this. I mean, really, other people do this all the time."

"You promised me we would."

Assessing the problems seemed like a waste of energy and we decided water and electricity were our highest priorities. We didn't have time to fight over aesthetic decisions. The bathroom and kitchen had to be functioning, every wall and false ceiling had to come down, and the wiring and drywall had to be finished before September. There seemed little point in debating the obvious; that we would deal with. It was the unforeseen that shook us.

Ontario Hydro took one look at the wiring and turned the electricity off until we had the poles replaced and a new service installed. "Too dangerous," they insisted.

"Too expensive," we responded. The candles were very romantic and we cooked outdoors, bickering over an ancient hibachi propped up on stones as to who was responsible for this life decision. We showered under a gravity-fed hose hung from the cedars. If we had survived in the mountains of the Yellowhead with the grizzlies on our summer vacations, we could survive here in Ontario. It was certainly harder for my family during the Great Depression in the northern bush. And farm life reminded me of bush camping. There was nothing hard about that when paychecks were coming in every two weeks.

The difference was that at the farm there were now rats in my kitchen instead of bears. Bears we dealt with by banging pots and pans and firing our rifles but no amount of noise or poison could dispatch the rodents. Cats were needed. Alice and Lefty, two not terribly healthy, mildly feral kittens came to us free from the pig farmer's barn and got right down to the task of matching Max, carcass for bloody carcass, stopping dead every rodent headed for my kitchen.

"Can't have a farm without cats," advised one old neighbour. "That's how the plague got started. Yous have got to have cats to keep the diseases away." I began to love the local patois and referred to the animals as "yous killers", as in "Get on with your job, yous killers!" Someday I would teach these phrases to my English classes in the city, I mused. The more locals I met, the more they began to live fictional lives in my head and the occasional evening parlour game of telling stories around the fire began expanding into a full time preoccupation with the lives of others and how they survived.

Indoors, we finally reached the bare brick. There was 1200 square feet of open living space on the ground floor. The basement beams were braced and replaced and the floors, under all that ugly covering, were pine. By this time we had run out of cash again; but, as it was summer, the real estate prices went up and we immediately remortgaged to buy wiring, hire an electrician and begin purchasing paint to cover the drywall. We left the windows as they were and I cemented and caulked and plastered all I could. It was a layman's job but the original house had, after all, been built without the aid of an architect or designer. We certainly couldn't afford one now. I loved the fact that the warped floorboards sloped and pennies and screwdrivers would roll into the corners and clink against the brick. The walls bowed inward and the ceiling angles were out six inches on the north end. It must have been built in winter when the only imperative was closing out the wind, not achieving plumb lines. Perfection continued to elude us but the affection grew logarithmically. Every wall presented its own problem, every doorframe a new and unchangeable slant. I banged in shimmies and learned to love the serendipity.

A nagging truth would hit me every few days as I watched my belly grow. The prospect of bringing a child into this foul smelling, dust-ridden building site was intimidating but neither of the processes was stoppable. In July, Ontario Hydro turned on the electricity and we had running water, brilliant one hundred watt bulbs and a functioning radio. We were almost into the 20th century. The Dufferin Health Unit, on the other hand, was not impressed with our unique septic system but, through a mercifully efficient municipal office, we were able to obtain a permit.

Glen, the local backhoe man, who loved to take the time to conflab using all the subjunctives, super pasts and idioms of our bizarre local dialect, came in to do the job. He spent a morning scratching his head, eyeing the results of our improbable skills and looking over the makeshift system that had been in place for the past twenty-five years since the outhouse collapsed.

"Why pay for an expensive cement septic and weeping tiles when a perfectly good old Ford truck would handle the honey, eh?"

"I don't know. It seems the Officer of Health isn't fond of this system."

"Couldn't have did it better myself back then. This truck did its work for thirty years and then served a useful purpose in the grave. Same should be said of us but can't be in most cases. Mind you, the ground can get kind of mucky up to the bootlaces. Wouldn't want that now would we?"

"Far too mucky for me."

I watched with great pleasure as the bulldozer plowed in the back fill to cover the miserable sewage-laded truck. I didn't care how many useful lifetimes it had lived, I wanted the regulation septic and Glen couldn't resist ribbing me about my need for a fancy Thomas Crapper and all the modern fixings.

"Never underestimate the value of a simple outhouse."

"We lived with an outhouse for years in the bush," I told him. "They've lost their charm for me."

"Familiarity breeds contempt," he philosophized. "One day you'll hate septics. Have to be pumped all the time. Back up everywhere."

It was his job to install new containers, beds and weeping tiles and he did it very efficiently, following all the rules and regulations of the Health Department, but his need for bantering over the job, pointing out the inconsistencies in building code theory and human practice, was highly contagious. There began the nattering about the differences in the ways of city and country folk. We found gleeful company in local gossip and endless delight in discussing the vagaries of weather, nature's cruelties and human ingenuity.

"Another professional guy, a lawyer I think, took to raising a couple of thousand head of buffalo just last year," Glen told me one day. "He's gonna make a success of it even if he has to go flat broke trying. Says he's gonna create the market for buffalo burgers." He smirked his sideways smile, the eyebrows on his forehead dancing. "Sometimes something like that can happen with horses—you have so much success breeding them you end up in the poorhouse. But hey, good luck anyway, really, good luck. I mean it. I really mean it."

Every day a new discovery commanded our attention: a dead pig under the refuse in the garage, a mountain of broken beer bottles, old tires, rusty bed springs, unopened subpoenas and parole papers.

"Wonder who these people were," TH would mutter.

"Wonder if there are any bodies tucked under the roses in the garden."

"Don't take up gardening until they've decomposed."

We made trips to the dump every day it was open. The farm wilderness grew around us and the fields were quickly overgrown by weeds with no cows on the property. Or so we thought.

As the summer heat began, we made the most fragrant discovery of all. One of the tenant farmer's cows had fallen through the ice over the previous winter and now, several months later, her bloated green carcass breached the frog scum on the edge of the pond. That day, we weren't sure exactly what the mass in the pond was, but as the wind rolled her over, four rigid legs burst clearly into view. Amid the willows and nesting mallards we watched in horror as she grew and decomposed in the advancing sun. There was no ignoring her. She had to be moved, had to be buried. But how?

We found several deserted groundhog holes twenty meters from the pond hill rise where the sandy loam was easy to dig.

With both of us shoveling for an hour, we had a fair-sized grave but the humour got more gruesome as we tried to figure out the geometry of getting the stinking corpse up the hill to its resting place.

"Alas, poor Ophelia, you are not so easy to bury."

The flies were out, as were the peepers and mosquitoes, so we put on some bush-strength repellent and our Farmer's Co-op rubber boots. I got a few lengths of nylon rope and backed my Volkswagen Rabbit down the hill. TH, rubber-gloved, climbed into the muck and began wrapping lengths of rope around the rotting ankles, knees and haunches. I attached the other end to the bumper and, when he waved me on, slowly accelerated and the old beast rolled over in the water. The carcass began to slide up the hill but when the full deadweight hit the dryer grass on the hillside the pus-filled hide gave way, slipping off the cow like a glove, splattering its soured flesh all over TH. I stopped and looked at the lumpy mess of maggoty cow coat on the end of the rope, cut it, dropped the chunk into the grave and backed down the hill again.

My husband was not in a good mood; he was transformed into a foul character from some gruesome Cronenburg flick. This time, without speaking or looking my way, he rolled the cow over, making sure the rope sunk deep into the rib cage, around the neck and over the haunches. Finally, the car skidding all the way, I pulled the beast into the grave and we began shoveling.

"I have never in my lifetime, in my worst nightmares...."

"Don't think about it, just get her covered."

"Plug your nose."

"How can you shovel and plug your nose at the same time?"

Thank heaven for afternoon rain. We stripped naked and washed under the flooding down pipe. Soon, the hillside turned green, the pond swelled with new life, the ducks were swimming in front of their broods, the frogs sang us to sleep at night and Green Cow Pond had a name.

*Green Cow Pond.*

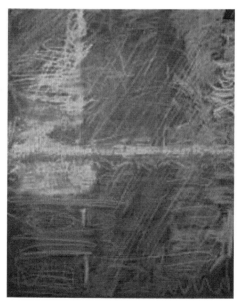

*Rainy night on Green Cow Pond.*

## Changing Heaven

The first summer we felt drunk with the opulence of the farm, the pandemonium of greenery bursting from the earth. We depended on an old push mower, a machete and a pair of hedge clippers to keep marauding nature at bay. Without the luxury of power lawn mowers, tractors and chain saws which came much later, hours of back-breaking labour were required. As the family gardener I concerned myself with the immediate acre around the house—enough so that we could sit outside to eat and have a place to unload the building materials that came every two weeks as our paychecks arrived. The rest of the savage wild unfolded as it would.

The bee-infested lilacs hung heavy over the house, the honeysuckle overgrew the paths, the rhubarb, wild raspberry, chokecherry and apple trees produced endless blossoms, then fruit. Sumac, beech, birch, cedar, mountain ash and poplar grew copiously around the back pond. Ubiquitous Manitoba maples overtook the collapsing cedar rail fence running around the paddocks. For generations the farm had sustained a hundred head of cattle that had eaten every new sprout. Now every root was wild with the prospect of producing seed. Ecologists today discuss the twelve-step program for field recovery in a very scientific, purposeful manner, rather like AA; instead, we just watched in merry disbelief as nature took her concupiscent course.

To add to the discovery, recovery and penury of our first summer TH managed to find an Appaloosa mare with what he thought were good breeding prospects. He had been daily at his Herculean task of mucking out the stables and once the stalls were cleared and scrubbed they seemed lost without occupants. A grey-dappled mare named Fayden came to us through one of TH's former students who worked at Woodbine Racetrack and was now on her way to university and could no longer afford to keep the Appy. Only ten years old, she was well trained and went both Western and English and for $1200 there was no resisting. An old Argentinean saddle was found at a farm auction and TH went riding every evening as I took to the garden.

"There is nothing so good for the insides of a man as the outsides of a horse." Was that Montaigne? And why do we all believe it? In a week I had fallen in love with Fayden and every night after dinner we would hang around the barn with our wine glasses listening to her chewing on her hay and nickering with satisfaction. We learned to nicker back to her. She was the first of our horses and proved patient with our steep learning curve; she was a good teacher of Horse As A Second Language.

Books on stable management and equine health joined the stack of new baby books and *Peterson's Field Guides* beside our bed. Rule number one of reading is follow examples: when the knowledge isn't there remember a million people have been at horse breeding and baby raising before and they must have something useful to say. We delighted in the richness of our newfound knowledge and endlessly discussed the protein content of grasses, poultices for founder, daily hoof care and worming. We kept Fayden off the fields and confined to the paddock at first. Coming from low-protein barn rations, where she competed with a dozen other horses, onto the fecundity of the farm must have been as much of a shock to her system as it was to ours. Within weeks she started to put on girth and trotted out briskly for short grazing times. Concern for her health came as naturally as breathing.

Normally ponies come after children but Fayden needed a friend and so Buddy came our way. Snow Pony Bumble Bee, his registered name, was a type B Welsh Mountain Pony, bay with four white socks, whose sire had won ribbons at the Royal Winter Fair for two years running. He was a feisty one-year-old colt owned by a near- bankrupt horse dealer forced to sell all his stock. We should have guessed that the horse business was not the place to make money but the pony was too sweet to leave to a meat broker. Besides, if we were going to breed Fayden we would need a teaser on hand. Buddy knew her cycles, curling his upper lip and sucking in the scented air, whinnying and prancing to announce his desire. Now, the minute I see a stallion with that rolling lip, (it's called flehmening, a $10 dollar word in my mother's books) I check to see which mare is in season. When the time to breed came, he would be worth the $50 we paid for him.

They bonded like lost lovers and we were pleased Fayden was not alone in the barn; herd animals are never completely happy by themselves. These two needed hay and good water, so the next priorities were obvious.

The old dug well had no pressure and it was impossible to feed a line to the barn. Each horse needs five to ten gallons a day of drinking water and for a while we carried that from the house. With every bucket-laden step I sympathized with women in the third world who did this every day to survive. Along with my enormous rounding belly my quadriceps began to take on a new shape. The definition on TH's back was visible under his T-shirts and the horse labour began to agree with him. It had to be done and it was one of the few chores he liked. The risk of letting two heavy animals down to Green Cow Pond in the winter was too terrifying to contemplate and TH started to repair the fences and worry about barn water. With a new baby due at the end of October, we would also need more water for doing laundry; hooking up the washing machine inched up my emergency list.

We phoned the local well driller and he came with his rig, pipes and an assistant and began a little informal dowsing. Any well-digger worth his salt carries wands in the cab of his truck and never has to drill twice.

"Never pay the price for those geological reports, Ma'am." He paced a few steps and I watched as the wand began to quiver. "It's like throwing money away. Don't need to pay a consultant to see if it's raining now do we? There's always water here for the findin'."

They drilled 180 feet into the Niagara Escarpment and hit an aquifer that blasted 15 gallons a minute and, until the pump and cap were in place, we enjoyed a mini geyser in our back garden. The Ditch Witch machine dug water lines to the house and barn and a new drop hydrant (no winter freezing) was installed.

The next day the wiring was in and the well started functioning. We dragged an old clawfoot bathtub that had been left in the garage to a sunny spot behind the barn, put a plug in it, and filled it with fresh water. Fayden and Buddy drank their fill and we gave them a good hosing down, their first baths of the summer. There was vast delight in the smell of clean horses and deep satisfaction in getting the necessities of living up and running. After the sun had warmed the refilled tub I took my clothes off and washed my sweaty skin and swelling feet; nothing had ever felt as cleansing as that soak. Bathing *en plein air* became a family ritual and we were grateful every day for the quality of our water. As well as reviving the body, the flow from the Niagara Escarpment made the best pizza dough, rendered chicken bones into ambrosia, and brewed the cleanest beer. All by itself, cold water from the tap cleared the day's grit from your throat. The gods have it no better.

*Buddy.*

## A Good Baby

That first summer flew into fall and I plowed around, mostly naked because nothing fit, like a Viking ship under full sail. I was tipping the scales at 210 and even at almost six feet that was a hefty girth; my doctor suggested I might be getting ready to give birth to a moose. My husband gained weight, pound for pound, as if to keep me company. In spite of all the constant hard work, and both of us returning to teaching in September, we managed to get to childbirth classes and ready a crib, some baby clothes and a gross of diapers. The kitchen was finished: stove, fridge, dishwasher, with a washer and dryer tucked under the stairs. We were ready.

Fall in Mono is Mardi Gras without the people, carnival without the noise. Trees flaunt banners of crimson, fluorescent orange, sienna, cinnamon, gold leaf. When the Group of Seven first exhibited their work, viewers who had never been to Canada complained that the colours were too garish, a spectacle overdone. Not at all. Our forests, after a frost, become crinkly underfoot but maintain a brilliant canopy of foliage until the winds take the dry leaves down. Each year I collected samples, pressed them in old dictionaries, compared the hues and debated the reddest eruptions. September, October, November have always been my favourite months: frosty nights followed by still-long days and winds that threaten then subside, unable to muster their maximum wrath until December.

We luxuriated in the warmth of Indian summers, the constant crunch of drying leaves, the carpet that built protection for seeds and wintering animals. Flocks of birds mustered, feeding on wild grapes, dried raspberries and blackcurrants. One evening, after dinner, forty cedar waxwings clung like early Christmas decorations on the chokecherry bush and stripped it bare. Another day dozens of colourful flickers, their red heads bobbing, poked through the soil with long beaks, filling for the flight south. Birds were the regular dinner visitors I enjoyed the most.

After all the straw was baled and sitting in the fields like giant muffins, flocks of geese would drop from their migration route and gorge on the grain left by the harvester. The corn silage field, too, was covered with birds—webbed feet marching, scrapping and finally resting for the night. Early morning they would begin their honking, rouse like an army about to enter battle and lift skyward following the lead goose south.

The beechnuts, rosehips, chestnuts and apples were a cornucopia for the small animals, oblivious to our presence, absorbed in their food gathering. As I watched the transformation that first pregnant fall I changed the way I felt about Ontario forever. I had been going back to school every September since I was five and had wrongly convinced myself that as well as being the end of summer it was the beginning of torture. No one can live in the country in the fall without feeling healed by the season.

No such autumn joy for my students who were perpetually nervous around me—fearing, I am sure, that I would rupture in the middle of discussions of narrative technique or cause and effect essay methodologies. My mother-in-law made me a paisley wool dress, shaped like a tent, and I wore it every day, rinsing it by hand on Saturdays and ironing it on Sundays. At mid-term, October 31st, a few days before Claire was born, a substitute came in to take over my classes. My belly could no longer fit between my spine and the steering wheel of my little Rabbit. I had seventeen weeks of maternity leave coming and I didn't want to waste any of it before the baby arrived.

Three days later my water broke after a particularly sleepless night and the world we knew before disappeared. After twenty hours of labour and a c-section, during which I told the doctor to take the baby out of my head if he had to, TH was finally able to cuddle me and the baby. He burbled about the miracle that had utterly changed him into a more purposeful person. As I slept off the anesthetic he busied himself counting toes. When I woke up my breasts were like concrete blocks and the only thing that could give me comfort was my child. At ten pounds she was perpetually hungry and that pleased me. She had the perfectly round head that caesarian babies do, and overwhelming blue eyes, the colour of morning. By the end of the first week we began to forget what life was like before Claire and we fell madly, head-over-heels in love with our new child. Sleeplessness, cracked nipples and laundry aside, it was perfect.

Canadian winters should all be prefaced by a new baby in a basket, horses in the barn, and only a few visits from family. That first winter as new parents was also our first winter as country residents but it seemed to fly by in a haze: work, sleep, laundry, dishes, cooking, work, sleep, laundry. For the seventeen weeks of my maternity leave I rarely left the house, leaving TH to drive to his college and do the shopping on his way home. There was little time to worry about more renovations, little time to ponder which way the road was going to turn. We were on it and choice flew out the window. But I must say we were very happy and conscious of being happy. My love of life in the country and of Claire grew with each new morning nursing the child. Nothing fazed me that first winter, not the iciest of northern blasts, not the road closures, not the howling wind as I went out to throw hay to the gee-gees. Motherhood evokes a state of mind all its own and nothing I had encountered before, or have encountered since, can hold a candle to it. When the spring of 1980 rode in we wanted to do little but focus on what made us happy: each other, Claire, the horses and Sweetfield Farm.

*Claire in 1980.*

# Childhood

From the time Claire was born, she played. Play was what our generation wanted to give back to childhood: she played in the kitchen, in the garden, in front of the fire. I wanted somehow to transform the emphasis on work from my own family into something more acceptable to me. Claire's preferred place for play was the barn while we did the chores. She participated in the discussions around the horses and incorporated their routines into her own. One of her earliest sentences was "Time to feed the horses."

As a toddler in her sandbox, with a herd of Little Ponies, Princess of Power horses and unicorns, she groomed her charges, fed them and "mucked out" their stalls made of plastic Lego. She would follow TH and me as we did the rounds, often pulling a wagonload of plastic friends behind her. "Let's do the horses." She was a strong-willed child, never one to accept being denied any of her desires, and it was a job just directing her into areas of "play" that kept her out of danger.

Her cart was stuffed with apples, curry combs and books because, as the horses were eating, she decided that was the time to start reading to them. One of her favourite books was *I Am A Bunny*. It was also first choice of the horses, she decided. Before she could read there was the mimicry.

"Hello, my name is Nicholas. I am a bunny. I live in a hollow tree." She would climb up on a straw bale and, in her hand, a pink pony with fuchsia hair would dance across the top of Buddy's stall or share his grain bucket with him.

"That's not a bunny, that's a pony."

"Hello, my name is Nicholas. I am a pony. I live in a hollow tree."

"Where do horses live? In hollow trees? I'll see if there's a hollow tree out by the manure pile we can put the horses in," said TH.

"Hello, my name is Nicholas. I am pony. I live in a wooden barn not in a hollow tree."

When she did learn to read on her own, after dinner as we went to check on the horses before the night, she would bring along a book to leave behind so the horses could read to themselves if they couldn't sleep. She often sang to them before bed.

*Old Stewball was a racehorse and I wish he were mine. He never drank water, he only drank wine,"* she would sing to Mango. *"His bridle was silver, his mane it was gold, And the worth of his saddle has never been told."* And, in all seasons, Good King Wenceslas, pausing before bellowing straight into the horses' snouts, *"Mark my footsteps good my Page, Tread thou in them boldly, Thou shalt find the winter's rage Freeze thy blood less coldly."*

The horses were very calm around her and she would often spread out a blanket in a stall and tuck herself into a corner to rest or share carrots and apples and stories with them as we progressed with the heavier chores—scraping bot eggs off the horses' shins and cleaning hooves.

My British in-laws, appalled at this filthy veterinary practice, were certain the child would pick up worms or develop some hideous leprosy-like skin disease. Never ones to have let their own children "muck about in the dirt" they found it hard to accept that this sort of activity could possibly be good in any way for their granddaughter. TH's father, Henry, forever had handkerchiefs in his pocket and was perpetually wiping Claire's hands lest she put them in her mouth. They were nervous around the animals and we tried to keep them out of the barn on their visits.

"Bloody horses, all this time with the bloody horses! The children shouldn't be around them. They're very dangerous." We managed to ignore their fears and Claire did her best to explain the lives of horses to her grandparents and her charm silenced them.

Horses sleep standing up and they lock their knees as they doze. On more than one occasion we would wake the horses as we carried Claire back to her bed at night and they would blink as Claire kissed them goodnight. Horse barns have that sweet scent of hay and straw and, although city people complain about the smell, there is little as lovely as the perfume of hay on the hair of a sleeping child. It bespeaks work and billowing raw pleasure and sends me crashing into La La Land the minute my own head hits the pillow.

Horse and child rearing demands a structure of little variance. Day in, day out, the child needs to be washed and fed and clothed. Every horse needs his hay and turnout time. Blankets in winter, regular worming and teeth floating (scraping with a rasp, as horses' teeth keep growing) and dentist appointments and vaccinations for the child, set a structure to the weeks and years that, far from being monotonous like laundry and cooking, is deeply satisfying. I loved being a mother to Claire, loved her ferocity and her dedication, which at times was not without its difficulties, but I always felt, that in the long run, this sort of horse care discipline was good for her character.

Horse people joke about this relentless feeding and mucking process: "You need a good strong back, size 19 neck, and a really small hat size." But I enjoyed it and those family evenings in the barn, even during the *"rude wind's wild lament and the bitter weather."* Like Wenceslas, I found some blessing in it and it's nice to hear a six-year-old tell you "it's time to read to the horses and we can't be late."

# The Loved and the Lost

Just one of the reasons many people find contemporary working life so unbearable is that they have lost contact with horses. Or so TH kept telling me and the baby. Claire needed to be raised with horses—it was as natural as breathing. The idea of horses and our love of them had burst into daily reality—the mucking out, feeding and care. And so we discussed the course of human and equine history endlessly with Claire as she accompanied us on the round of chores, tucked into the backpack strapped to one or the other of us.

Earliest man, we told the child, his nature daily occupied with concerns for water, food and transport, would have innately sought a relationship with the horse and nurtured it. Survival and procreation were made easier by mobility. Stone Age cave painters in Lascaux and Chauvet left murals of herds on their walls. Primitives must have marveled at the speed, grace, and kinships of the beasts and recognized their curious social natures, their possibilities for domestication. The need for horses must have been realized just after fire and just before the wheel.

"Horses change the way we relate to the earth. They change who we are," rationalized TH as he bought Claire yet another picture book on horses.

There is archeological evidence that Eurasian steppe dwellers first domesticated the horse near Dereivka in the Ukraine over 6,000 years ago. The skull of a seven- or eight-year-old stallion found in a burial mound reveals the characteristic wear patterns in teeth caused by the bit. Antlers with bore holes that would have functioned as cheek pieces were also found in the grave. That village had been built around a cult stallion, and nations and cultures thereafter followed the pattern.

"Better to make a cult of the horse than any other kind. Think if there was a head horse in Rome, a horse in the White House, a head horse in China."

Evolution had left horses with a diastema, the gap between the front incisors and the rear grinders, which early herdsmen quickly understood could hold a bit and bridle. With a top speed of 70 kilometers an hour, horses were prized more as transportation than as food. They were highly adaptive, lived on grasses, could bear weight, carry sustenance and shelter on their backs; they could be raced and they instilled power. Having mounts transformed societies.

I became obsessed with telling horse stories to the baby.

The image of the horse appears in crude petroglyphs, their totemic power deeply felt. In 1400 BCE Assyrian kings rode horse-drawn chariots in lion hunts. A hundred years later reliefs were carved in Egypt showing Ramses II on a war chariot. Gods hauled the sun and the moon in horse drawn chariots. Before the Bronze Age, the Battle Ax folk conquered Sweden on their horses. (They were related to my mother.) The ancient stone cists at Kivik in Scania show charioteers. 2,400 years ago, the Greek Xenophon wrote his horse-training manual that helped develop a mobile culture. Horses graced the Acropolis in 490 BCE; the equestrian statue of Marcus Aurelius in Rome, constructed in the 2nd century, became a model for all politicians and all equine statues thereafter.

For most of the past three thousand years people would have found it hard to live without the horse; in the development of social history from the earliest agrarian societies to the subjugation of nations by modern warfare the horse was key. Without horses there could have been no centaurs, no Trojan Horse, no Roman Empire, no Boudicca, no crusades, no chivalry, no St George to slay the dragon, no trade for the Persians and Byzantines. Christianity could not have taken Europe, Chaucer's pilgrims would never have left London, and the Renaissance would not have travelled north. Chevaliers and troubadours would have had less to prance about. Without his dozen horses and mares in the hold of his ships, Columbus would have been stranded in the water in 1492. Richard III would not have been able to cry, "A horse, a horse, my kingdom for a horse." Democracy would have waited a long time; the humanities would not have travelled. Attila the Hun, Alexander the Great, and Napoleon would have been without their war horses. Pisarro would never have conquered Peru. The Light Brigade would not have charged. There would have been no invasions, no migrations.

World War One was dependent on the horse and there would have been no peace without draft horses. For parade, prayer, pillaging, pilgrimages, politics and plow the horse has been with us, taking us, for better and for worse where we wanted to go.

From Paolo Uccello's *The Rout of San Romano* in 1456 to Picasso's *Guernica*, artists have tried to capture this power. For me, art galleries become more animated when I search out any one of a thousand horse painters: Simone Martini, Albrecht Durer, Pieter Brueghels, Caravaggio, Stubbs, Gericault, Degas, Chagal or Braque. They loved the horse and I love what they saw and painted. The only reason I could get my child to galleries was because they had pictures of horses.

There is a particular painting in the Getty Museum in Los Angeles attributed to Hans Holbein in the 1520s. It is a painting of a horse and rider in motion entitled *Allegory of Passion* and it has a line inscribed from Petrarch's *Canzoniere*–'E cosi desio me mena.' (And so desire carries me along.) In that same collection there is Potter's *Piebald Horse* and Gerard Ter Borch's *Horse Stables*. I always go back to these animals in my head and, when I am in London, to Edward Landseer's compassionate horse portrait *The Arab Tent* in the Wallace Collection. Degas' horses in the Norton Simon museum in Pasadena—while magnificent and not to be missed—are of stressed-out beasts, wire-tight thin racers, lacking the calm grounding of my favourites. Horses are an essential gallery staple, galloping through history as they do, and every major collection has at least half a dozen worth spending time over.

Settlers would not have settled, the mail would not have moved. Paul Revere would have had to run on foot. Social order would not have been so understood; the poor had chickens, mules, cattle and oxen; the powerful and the righteous had horses. The Greeks and Romans knew the distinctions and that notion lasted straight through to the duster. John Wayne would have had no presence delivering his lines standing on the ground. The west would not have been won; Hollywood would have been without a thousand movies from *Ben Hur* to *Gladiator*. No *Black Beauty*, no Rhett Butler, no *Wuthering Heights*, no *Black Stallion*.

Composers would not have been able to hear the clip-clop of walk, the jigging pace of trot or the three beat canter. Orchestration would suffer. There would be no *Ride of the Valkyries*. Christmas would have no sleigh bells. Libraries would be short at least a million books. D.H. Lawrence and Cormac McCarthy might have thrown in the towel. I refuse to believe in the Apocalypse but if it ever comes it will have to arrive on horseback.

*Mango standing for her passport photo.*

# Studies of Plant Life

My husband went out that spring looking for more horses we could ill-afford, Claire was five months old, and I had an insane burst of April energy. A nearby farmer agreed (in exchange for some cow pasturing time on our north field) to turn over half an acre, donate a few tractor buckets of well-rotted manure and harrow my first vegetable garden. In May I was contemplating a ready plot of dark, fertile land large enough to feed a family of twelve for a year. It wouldn't all produce, I rationalized, and with seed catalogue and ignorance in hand I went to work with shovels and hoes and a three-pronged rake. I ordered three types of seed potatoes, carrots, spinach, chard, onions, turnips, snow peas, tomatoes and lettuce, beets, celery, cauliflower, red and green peppers, broccoli, Brussels sprouts, asparagus root and raspberry canes, zucchini and pumpkins. My baby would eat everything. I even tried exotica like salsify that, at that time, I had never cooked but the blurb in the catalogue made it seem like ambrosia. I had just come through renovation, childbirth and nursing; how hard could gardening be?

I hated reading gardening advice books. They all seemed too restrictive and technical with their zones and fertilizers and staking and pruning. After a few cursory glances I pushed the stack aside, realizing I should have done that the winter before I started; the books lingered on my shelves like forgotten friends as spring plowed forward faster than I could read. Reluctantly following a makeshift grid rather than scattering seed to the wind, as my nature would have dictated, I ambitiously planned four-foot square raised beds; I dug trenches and laid down straw between the rows to keep the weeds at bay. I planted the seeds out of the box as I grabbed them. Full sun? Partial shade? Sandy soil? It was all the same to me. By June I was in my garden patch with the baby two or three hours a day. Hubris was watching from behind the cedar hedge.

We were already harvesting spinach and lettuce that Claire ate straight from the ground. Avoiding pesticides, I whacked at white moths with my badminton racket and squished potatoes beetles between stones. We made dinners of spanakopita for a dozen, followed by overwhelming amounts of salad. I froze cooked spinach in bags and peas on trays as fast as I could shell them. Runner beans with butter and waxy new potatoes were sparring with zucchini flowers and baby beets as my favourites. The zucchinis that grew to the size of footballs TH kicked over the fence into the compost heap for the raccoons to fight over. Empirical learners are always like this—which brings me to a reading rule: if you haven't read about it, prepare for problems.

By the time September rolled around we had to get Claire off to the babysitter and ourselves into the classroom. My garden was overflowing with unmanageable ripe produce. I put several cardboard boxes full of tomatoes and other perishables in the trunk of my car and left them in the English Department office with a Help Yourself sign. I filled up boxes for my in-laws and gave produce to anyone who drove up the driveway. It was, my mother told me, an absolute waste of time and energy and seed money. "Only an idiot would grow a garden to give it away."

The following year I toned down my act, returned three-quarters of the plot to grass and limited myself to spinach, tomatoes, snow peas and a small number of immediate consumables. I re-read the vegetable garden section on my bookshelf.

I began planting a few nasturtiums and other edible flowers that I could pick and throw into salads and, even if we didn't get to eat them, they were pretty. The tiger lilies grew to a beastly size. Asparagus root had taken hold and for two more years we gorged on sweet green stalks sprouting through the weeds. The next year the neighbour's cows broke through the fence and, one particularly wet day, we awoke to fifty head of cattle knee deep in the muck of what had once been my garden. The asparagus bed never recovered from the trampling and I decided to focus my efforts on the herb garden, herbaceous borders, perennial flowerbeds and maybe a few trees.

Vegetable gardens on the scope I had first imagined mine were useful when feeding hundreds but my attempts were wildly optimistic, considering I had neither the desire nor the time to develop passable skills in canning, drying and preserving foods for the winter as every other female member of my family had done. For years to come my mother continued to harp on my incompetence every spring and every fall. She wanted to send me to Glastonbury for re-education on fast growth and early harvesting, to Harvard for an MBA in time management, and back to my *Fanny Farmer* and *Joy of Cooking* for lessons in canning. Vegetable gardening taught me a little self-control and my hide thickened to criticism.

*Giant tiger lilies.*

# Voice Over

My intensely practical mother was nonetheless prone to odd bouts of wacky mystical belief. She thought I should cover all my plants with plastic pyramids and suspend trays of "life-giving" tomatoes over my wood stove in my spare time. She believed in flying saucers, Filipino psychic surgery, various west coast independent churches, the Rosicrucians and personal divining (if you swing a watch over your clothes the universe will tell you what to wear). She changed her bank account numbers and her name several times in the belief that every letter had some cabbalistic power and she would benefit if her middle initials were F.S. (Financially Secure). One of her more interesting forays into the mysteries of the occult took place in an innocuous-looking commercial building in New Westminster, British Columbia. It was an Oriental Fundamentalist Christian Church, where members spoke with the dearly departed, and there she met the Second Husband.

When she was in her forties and my father found other women more interesting, my parents separated and spent several years trying to divorce and sue each other over imagined hidden assets. It was never a marriage based on trust and they succeeded in wearing each other down, making a few lawyers richer and creating mountains of bitterness neither of them knew how to handle as they aged. My father went off with ever-younger and sleazier women. "Always wanted to trade in a forty for two twenties," he so wittily joked. He made embarrassingly flirtatious passes at my friends, spun comments about women's breasts that could have landed him in court. I was perpetually on edge when I was with him, fearing social gaffes that would end in police charges. He regularly told women to shut up, keep their opinions for the kitchen, get their legs open, aprons on and lips buttoned. After decades of this, my mother had learned a few lessons in subterfuge and smiled when men spoke; I suppose that was what attracted the Second Husband.

The SH proved to be even more bizarre than my father. My mother announced their marriage to me over the phone one day (I had never heard of him until the wedding) and so I sent an appropriate gift of a duvet with a silk cover and went through the supportive dance about doing what she wanted to do and I hoped she would be happy and have a pleasant retirement, etc. I decided to go out to Vancouver and meet him although, even over the phone, I could tell that this might not be a meeting of minds.

"He's a doctor. Not a grease monkey like your father. He's educated like our Swedish family, educated like my children. Not like your father. My new husband is from Singapore. He lived in England. He has two children in university. His wife died of cancer, poor thing. He needs someone around the house." I tried to get the whole subtext of what she was trying to tell me about her new husband but it was not all that clear to me.

"I want you to wear a dress. Please wear some lipstick." Still not clear. "And don't talk too much." Getting clearer. I hoped that my mother's second marriage would be less confining than her first but that was not the case. New levels of paternalism were in the offing. "Do your best not to embarrass me with too many ideas," were her last words over the phone.

Dinner in their new house was about as tense an affair as I can remember. I wore a dress, some bright pink floral thing, I had received from my father's second wife as something to wear at *her* wedding. It was a costume I wore for stressful family occasions when my black stretch pants and second-hand men's tuxedo jackets were deemed inappropriate. I tried my best to adopt the role of the Toronto WASP English teacher my mother wanted me to be. I was not even close in my imitation.

When I arrived at the house, my mother thanked me for not wearing jeans and told me to take my shoes off. I began by politely asking him questions about his practice. "Oh, I've retired now. My main business was in Singapore and I don't practice here." I took that to mean he wasn't licensed to practice in Canada. His upright, cold manner told me he would be asking the questions, not answering them.

"Brain surgery," my mother answered. "He did special things with the brain. When I told your father that, he said he didn't believe me." I had doubts myself.

Both of his children would study medicine, he assured me, as only medicine would provide them with the satisfactions one deserved in life. He commiserated with my mother that I had been forced to take up teaching and began to question why so much tax money had to go to education budgets. When I ran out of answers for him and had finished the tour of the new house in West Vancouver I turned to my mother.

"What about your big garden at the old house? Did you plant anything? I've cut back this year, myself. Did you sell your house? Is it rented?"

"Your mother's house is rented. The garden is under the care of the tenants. She has too much to do here to think about those unimportant things," he answered.

"But you love to garden!" She didn't answer again and deferred to the SH. If we couldn't talk about gardening, I wondered, what would we be left with? I watched as he cut my mother's food and apportioned her a large serving of celery and rice.

"She has enough to do just keeping the house and the lawn here."

I focused again on my mother with some determination. "This must be the first meal you've ever cooked without potatoes. Grandma would roll over in her grave."

"Potatoes have poorer roughage qualities than brown rice," he answered. "Your mother has learned to eat rice." He spoke for several minutes about the history of rice without once looking at my mother.

"Yes," she finally answered, "after all those years of peeling potatoes for your father I now eat rice."

Finally, it sank in. This new marriage was all about revenge. Revenge on my father. She had taken to a completely foreign existence where she would not be required to live out her old life. She would have to work, yes. Clean, cook and provide, yes. Listen, yes. Talk—again, not too much talk. She would do exactly what she was told to do.

The Second Husband was a different sort of bully, a polite one, one who had all the answers. He wasn't as rough-hewn as my father. He was more formal, more reserved, but the infantilizing process he unleashed upon my mother was no less egregious and damaging than the marriage she had left behind. But it gave her some sort of power over the painful memory of my father—if not over her own life. She was able to belittle my father for his ignorance, berate him for his lack of social skills, his background. He may have left her for a younger woman but she now had a smarter, well-bred husband.

She would speak to my father and *tell* him all this, for they still inexplicably spoke once a month over the phone. She would tell him what she wanted him to know: she had moved up in the world, she had married a doctor. The SH was a Christian: his wife had suffered greatly and died of cancer, but they supported each other as good Christians should. They were not peasants—not pagans. She was needed here (and did more work than my father's two twenty-year-old bimbos could ever imagine). She did useful work and it was appreciated. The SH had two children (as many as my father and that meant she now, technically, had four). The life she had now was socially better than the life she had suffered with him.

Their new house was in the British Properties and her doctor had been to England and learned all the important things about being English. The Asian British were more British than Queen Victoria herself and in colonial British Columbia they were even more Anglo. The message she wanted to give to my father was that she was better-off, she was happier, more successful now than when she was with him. Something like that was the message. Her new husband had to save his delicate hands for brain surgery; he didn't fiddle around with car engines in his spare time like my father did.

The perversity of the logic of this dinner, and the ensuing pain and suffering, began to get lost on me. I could hardly focus. I was beginning to feel ill before we got to the jelly desserts. I did my best to behave for the rest of the dinner but was relieved when the taxi came and I found myself in the airport bar waiting for my delayed flight back to Toronto and the sanity of the farm. I changed into my stretch pants and an old T-shirt and trashed the pink dress in the airport lounge garbage. That was the end of that kind of pretentious nonsense for me. "Why do women do this to themselves?" I asked the bartender as I unwound my story into a gin and tonic. He had no answer.

Thank heavens the marriage was dissolved. In two months it was over and my mother was back at her house in Langley, back visiting me at the farm and my brother in Ottawa—peeling potatoes, complaining about how she was always hungry after eating rice, pottering in the garden, complaining about the immigrants.

She had also recently read about Madame Blavatsky in one of the occult magazines she subscribed to and was delighted to find Yeats on the bookshelf at the farm. She puzzled over "Sailing to Byzantium" one night with me on the porch as the bats flew around our heads and she decided Yeats was far too obscure to be understood; but table knocking and Ouija boards, real séances— now there was something we could talk about. She refused to accept that these were parlour games and regretted that I had not studied the Tarot deck in university. Perhaps I had taken all the wrong courses. Why even the SH, who studied medicine, was a great believer in messages from the other world. He was perpetually in contact with his dead wife. Perhaps that was why the marriage ended. My mother was a jealous woman.

But she took to gardening again and we discussed tomatoes and laughed about my failures. When it became clear to me that my mother was quite nutty, if not totally disturbed, the humiliations and abuse were not so deeply hurtful, though I was still not ready to introduce her to my friends. Over the many months that she came to visit with us I never introduced her to TH's parents. In fact, we worked hard to keep all our relatives from converging on the farm and creating some horrible scene I would have to relive in my head thousands of times for the rest of my life. Call it selfish, call it self-defense but there's only so much weirdness a person can put up with and I had reached my limit. Her bitterness and unhappiness were her own and my part in them was small. She would always prefer micro-cults and friends who promised to somehow be in touch with the dead, so painful was it for her to live with the walking and breathing. But I learned to live with her visits—indeed, to love her for the good that she tried to do and forgive her suffering—and, to a certain extent, enjoy our time together as long as we focused on the farm and nattering over the vegetable patch and feeding the family.

# Winter Studies and Summer Rambles

The Christmas after Claire turned five our babysitting arrangements became more complicated and between our jobs—more renovating, laundry, sick and ageing parents and mucking out the horses—the world seemed to spin out of control and I reached my level of maximum stress and incompetence. I faced stack after stack of papers, lecturing sixteen hours a week, seeing students, sitting on committees, and marking essays late into the evening. I seemed to be spending sixty hours a week just getting through the maintenance. I shared an office with a dozen other disgruntled professors who complained, like the doomed teacher in J.M. Coetzee's *Disgrace*, that students were post-everything and that teaching any text with historical or literary content was almost impossible. One teacher was using exercises from an old Grade 6 grammar book to get his remedial first-year students used to the idea that subjects and verbs had to agree. On top of that all the college teachers in Ontario were out on strike for four weeks; two of us without paychecks made my mother's suggestion that we eat the horses seem like a good one. Our overdrafts hit their limit. Unhappiness seemed to abound.

I became an obsessive list maker (for me it was an art form), a just-in-timer, who collapsed at the end of each day. I found myself in the 24-hour supermarket aisles at 11:30 pm filling a cart, weeping as I passed through the checkout. The commuting, the frustrations, the expenditure of energy had finally worn me down. Anyone who looked at me sideways I would demonize and want to spit at, and yell like my grandmother did, "Smell your own shit!" At semester's end the whole family had barely enough spirit to cut down a dismally small pine and string it with a few pathetic lights.

"It's pretty minimal," said TH, as he wrapped a few toys in newspaper and secured them with duct tape. "Gift wrapping was never my forte."

"Very postmodern."

His parents came for over-cooked turkey, mashed potatoes, stuffing; we came to call these "white" dinners, they demanded them with such seasonal regularity, such unrelenting sameness. How could something so bland become so important? There was absolutely no satisfaction in anything. I never wanted to have another Christmas. I didn't want to ever see another relative or learn more about child rearing. We had passed the terrible twos, the needy threes, the sponge-like fours and now we were into the greedy fives. It wasn't fun anymore. We seriously thought of selling the farm and moving into an apartment in Toronto.

New Year's Eve we stayed home, contemplated our madness, and made plans: one-year plans, five-year plans, ten-year plans and things we could leave for retirement. We were forced to see the arc of our lives: in for a penny, in for a pound. It was one of those ugly realizations Blake talks about that experience of the fallen world heaps upon us. Innocence would never return.

When semester started in January the English department was unsuccessfully trying to recover from the hostility of the strike and I began getting ill, one bronchial infection after another, high fevers, asthma attacks. Every time I took Claire to day care, in every class of students, there was at least one person coughing and sneezing and I carried around the same infection for months. My medicine shelf was full of antibiotics, antiasthmatics, Tylenol. Finally, one morning, up at six to take a pee, I realized I could hardly breathe. The thin whistle of air I could suck into my bronchial tubes was not reaching my lungs and I choked as I exhaled. Two of my ribs were cracked from coughing and even though I was using my inhaled steroids and a Ventolin mask the vise-like grip on my chest did not let up. My inflamed tubes were gluing shut with infection, my fingers turned blue; the ground would not stay under my feet.

"I'm taking you to emergency. Try to breathe slowly. You have to keep breathing." TH drove like a maniac down the icy run on Highway 10 after we dropped Claire at a neighbour's. In the hospital, hooked up to IVs and oxygen, the prednisone and antibiotics dripping into my veins I began to hallucinate—herds of animals were being loaded onto trains in my living room. Swarms of tourists were pulling at my handbag.

"Let that go!"

"I'm right here beside you."

"What time does our train come in? There are so many trains in this station."

"There are no trains, relax, keep breathing."

"Is the luggage here? The dog? Where is Claire?" In the tunnels, if I blinked it was morning; then again, it was night. The moon shone, the waves crashed, there were stampedes and fireworks.

"It's only the drugs."

"I'm hanging out to dry. My fingertips have clothespins on them. I'm wired to the line by my nose."

"It's only the drugs. That measures your oxygen. It's not a clothespin. Leave that alone, it's your oxygen."

"What nonsense!"

At the end of the week my lungs had cleared enough to lower the dosages, my husband came back into focus, I stopped swimming through train tunnels.

"Your body is trying to tell you something," my astute doctor noted. "You need to cut back and keep this under control."

I started to slow down. It took me three months. I tried to look forward to the pleasant things on the farm; life's cruelties, as they came, we would endure. Count the pleasures. Travelling had taught me to distrust the Canadian virtue of endurance until death. I didn't want to breathe my last on some Arctic ice floe eating the flanks of our dog. We learned to stoke the fire in winter, cuddle up with books on the couch with the best view in the world and drink wine as we watched the smoking blue snow whirl across the drifts.

Claire began numbering the noble but aggressive blue jays that came for the sunflower seeds all winter and her learning kept us going. Max, my constant companion, took up position near the stove and Alice and Lefty, the handicapped handicat and the pugnacious mouser, slept on top of him. Sweetfield became the measure of all things, my only comfort in the storm.

After some time off, teaching came into focus and I felt myself no longer on a frantic mission to save the unread; I was just in a job like any other.

I watched in sadness as the same working disease hit our friends who ended their marriages, lost their homes, betrayed their dreams and abandoned their children. I was not alone. The eighties were a field day for lawyers, accountants and analysts. What an utterly bizarre world we had created. I became convinced that our generation had succumbed to a collective depression, the natural result of our youthful optimism and unbounded desire. The farm became holy, where I retreated like Quasimodo screaming for sanctuary from the horror of the world outside.

I took to living one day at a time, not too much planning. My body realigned itself with some other rhythm of the universe, not the mad one I worked in. I spent three months talking to a psychiatrist about the forces that were driving me and she helped me start making distinctions—huge ones—between what mattered and what didn't. I knew where I was happiest, where I was needed the most. I had decided not to choke to death just yet. If I focused only on the farm, family, painting and one book at a time, surely my health and summer would return.

*The Movement of Clouds.*

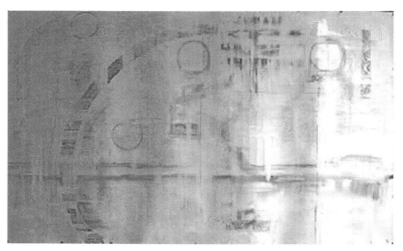

*The Spiritual Universe.*

# World of Wonders

R ebirth came for me the following year in the form of another pregnancy. Second children are always easier, people told me; my mood lifted and I found myself more relaxed, healthy and confident. I cut down on family visits and took to "holistic marking" (an educational euphemism for using generic marks sheets and just circling the most egregious errors) for my five composition classes of forty-five unprepared students. I looked forward to my advancing pregnancy. This time we would know how to handle projectile vomiting, loose bowels, diaper rash. We would limit our activities, get more sleep, and not worry so much. When Caitlin was born, another c-section over ten pounds, TH could only ask, as the surgeon let the slimy baby slip into his waiting arms, if she was okay.

"Ten fingers? Ten toes?"

"Perfect. Perfect in every way."

Claire was excited for the first few weeks, then wanted us to take the baby, miraculous though she was, back to the hospital because babies take up too much time. Her preoccupation with the horses and her new classmates in September eased the anxiety and she accepted the state of lifelong sisterhood and mild sibling rivalry. Babysitters came and went, the horses grew, work interfered with the lives we knew we wanted to lead but children, the farm, "the complete catastrophe" as Zorba the Greek called family life, made it all worthwhile. Our lives ran as smoothly as any three-ring circus could, and the kids grew up with a great sense of responsibility for themselves and their horses, Max, and the cats. The authenticity of labour in a family is something understood by children early; the value of time, the pleasure of wood fires, snow days, the satisfactions of healthy horses and the cruelty of death are life lessons best learned firsthand.

We shielded them from none of that. When Max developed a mouth cancer and had to be put down at the age of twelve we said our goodbyes, wrapped him in his blanket and buried him with his food dish. We had a full-day funeral and looked through all the pictures of him chasing groundhogs, sleeping with the cats and patiently sitting in the sandbox as the girls made castles around him. They made him a cross and a cairn from stones gathered from his favourite groundhog-hunting field. His grave, marked and visited regularly, never fails to bring tears to our eyes.

What we did want to protect our children from was endless channels of television, shopping malls, ubiquitous advertising, the soul-destroying parts of modern life. They had survived without Nintendo, with only two channels on a twenty-year-old television, and without the need to follow every fashion victim to the sales counter. There would never be a shortage of books, videos, magazines, radio and mail order forms for necessities. They both learned to travel: a sabbatical year touring in France, trips to Vancouver, Los Angeles, New York, London—but we always returned home to the farm.

When the girls did finally have to travel to Toronto for high school, neither fell into it very quickly; both expressed shock. It is not that life is without problems in the country: a boy in Caitlin's class was killed in a farm accident, nasty cliques of kids teased and belittled their churchless lives, disc players got stolen, teenagers drank too much, did drugs and drove their cars into ditches, but, to a large extent, the girls maintained their wonder, a sense of awe about the world that few city kids ever develop.

Of course it is not possible for everyone to close down their cosmopolitan lives and rush, the moment of conception, out to the countryside; however, it doesn't take much to see that the modern world has deprived childhood of its glow, lost the marvels to the banality of logos on T-shirts. Seven-year-olds boast a false sophistication, fourteen-year-olds get silicon implants. Children of friends have come to the farm and declared themselves bored after twenty minutes: no video games, no shopping.

Many children grow up afraid of the night sky, afraid of animals, afraid of walking in bush. The middle class sends their children to summer camps in Algonquin, or to the zoo, but the vast majority of young people I have taught in the east end of Toronto have little experience of the outdoors, little understanding of their role in nature. It is tremendously sad; it is a part of life not lived.

Caitlin learned to count by numbering fence posts and to multiply by figuring bales of hay stacked in the barn. She learned a love of biology from animals, about ecology from trees and ponds. I remember a teacher arguing that if a student learned a computer programming language, that should be the same credit as learning French. as if any knowledge—regardless of its cultural context, regardless of its intrinsic value, its saving grace—was equal to any other bit of information. Learning to recognize a bird is not the same as hearing one sing, watching them migrate. Country childhoods do not guarantee success or constant happiness in this world but, like the first rule of medicine, they do no harm.

*Ernie learns to ride.*

*Giant ducks on Green Cow Pond.*

# Dinner at the End of the World

With white paint finally covering every wall and the remains of the barn renovation scrap pile burnt and cleared away, we decided it was time to celebrate not only our second baby, the horses and our survival, but also the friends who had, after initial bewilderment, supported and helped us through the crucial first phase. Food is the only way to celebrate. We thought we'd start an annual summer fest and invite everyone the first Sunday in August. It would start at noon and, we hoped, end by eight; we would walk and cook and eat outdoors.

We photocopied maps and invitations and phoned all our friends, our colleagues, some of the local farmers and new folk we had met in the township.

The pig farmer down the road sold me a live forty-pounder that fouled the trunk of my car as I gracelessly dropped it off at the butcher. Slaughtered and cleaned, it was delivered to my fridge on Wednesday. Uncle Leo, by way of apology over the threatened pig farm purchase incident, sent us a belated housewarming and wedding present of twenty frozen salmon on an Air Canada flight. In blissful ignorance earlier that spring I ordered a hundred duckling eggs, read a pamphlet from the Ministry of Agriculture on *Raising Ducks the Modern Way* and, lo and behold, a few months later Green Cow pond was covered with a contented waddling flock. I had become emotionally attached to the birds over the course of feeding them and now, out of perverse farming pride, was obliged to kill and cook the birds I had so lovingly named: Peking, Orange, *Foie Gras*, *A la Moutarde*, etc. I brought a dozen or so to get plucked and cleaned at the poultry factory north of Shelburne and the rest I left for culling in September. Friends offered Caesar salads, couscous, pesto and desserts. We were set for a feast.

On Friday we drove to St Lawrence Market in Toronto and stocked up on good olive oil, olives, cheeses, fruits and more vegetables. The Italian baker in Caledon (who baked every day) set aside twenty fresh focaccia loaves that would be picked up by a friend on her way and my husband hit up the Vintages store at Queen's Quay for far too many cases of expensive wine. On Saturday morning, in preparation for the pig, we dug a pit two feet deep into a small ridge of dry sandy soil where we built a large fire of applewood and maple that burned all day. It didn't seem all that difficult to feed a hundred. Tribes had been doing it for millennia.

I salted the cavity of the pig and filled it with whole garlics, thyme, bay leaves, rosemary, sage and parsley from the garden and stuffed it with three pounds of sausage meat, five chopped onions, two handfuls of walnuts, raisins, cranberries and dry bread. I stabbed at it with a darning needle and heavy string to sew it shut. We wrapped the whole pig in four layers of heavy-duty tin foil like a Christmas present and, around nine o'clock in the evening after the bed of coals was ready, we placed the packaged pig in the fire pit on a large grill and covered the pit with a sheet of metal. At six in the morning we turned the pig over and left it on the other side till about 11:00 am. The salmon we threw on the warmish coals.

Home raised ducks are leaner than those frozen things and I precooked the birds a day in advance so most of the fat had been discarded. (It should have been saved for my mother to make soap but I recklessly threw it away. She would have died to know that we were giving all this food away instead of selling it to our friends.) On the day of the party I roasted the ducks for another half hour, rubbed them with coarse salt, five-spice powder, soy sauce, black pepper corns, brown sugar, one cup of port and the grated rind of four oranges. Basted a couple of times, the skin of the duck was sticky and crisp; however, the remains of some of the duck skin somehow ended up in the blades of my lawnmower a few days later.

We rented long tables and put sheets and tablecloths down and lifted the pig onto the center table, the salmon on one side and the ducks on platters on the other. Friends spread out the salads, breads, cheeses, etc. and were willing to follow some semblance of order set down by ancient Italian custom. I once read a Bedouin recipe in the *Manchester Guardian* for cooking a whole camel stuffed with a sheep, some chickens, and couscous—enough to feed five hundred. The camel takes two days in the desert sand but the idea is the same the world over. My aunt and uncle had been cooking salmon in sandpits for decades as the natives did before them. The trick was to plan ahead and work in well-lubricated groups. A hundred of us ate and drank for ten hours; it was a divine lunch.

Word of the dinner party spread and the following August the list grew to 150. Friends called to see if they could bring friends: teachers always know writers and actors out of work and they, too, all had hungry friends in town; half the cast of a comedy show were good buddies of a colleague; the farmers had summer help who needed to be fed; people from my past, whom I was certain had no use for me, called; Claire had play-friends who had parents. The third party got way out of hand (close to 200) as neither TH nor I had yet learned to say no; people we didn't even recognize were showing up. Summer Fest had gained some underground *potlatch* status and so our third summer was our last. The next year we went to visit friends in Muskoka that August weekend and sensibly cooked only one salmon in the sand.

After that, the dinner parties became somewhat smaller affairs, although yearly we threw something that required table rental. Sunday lunch was our *métier*, primarily because the driving home was easier for our guests and also because the hostess was always in bed at sunset. I liked to help out at other people's parties; my friend Val had been doing New Year's Eve at her house and I helped out with that cooking but it was still hard to keep my eyes open past ten. Gone were the days of dinner parties that started at eleven pm and ended at three in the morning. I was now totally on the other side of the clock and I still can't imagine doing now what seemed so simple in my twenties.

I took an Italian language class in which we did nothing but talk about food and so, in hopes of winter months of retirement in Italy blissfully translating the poetry of Eugenio Montale, I began making gnocchi and pasta with my machine while memorizing verb charts. The pastas we served with the usual grilled red peppers and local goat's cheese, recipes that are ubiquitous in these foody days. Great olive oils and imported cheeses were now in our local Shelburne stores; tarragon vinegar, cranberry, cider, sherry and balsamic vinegars were an absolute necessity, with the added bonus of learning the Italian words for things one loved to eat.

Some of the best food in the area was free or just next to free. My friend, Susie Brown, the maven of real estate in Mono and Mulmur, brought me two grouse (*brontolare*) that had blindly flown into her picture window and cracked it. They did well on the grill after hanging and marinating for a few days. My overgrown herb garden never let me down. Farmers' markets in the summer provided cheap bushel baskets of local vegetables as well as jams, chutneys, jellies and sauces with such variety we could have been anywhere in the world. The natives knew that squashes grew well here and there was always peaches-and-cream corn and, for a few dollars, we would eat our fill all fall.

There was delicious labour to be had in foraging and eating indigenously. The brilliant growth of mushrooms which overtook the floor of the back maple forest each spring had earned me a nice tab at a few of the local restaurants where the chefs were only too happy to take care of my overabundance. One morning, while walking with my friend Babette, we were forced to take off our shirts and tie the sleeves and tails together to make pouches, which we could fill with kilos of the tasty morels before the slugs got at them. Walking back to the house, half-naked carrying shirts of mushrooms, filled me with joy. The taste of gleaned sweet wild asparagus, even half a dozen, could not be matched by any green-grocer in Toronto.

My husband was an avid barbecuer, oenophile and cookbook reader and planned holidays around places where chefs were creating miracles and vineyards were perfecting new wines. He stood by his love of wood fires (no propane for him) and grilled sirloin to perfection. Armed with a great pinot noir, and Lesley Chamberlain's *The Food and Cooking of Eastern Europe*, he marinated beef while quoting from her two other books, on Nietzsche and Freud.

The one question TH perpetually asked before guests arrived was "Is there enough meat for all of us?"

"I bought almost five pounds. We're only six people."

"I like to think in terms of at least one pound per person."

"We're having three other courses!"

"Don't get all vegan on me. Next time I'm cooking more."

"Next time cook the whole bloody cow."

We ate al fresco from Easter to Thanksgiving and barbecued in our winter parkas. We mixed things that would make Brillat-Savarin roll over in his grave. Food was always improved by fresh air, your own ingredients, fine wine and a few inspired lapses in taste that are pleasing to the spirit. I had learned never to fuss too much; when you're poorest that's the best time for a largish peasant lunch.

One of my favourite ways to end a meal was with cheap boozy fruit. I used whatever was in season and slightly past its peak: strawberries, raspberries, blackberries, red currants, peaches, plums (or any combination thereof) and cut them into slices in a large bowl. With a dash of pepper, or a splash of balsamic, some sugar (depending on how sweet the fruit is) or leftover wine to sit in the fridge for a couple of hours before dinner—nothing could have been easier. I served this with custard, over dry bread or cake, with cream, polenta and even oatmeal porridge, but my favourite, by far, was Cream of Wheat made according to the package directions with a half a cup of icing sugar added. It reminded me of the porridge my grandmother used to make: cheap, filling and warm. You wanted to sleep after eating it.

There is no better gift in this world than the gift of food and companionship. No better way to celebrate the rites of passage, the season, our successes and our failures. Every parent on the planet knows the pleasure of feeding children; every child grows up remembering the dinner table. When all else is gone, memories of dinners remain.

## Green Grass, Running Water

Walking off numerous large meals led us to appreciate the geography and history of the Niagara Escarpment as well as our place in it. Across from the farm there was an entrance to the Bruce Trail that led north to the Boyne River Conservation area and south to Mono Cliffs Provincial Park. Dufferin County is called the roof of Ontario, and has several townships. Mono, pronounced MOH-nuh, incorporated in 1850, is the most southerly. There is speculation as to the origin of the name—the daughter of the Shawnee chief, Tecumseh? named for the Welsh isle of Anglesey, Mona? or, (my money's on this one) from the Gaelic word *monadh* or *monagh* meaning hilly.

I found out that our farm, bought with such ignorance, was on a wild and delicious ground, a ridge where the Niagara Escarpment tumbles, like a line of falling dominos, from the far tip of Tobermory on Lake Huron through Wiarton, Creemore, Mono Mills to Cataract, Terra Cotta and Georgetown. Lengths of jagged cliffs run past Lake Ontario to Niagara Falls dividing the southern part of the province into rivers flowing east and rivers flowing west. The high wetlands give rise to the Nottawasaga, Boyne, Pine, Noisy, Pretty and Mad Rivers, which plunge downward into the waters of Lake Huron, Georgian Bay and Lake Ontario.

The rocks contain a record which can be read back to Paleozoic times: ancient trilobites, molluscs and corals reveal themselves in loose croppings, raised outliers, in kettles and the rocky rows broken by the farmer's plow. We could walk from the bluffs of the proglacial Lake Iroquois waterline through Rock Chapel Park and the Royal Botanical Gardens into quarries and caves, past Rattlesnake Point, through the Badlands of Queenston Shale, the Hockley Valley, and the Violet Hill Meltwater Channel, up to Craigleith Provincial Park over the ridges of Blue Mountain and into Bruce's Caves, resting at the Slough of Despond, the north shore of Devil's Monument or at the beach at Lion's Head.

Along drifts, past sinkholes, over meanders and misfits, the 800 kilometers of the Bruce Trail curved through farmers' fields, around grazing horses and protected parks and dropped the walker into areas of incredible beauty. These unexpected places inspired twists in the cranium. The curious could follow wolf prints in winter snow or rest and admire the wild orchids of summer, and emerge restored where natives, traders, settlers, gypsies, fugitives and freedom seekers once ventured—herons, geese and hawks overhead, snakes, voles and rabbits sharing ground.

I had reached a point in my life when my own history seemed of less interest to me and I became curious to find out about the people who used to share this landscape. The first peoples here were the Petun, followed by the Hurons, the Ojibwa and the Iroquois; there are still traces of Chippawa encampments and unexplored sites and histories that are being researched in Native Studies departments throughout Ontario. The Europeans, when they started immigrating, were rigorous record keepers. One such man, an Irishman, Michael McLaughlin from County Tyrone, settled here in 1819. In 1820 the Surveyor General of Upper Canada ordered the land surveyed by Samuel and Ezykiel Benson. Many of these records reside in the local County Archives and when out walking I can still find markings, often just cedar stakes in the ground or blazes on a tree, that were left by surveyors not so very long ago. Walkers find many of these roads remain incomplete and dead end near the cliffs or in the middle of marshy ponds. Straight lines on paper rarely translate in the landscape. But this land was viable for farming and the Northern Irish, the Lowland Scots and a few English were frantically buying good land from the Crown, from surveyors and speculators, and marking that land with their labours and their conviction. Sweetfield was one such farm.

The Protestant and the Catholic farmers continued their old world feuding across the town lines of Dufferin. In 1866 the Protestants mounted an armed battalion of over 400 men and prepared to rebuff a Fenian raid that existed only in their fevered imaginations. For years there was the fear that the Popish bullies would come and steal women, cattle and grain. The Orange Lodge, loyal to monarchy and the Protestant church, still marched in Dufferin as recently as July 12th, 1962, to celebrate the Battle of the Boyne. The parade of marchers was three miles long with 91 lodges represented. To the local schoolchildren the Boyne River, site of some of the best fishing holes in the county, seemed an unlikely setting for a battle. We loved to name things in Ontario after homelands in Europe but we don't teach the same European history here. Nor should we. Most of the kids were totally mystified by the confusing marching rituals and when their grandparents died so did the parading, and one hopes those animosities will never be rekindled.

Our serendipitous purchase had led us right into the heart of a bizarre set of stories, imported and locally bred: a history that included a set of mastodon bones recovered from a farmer's field and subsequently stolen (the subject of a novel, *Perpetual Motion*, by Graeme Gibson); missing (or were they kidnapped?) children turned native; tales of ghosts and leprechauns, frozen corpses and ghoulish wakes; ferocious churchmen and pious housewives; gypsies and temperance wars. Many of these events were commemorated in the names of places such as Temperance Creek. TH and I privately named other places Incest Corner and Axe Murder Cross Roads and Burn Your House Down Hill when we heard the tales the farmers told, but these place names never made it onto the local maps. It still shocked me how narrow-minded, vicious and unforgiving people could be after generations of working the land. Tales of farmers burning out their neighbours, castrating prize bulls, stealing livestock, electrocuting horses and poisoning wells were not uncommon. Alice Munro, an Ontario neighbour of sorts, tells stories of just such families. Farming destroys more than the body, it often twists the soul and we had been fortunate to find a few friends who had managed to turn agriculture and horse breeding into a relatively happy and untainted life.

Schoolchildren all began genealogy projects if their parents had been here more than two generations and the local historians were hard at work recovering stories from early newspaper accounts, now that finding missing relatives had hit such a fevered pitch. Archeologists were going over bones in unmarked graves trying to piece together oral history and fact. These were all spun into tales that residents loved to retell, that the local newspapers reprinted, if in somewhat revised forms.

Walking the trails from the source of the Humber River to the Boyne Conservation Area we found wooden markers and plaques, gravestones that commemorated four deaths from pneumonia in the same month a hundred years before. Every pathway ended beside a church, rebuilt to house weekenders, its congregation now composed of mountain bike clubs, horse riders and hikers. Now photographers, painters and sketchers line themselves up along ridges overlooking McCarston's Lake or along a cliff edge, the landscape inviting the viewer in for a better glance at history, a moment to better understand themselves.

Walking in landscapes relatively free of development has a peculiar effect on many people. Given who we have become, many find it strange to walk in the bush or even on grass if their whole lives have been spent on concrete. One friend was terrified of being bitten on the ankles.

"By what?" I asked.

"By snakes, insects and small animals, of course! I can't walk on the grass. That is why there are signs everywhere downtown. Don't walk on the grass!"

It was hopeless to explain anything and in the end I rode her around on the back of my tractor, assuring her that nothing would jump up and bite. She refused to accept the notion that these animals were more afraid of noisy us and only the most silent and stealthy of naturalists could watch them with any luck. Afterwards we met only in restaurants.

We had two great friends, Heather and Rupert, expat Canadians (there were over 300,000 in Los Angeles) who worked in the film industry. They were regular visitors and on one occasion they brought a cameraman who was working on a project with them. He had never been to Canada, never been much outside of Hollywood for that matter. Our farm had an unnerving effect on him. During lunch he kept looking out the window and reframing things with his fingers forming a square, the way that everyone who tries to capture images does. The activity got more and more manic as we walked after lunch and within twenty minutes he was frantic. He made his mystical finger signs over the cows in the far field, over the dog jumping the fence line, over the horses as they grazed, over the pigeons as they flew out of the barn, over Claire picking up stones. Every glance became a frame, every moving object a story.

Finally, he began gesticulating wildly. "This is all *real*," he would shout. "Every fucking inch of this is *real*. Look at that forest! *Real!* Look at that hawk! *Real!* Jesus Christ, it's all *REAL!*"

We finally bundled him up with a cup of tea before it was necessary to call the Clarke Institute and Heather and Rupert headed with him back to the airport. I'm sure he never wanted to come back to Canada again. Just too damn real.

Our area had become a haven for New Age clinics, holistic therapy centres, Tai Chi retreats and businesses that exploited our need for nature. Walking meditations had become life-saving for city people and the Bruce Trail Club was now so large you never met the same folk twice on hiking days. It costs some people a small fortune to dress for weekends, to take the certificate course in flora and fauna, to buy the interpretation guides and maps and book the time. I preferred to wander until I was lost and able to breathe in very deeply, without instruction.

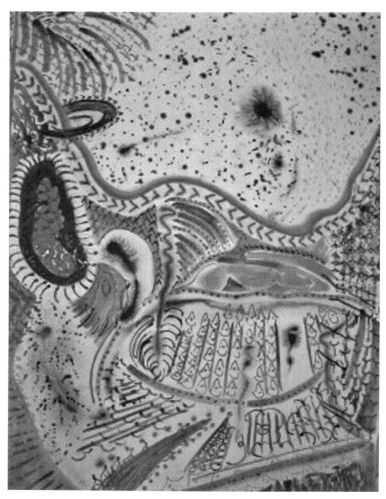

*Landscape changing.*

## Not Wanted On The Voyage

Barry Trivet's hatred of city folk was taking a toll on his family. He knew that but there didn't seem to be any way he could bottle up his feelings. Every time some new city banker or accountant or professor bought a local farm Barry lost the friend who had previously owned it and he felt a part of himself being ripped away by every moving van that went further north. And, with each farmer that left, he lost some part of his power, his position, in the community. The old timers called him the unofficial mayor and his good wife, Charity, sewed a pillow sampler with "Mono's Unofficial Mayor" embroidered in red and gold and he kept it under his feet whenever they watched television late at night. He resented the fact that the farmers had to move when they saw more money in bank interest than they could ever earn in farming and he resented the fact that the new folk all had jobs and money and fancy trucks and some damned city attitude that they could live the country lives they wanted to live. And his anger blossomed in every member of his family.

"We can't live how we want to now," he told his wife, who nodded her head in Presbyterian agreement. "They just don't understand how it was. They don't understand all the hard work raising five kids. You can't just up and plant perfectly good fields into trees. Farmin' ain't a hobby!" He jabbed the beans in his bowl. "They don't even keep their fences straight 'cause they ain't got no cattle."

"After my family spent generations building cedar fences and clearing fields and blowin' up the stumps to get a crop into the ground these people move in who ain't even farmers! Something has to be done." She could tell by her husband's brow that he was thinking about what to do—about fixing it so that real people didn't have to move and so that city folk wouldn't take over the farms for "no damn good purpose." It was all he talked about over their boiled dinner and bowl of jelly. It was all he talked about as he watched television and all he dreamt about in fitful sleep. "Those damned city folk."

He made plans to deal with them. He tried every day to think of some new tactic to thwart their obvious pleasure in the hills and valleys in Mono. He reported them to the fence viewer and insisted that all the neighbours build good cattle fences whether they had cattle or not. That was good for a few years until the bloody council was taken over by city folk and the fence law changed so that farmers had to fence their cattle in and city folk did not have to fence them out. That really got under his skin. Not only did he and his family have to birth and breed and castrate their stock but now they had to pay for all the fencing as well. It just didn't seem fair to him, not fair to him and not fair to his family and not fair to his wife whose family had worked hard all their lives. "Been here a century! It's just not fair."

It got further into his worn fingernails that the bloody bankers were eligible for farm tax rebates even though they didn't farm the land. Whenever he could, he reported his neighbours to the investigations office at Revenue Canada and gave them all the information he could about what was wrong with the government, what was wrong with the tax laws and what was wrong with his neighbours. All his suspicions he built into major infractions.

It galled him that agricultural land owned by a movie director qualified as farmland just because he had a few longhaired Highland cattle to show off at the Royal Winter Fair. "It's not bloody farmland if it's not owned by a farmer!" He would curse at the civil servants who would quote him chapter and verse that farmland was farmland even if it was owned by a non-farmer. "It's a bloody hobby, not a farm! They don't even live here full-time!" Ratepayers were ratepayers even if they only lived there on the weekends he was told. He called the Ontario Federation of Agriculture and complained about his new neighbours, he called the town and complained about their barns and their house extensions and their plans for swimming pools and saunas. He called the Niagara Escarpment Commission even though he hated the idea that some other provincial body could dictate how things were going to be in his part of the world.

As his vituperation grew too much for his frame he passed it down to his children who also grew up hating city folk and their children. When the lot on the corner was sold to a real estate agent he fought her development permit all the way to the Ontario Municipal Board, so angry was he that a perfectly good field could be turned into a two-storey ranch home. "It should all stay in crops and it should stay in families not in corporations." He could hardly listen to the news or deal with the stories in the local newspaper about artists and breweries and golf courses taking over his land. He saw it as his land—not that he owned it all—but because he had farmed it and that gave him the right to make decisions about how it was going to be used.

Charity had taught at the one-room school when it existed before the city folk had started demanding larger and larger buildings with gyms and cafeterias and bus drivers and even French classes! She left her teaching then, when the younger women came up from Toronto to take over the schools, and soon all manner and colour of children were mixing with their own. In spite of the fact that he taught them that the Trivets had opened up this land and given its soil the first turning, the young Trivets were being left behind in school. They were not given any special treatment, except on show-and-tell days when they would bring in the first deeds for Crown Land that had ever been issued in Dufferin

County. They could not handle the French and the new curriculum which, given no respect at home, earned no place in the heart of the youngest child who declared, when her elder brothers dropped out of school: "Me too! I'm not going to school with any of these kids. I hate them and they hate me!"

The children were regularly taken out of school for spring haying time, and again in the fall for baling straw. Over the winter they missed the school bus when the cattle had to be fed and in May, when calving began, they didn't make their exams. When confronted by the principal about the children's absences all the Trivets announced they would keep their children from school as long as drug dealers from the city kept bringing marijuana into Shelburne. The town was going to ruin with every new house that was built and every new resident from the south bringing in all manner of stupid ideas.

"Don't worry about it. We still own more land than the rest of them. They may close our little school but they can never take away the land, and they can never take away the bones of your grandfather from the cemetery," Chastity told her grandchildren and attempted, as best she could, to home school them and prepare them for correspondence exams.

"It's the city folk!" Barry Trivet scolded the young teachers when he went to pick up the last of his seven grandchildren from the school. His three eldest boys had moved away and there was only one left now, with his sickly wife and all her children, to take over the land and keep the proud name of Trivet on the town tax rolls.

"How can they make a living? How can they put food on the table with the price that cattle are fetching? Every day I take my tractor down the drive is a day I lose money," Trivet whined to his wife. "What kind of pay can they get for plowin' and seedin'? The only good crop these days is a square bale of hay that gets sold for three times what it's worth to some city guy with horses who don't know any better. You can't even eat the damn horses and you certainly can't graze the golf courses."

So, instead, he continued reporting everyone he could for real or imagined breaches of codes that were no longer on the law books. He threatened the city folk with closing their lanes and plowing them full of snow in the winter until some young punk opened up a snow plowing, pool and grass cutting business and no one even asked him to clear driveways any more. No one asked for his bulldozer and no one called for his advice. No one consulted him before they tore down a barn or put in a new septic bed. No one.

His son took to boarding horses and raising dogs and looking after farms when people took their vacations. "It's a humiliation," he told his wife, "a humiliation! When farming is a noble profession the kids have to take anything they can get to carry on."

There were more small skirmishes in the town council chambers when folks moved in and skirmishes when he had to apply for building permits to move his own driveway. That was another blow to him. "I built these roads, I built these houses and barns and now some stupid lawyer tells me I have to apply to council for a permit on my own land! On my own land!"

It drove him mad and he took it out on the children and grandchildren who all eventually decided to sell up as their neighbours had done. One by one his children sold off the land he had given them, sold off their birthrights, and it galled him and it turned Charity to frequent bouts of tears and long days of writing letters to dead relatives. She stuffed the jars by their gravesites with sad tales of how the good old days had gone, how family values were left by the wayside and now even the old church was sold off and turned into a day care. Some days she would find in the paper some long-time-ago friend had died in the Dufferin Oaks Seniors' Home and she would go to the funeral and mourn for far more than the death of a member of the Women's Institute. The 4H Club had so few members it hardly seemed worth running anymore and there was no way she could convince the teachers, in spite of her frequent visits to the schools, that a greater part of the curriculum had to be devoted to practical country skills. All the kids wanted were more robots for the computer club. "Good learning time was being wasted and things should get back to basics."

"We can't do that, Mrs Trivet. We have to follow the Ministry guidelines. We have to teach all the courses kids would get anywhere in the province. There's no time left in the curriculum for much else." And so she watched as farm skills were reduced to a once-a-year visit to the Dufferin County Museum and Archives, where spinning and weaving and knitting were mere tourist attractions. And she began to curse, as her husband did, the changes she could do little to stop.

The same week his grandson was arrested for drug trafficking, Charity had a small stroke and Barry had to leave her in the hospital for observation. A few people came to visit and there were some flowers but he felt he had come to the end of his line. His son would carry on as best he could with the cobbled-together jobs but he would leave him something. They would both die, Barry knew that: both he and Charity would lie down beside their grandparents and parents in the Shelburne Cemetery and few people would come and leave letters in the flower jars by their graves. No one would have anything to say. It had all been said so many times before.

The suite they were given in Dufferin Oaks had a plaque put on the door: CENTURY FARMERS 'Barry and Charity Trivet', and listed in print too tiny to read their genealogical charts and a little map of their part of Dufferin County. The money from the sale of the land, over two million dollars, went to the son and his sickly wife and their remaining children and they stayed on, as best they could, to keep the family name on the tax rolls of Mono.

*A fragile household.*

# Who Has Seen the Wind?

The symphony of wind through forests, the *shrrrr* of leaves and needles, makes air visible. If you can't fall asleep to the sound of rushing water or the lick and slap of your partner's finger on the page of his favourite fiction then wind is the next best soporific and fresh pine a divine aroma. The need for deep sleep takes precedence over much else in our lives and the habitat at the back of our farm offered a possible site for a tranquilizing forest plantation. What had once been a natural migrating corridor was now rocky pasture and we wanted to return it to the wild and to the calming wind. We contacted the Ministry of Natural Resources to enlist in the tree planting program.

Much of Mono Township, like other areas settled in Canada, had been clearcut to make way for crops; even hilly, almost inaccessible ridges had been cleared for grasses and cattle grazing. House building, cooking and heating consumed a lot of trees and many of the old farmers couldn't see the point of replanting when the open space could be used for pasture.

When the forester arrived to examine the soil and drainage in the back thirty acres she brought with her aerial photographs of our area and the plan for the Niagara Escarpment. At the time our biosphere had not yet been declared a preserve and there was much to be done to reforest, conserve and enhance.

There was a seven-acre marsh on the southeast corner of the farm (that wonderful word 'swale') that provided nesting for several species of warblers, ducks, red-winged blackbirds, herons, bobolinks and geese. There were snapping turtles, salamanders, frogs and toads as well as butterflies, dragonflies and dozens of species of small animals. Dogwood, sassafras, wild blueberries, pond lilies, gooseberries, thorns, nettles, primroses, buttercups, wild orchids and strawberries were evident every spring. Ferns (ostrich, hart's tongue, smooth cliffbrake, green spleenwort), mint, chamomile, cattails, dandelions, mosses and over four hundred species of other delicate plants surrounded the marsh.

Such splendid wetlands had often been drained for pasture but no amount of previous trenching had been able to redirect the robust flow of underground water that welled up and headed into Sheldon Creek. In wet years (more than 850 mm of rain) it was a large pond and in drought seasons it shrank to a couple of acres. We wanted to keep the swale as clean and biologically diverse as possible. We deepened two sections of the pond by bringing in a back hoe and building an ice bridge over the swamp in February and then cut a narrow trail along the upper ridge for access to the maple wood lot, but the rest had to be inaccessible to all but the eye if the nesting birds were to thrive.

The rocky twenty acres to the north, grazed bare by generations of cattle, we wanted to return to forest and so we ordered 6,000 red and 1,000 white pine, and a few hundred white ash. We called it Claire's forest. The Natural Resources crew arrived and in two days the tractor plowed the trenches and seedlings were dropped into the soil. We left an access road between the furrows so that in twenty-five years we could thin the plantation. For a few pennies a tree and very little labour we had planted a link from Mono Cliffs park to the Boyne Conservation reserve. The pathway between the trees was full of milkweed and we soon named it Butterfly Alley for the monarchs migrating from Mexico. For the first few years they came in the hundreds but, unfortunately, the number declined. The devastation of the Mexican forests, the breeding ground for the monarchs, was a disaster. Wanting some of nature's original songline, we persevered with our planting of forests.

The second plantation of 4,500 trees we called Caitlin's forest. We planted rows of tamaracks, European larch, red oak, poplar, spruce, red and more white pines. These were planted (some by hand) in loopy circles around the front pond and over the sandy eroding hill to the north leaving narrow access trails. Always on guard against encroaching civilization we were now completely surrounded by a wall of trees. We lived in total privacy, in a sanctuary for wild turkeys, foxes, coyotes, rabbits and us.

The paths through the plantations became natural routes to follow on foot and on horseback and so I invested in my first riding tractor. Keeping the grass down around the new trees was important to ensure healthy growth and a path served to remind the groundhogs that they shouldn't dig burrows where the horses galloped. The weekly summer ritual of clearing the trails, checking for damage, moulds and tent caterpillars became part of my routine. Early mornings, while the rest of the house was still asleep, I would get away on my tractor and spend an hour with the birds while meandering along the trails with my machete and clippers, neatly storing good kindling in my wagon. I trimmed back the beech and clipped the thorn trees high enough to avoid the heads of trotting horses. For our tenth wedding anniversary my husband bought me a chain saw and a logger's hard hat (no diamonds from him) and I would daily retire to the delightful refuge of my gardening equipment shed where I planned out my garden. From the shed and the kitchen much goodness and contentment sprang. For Christmases there were shovels and hayforks under the tree, hoes and wheelbarrows "For MOMMY!" For another birthday I got a new set of binoculars. Now I was fully equipped to look after the forests. As the trees grew and the soil changed, grouse came to nest and a flock of wild turkeys made home there; the more we cultivated and managed the wild, the more wonders it produced.

When old trees came down in the storms, trunks six feet around, we dragged them by tractor to where they would form a good cross-country jump. Brush we cleared to towering burn piles. I developed a bird's eye view of the farm, imagining where all the necessary parts of this Eden we were creating would fit. I was reading Diane Ackerman's poems about pilots ("silvery jet blades slicing the day open like the carcass of a wide blue animal"), horses ("their tails held high in long division signs"), birds ("tiny beak, when it bit, focused the whole of her feathered dream onto one sharp point") and her lines recurred to me as I worked with "running water and the blossom urge". After days like this, like Ackerman's pilot, my head felt fresh, "like an abacus cleared after a large sum".

We needed the barn and paddocks renovated and some pasture, hay fields and grain. I imagined a water jump, a toboggan hill that would double in the summer as a bank jump, some open meadow gallop tracks, a sandy dressage arena, and a grassed stadium jumping area. When horse friends came to dinner we would walk and fantasize about hedge jumps, rock walls, devil's dikes and leech ponds. Every time I hiked along the Bruce Trail, or walked through local farms I imagined herds of contented athletic horses testing their mettle and the courage of their young riders throughout the Township. It was bizarre, in that I was not a rider myself, how much pleasure I derived from providing that possibility for others. I thought of myself as a savage gardener, a tender of the wild rather than a refined horticulturalist, and every wild garden needs animals to animate it, give it a purpose beyond our own aesthetic satisfactions, and our few horses filled that prescription. As the gardens, forest, and children grew, so did our involvement with building places for horses.

*The big barn.*

## As For Me And My House

Breeding horses rooted us even deeper into the land and I decided I had to get the history of the place straight in my head. I had a lot of questions unanswered. At the Dufferin County Museum and Archives I combed through the files and tracked down the story of our house. The land had been bought from the Crown by a Walter Scott in 1871, one of the many branches of the Scott clan that claimed relationship with the Scotts of Buccleuch dating to 1130. This branch included *Sir* Walter Scott, the novelist, and the old timers around here still refer to our farm as 'the Scott place'. There were other Scotts from Lincolnshire, Scotts north in Proton Township, Scotts to the south, but the complications of his family tree (he was one of twelve children) were more than my feeble mind could handle.

Our Walter Scott was a stonemason (he and his relatives had a hand in building Mitchell's Church and the church at Relessey nearby) and he apparently started to dig the cellar in 1874, and a good six-foot deep, three-foot thick concreted field stone cellar it is. I repointed the stones and replaced the old wooden stairs with concrete but, other than that, it was as he built it. His wife obviously had her root cellar down there and I grew a fine bunch of mushrooms below ground until I decided I didn't want the scent of horse manure wafting up from the basement anymore.

Finally, it was quite civilized, with a new furnace and hot water tank, reverse osmosis water system and electrical service. Old Walter would have approved but probably not his wife who needed the cold cellar for her vegetables and preserves. Good stonework is hard to beat and the walls were a joy to whitewash every few years. He obviously had some help building the rest of the house and the barn as several houses went up on this line in the same Victorian Gothic style very quickly.

The Buchanans and the Halberts, the Montgomerys, the Avisons, the Summerfields, the Thompsons and the Forseyths were all neighbours, and community development and barn bees were the norm. William Dynes, who once lived south of the Granger schoolhouse a few doors away, was our first Member of Provincial Parliament as well as being the postmaster and organizer of the first Farmer's Party. The once busy corner, known as Granger, was marked by a reconstructed Catholic Cemetery but the main church and post office were, sadly, no longer.

The work of the first area settlers in Turnbull Settlement (now called Mono Centre) was dutifully recorded by Jean Turnbull (5th generation) in her notes and her chapbook *Still Burns the Flame*. Lists of the congregation and the hearty women of the auxiliary of Burns Presbyterian Church in the heart of that hamlet, and the energy they devoted to developing their church, cemetery and community, was reading I avidly consumed.

The records were full of stories about Scottish and Irish immigrant farmers who made their way to Mono Township: the Lundys, the Pattersons, the Larges and the Laidlaws amongst others. One such family, the Turnbull ancestors, John and Martha, had run a market garden in Brooklyn, New York, when an outbreak of yellow fever began to kill a number of children in the area. They decided that living in a homestead with good water would become one of their priorities. Memories of cholera in the old country were too fresh in their minds and the relentless daily funerals in Brooklyn finally drove them out. Still others came along old Loyalist routes, via Montreal and Halifax to York, then up the road to Mono Mills, carrying children on their shoulders and a few provisions and tools in ox-driven carts and horse drawn carriages. A few were military men and their families: William Glover, John McQuilkin and Noble Wright were granted land after the Battle of Waterloo for good service. In Muddy York the settlers found the papers full of tales from the traders and surveyors of some "new land" which was being explored north of Lake Ontario and South of Lake Huron. The elevation of the land promised a long frost-free growing season and the combined appeal of water and sun brought many settlers. Crown grants were given in 100-acre parcels. The maps at the time show very little except a vague boundary around an area called the Home District. The surveyors had noted the rocks, forests, and excellent springs in the area and many immigrants decided that Mono was where they would take their families.

There were no roads and the only way in was by horse and cutter during the winter when the rivers, lakes and marshes were frozen. A house would have to be built; others from their home churches would have to be encouraged, by glowing letters, to join them in the wilderness. The first few pioneering families went ahead to open the land, set up the church, start a school and organize the Mono Agricultural Society. Anyone who farmed in this Township in the 19th century deserved honourable membership in the archives for bravery alone.

Some of the sketchy stories of these early farmers, and especially the lives of the Scotts who constructed the house in which I worked, ran around in my head and, as I fought blizzards to the grocery store or cleaned the mudroom or parged the barn walls, I wondered about their lives. Roasting a turkey or relining a horse blanket reminded me of those men and women whose labours inhabited the nooks and crannies around every stone. They were people I wish I'd known and I quickly took to living with their ghosts.

## Left Hand Right Hand

The first thing that made Martha angry that stormy December morning in 1848 was not the ferocious weather or the rudeness of the locator, Mr Raven, whose vague directions annoyed her, but it was the fact that John had not bargained hard enough with the horse dealer over the price of the cutter and the team. In Scotland no one paid two years' wages for a horse but here in the outpost it seemed that they could ask whatever earthly figure they could imagine for four-legged transportation. Three hundred dollars for the pair—why all the land was barely more than that! Thieves and scoundrels all! The sooner the cabin was built and she didn't need to depend on the honesty of others, the better off they would be. Never again would she loosen the pouch tied to her skirts to feed another man's greed and drinking habit. These horses would do forever, or at least until they could start breeding their own.

"We will be leaving this morning," she announced to John before the light broke through the windows of the Settler's Inn south of the Credit River. "And we'll not be coming back for the cow tomorrow. We'll drive her in with us today."

The husband's ears were sliced open by his wife's demands though he could barely see her in the darkness of the chilly room.

"The Irishman, drunk in the next room, carousing till early morning and knocking over tables in the most aggravating fashion is now snoring so loudly the walls shake! How on earth were the children supposed to sleep? And those two surveyors whose muddy chains and boots had been left in the hall for all and sundry to trip over as they entered the filthy dining room—where were those men raised? The bread is so hard we're lucky we didn't break our teeth—the victuals so ill prepared I had to mash everything before the children could get it down. Not one more day John, not one more day! I have pots of my own for cooking my oatmeal and a flint for my fire."

Her husband rarely responded to her conversations with more than a grunt so accustomed was he to her scolding.

Her children, descending from ten-year-old Young John, to Thomas, through Jane and Alexander to the baby, Martha, had barely slept and she had difficulty waking them now.

"I'll not be keeping the children in this establishment for one more night, my good husband. We will be at the homestead by evening or we shall take these babes back to Brooklyn in the morning to die of the fever. Now get out there and make sure that locator has roused himself from his stupor to guide us in, or I'll be there to twist his socks onto his toes myself in the next hour."

Martha, her thick eyebrows and jowls dancing to the tune of her anger, met no resistance in him and he set out to fetch the locator who had been sleeping at the surveyor's hut. His promise had been that the land by the rocks was no more than four hours through the bush but the wind was high and John was not certain how much headway the horses would make if the blizzard grew stronger at the top of the hill. Carrying the full load presented dangers to both the horses and the children. Nevertheless, he knew there would be no more resting in this inn of ill repute for his determined wife.

"I shall finish the tying on in the shed when the children are dressed and the victuals are prepared. Don't be longer than an hour readying that cow, John, or I shall truly be turning back to the south."

The children were anxious and excited, full of apprehension about the cutter journey and tales of the Indians they would have to barter with, as the sled had barely enough room for the necessities beyond the first few days. John would have to make many trips to the stores, many trips to mills and suppliers before they would be settled, but the most trying of the journeys was surely the first, bearing as they were all of the children, hay for the animals and their provisions. When the road would open—that is, when there were enough men in the area to construct a road—John had promised to build a larger trap or a boxed carriage with room to bring in the furniture they had left behind in Brooklyn. That would have to wait many years until the cabin was built and he could not waste time worrying about that, for this day's journey made pressing demands.

The only piece of furniture that was to come today was the table. Martha said she could do without beds and chairs but she could not function without her table. Yesterday they had reset it on the back of the cutter, upending it and tying the legs securely to the top iron of the runners. Under the table Martha had meticulously packed a few dishes, her boiling pots, a large copper kettle, padding those with hay to prevent any breakage—hay that would be fed to the horses when they arrived. The shovels, rakes, hoes, scythe and axe she had bound to the side of the table legs as well as a few knives and other implements for trading. The few blacksmith tools had gone in with the saws and cutlery and if these two fine horses her husband had bought dared to slip a shoe on the journey there would be much untying to get to the cache of nails and hammers. There was not an inch to spare under the table. The blankets, clothing, seed baskets, water jugs and four tins of pipe tobacco were braced inside the table and covered with a simple mattress and canvas tarpaulin. The children would ride tucked between the legs of the table out of the wind, the eldest on the sides and Alec and Martha, the baby, within their legs.

The packing and loading of these bare necessities had taken her most of the previous day and it was with some fear that Thomas, yelling and jumping about, joined the others in the cutter.

"Hush your mouth! Listen to your mother." She would drive the team following the locator, and John would snowshoe behind, leading the cow the four hour trek into the bush—but at a pace only as quick as the poor beast could manage.

When he returned with the locator, all the horrors of drink and sloth the Presbyterian minister in York had warned her were rampant in the new home county seemed wrapped up in the narrow yellowed pallor and twisted lean frame of their guide. How God had sent one of his most pathetic creatures to take her and the family into the wilderness was a trial she would address with him in the next world. Surely goodness and mercy were hers in the afterlife for they were not to be found on this Ontario morning. She touched the Bible she had tucked next to her bag and remembered the injunctions in the sermon "Hard Work Wins Progress" the minister had delivered weeks before.

"There'll be no problem, you can rest assured. I've ridden the trail many a time and I'm sure I know your marker if it is the one by the spring at the rock where you say," Mr Raven assured them. His old horse seemed too knock-kneed and sway-backed to carry even the small bag of meat and bones he called his master let alone the chains and markers, axe, bow saw, rifle, ropes, water, and food the locator so carelessly flung over the beast. "I'll be back before nightfall and you will all be safe in the lean-to before the sun goes down."

"God willing, sir, God willing." John looked up at the overcast sky, and prayed to the small patch of blue. He consulted once again the map he had been given with the Location Ticket and hoped that the terrain bore some resemblance to his memory of it of two summers ago. Even now, in the deep of winter, he was certain the spring would be flowing out of the escarpment rock.

"We will be there by afternoon," Martha told the children. "Now, not one wee peep out of the lot of you till we're safe in the shelter. No one eats from the lunch box until I say and, Thomas, you hold tight to little Martha so the poor bairn catches no chill on this heinous windy path. We'll be too busy building to take to nursing sick ones when we get to our land." The instruction from the ministers not to attach your spirit too strongly to children who might well die on the journey stuck in her bonnet. The children sat hunched between the legs of the table, unwilling to cross either parent's will at this moment in life. They had been to the outhouse and hoped their stomachs were up to their mother's wishes and the jostling of the cutter. So much had been said about this journey, so much food and good water and game awaited them that their fussing could wait. John, the eldest, the inheritor of his mother's brow, kept a steady eye on his siblings. He watched as his father brought the cow from the stable, his mother whipped the horses on and the guide jerked his mare down the road. The runners were smooth, gliding quickly over the well-worn frozen snow close to the inn.

Martha wrapped and tied her muffler one more time over her face once the horses were off at a good clip and she could manage the reins with her left hand. She glanced back briefly at her brood and headed after the locator, straight into the wind. At the top of the hill the sweat on the horses began to freeze and she pushed them into a quicker trot to keep them warm. "Move up there! Mr Raven, get her moving! I'm not keeping these children in the wind, freezing their faces for longer than promised." The locator kicked at his mare.

John ran behind with the cow, pulling the beast and lashing her on with a birch. When they reached some treed shelter at the end of the frozen marsh Martha would allow the children to eat and her husband to catch up. The cutter trail was clear enough for him to follow.

For three hours they travelled against the wind between stands of cedars and around boulders that scraped the runners, due north, until finally, at the end of a high ridge, they turned along a never used route, marked only by a blaze on a tree, and headed eastward. Martha watched as the northern sky cleared and patches of brilliant sun reflected from the snowdrifts. The crows and jays cried out from the tree branches. At the top of the ridge she looked back and saw her husband at the bottom of the valley, an hour behind them, whipping at the stubborn cow but in no danger of getting lost.

The locator had stopped to sip from his flask and comment on some bear tracks but Martha frowned at him. Bear tales would worry the children and his flask should be hidden away. As long as he got them there what would she care what drunken state he was in on his return journey? If he did not sin, she reminded herself, he would not repent, and without repentance there could be no salvation. Temperance meetings would be on her list as soon as the cabin walls were raised and she found a good neighbour's wife willing to enlist in God's work with her. She paused and checked on the children as the horses caught their breaths after the last heavy rise.

"Wee John, give each of the little ones a piece of bread and salt meat to chew on and some milk from that jug at Thomas' feet. Chew the bread before you put it into Martha's mouth. Dip it in the milk if it hasn't froze." The children ate hungrily. "Eat slowly and thank the Lord for his blessings, then put your mittens back on. We've another hour at least to travel."

The horses clipped over a shallow frozen creek, the cutter cracking the ice as they slid onward. John's feet would surely be wet she thought but it will keep him moving for the dry boots and woolen socks in her possession. The locator waved his arm, indicating a short journey further and to the right. Martha gazed across the horizon; the thick forest of elms, the sturdy maples, beech and pine were plentiful beyond the imaginings of the normal Scotswoman. Never had she seen such fine timbers, such straight and sturdy beams for construction, so much loose limestone and rock for building. The cedars would make good roads, and there was much dead wood for cooking and heat.

In due time, after the lean-to was built for the night, after her locator was back on the trail, after her husband arrived with the cow, she would give thanks to her Maker and the Maker of all this wilderness; she felt a kinship for the stone she hurried her horses over and never had her eyes seen such opportunity.

One year later, when the cabin was built and she had taken to schooling the children (there was little time for childhood games) Martha found herself pregnant again, the first Scottish child delivered in the town of Mono. She gave birth, unaided, in the early morning and the same day a tree, with a twisted and heavily knotted trunk, had been felled too close to the cabin and landed on the roof. Part of the cabin collapsed and John was near the end of his wits with the labour. They had heard from a travelling seller that some Ulstermen had gone south or even back to Ireland, finding the heartbreaking conditions beyond their constitutions. John, depressed by the errant tree, thought perhaps it was too much for the tiny baby to survive more wind but Martha, a true Scot, would have none of it. She grabbed the axe and began to chop away at the offending limbs the moment the newborn fell asleep. There would have to be more shakes cut for the roof and the cabin to be repaired; she had now eight stomachs to keep full and there would be no retreating from a little accident sent to try them.

"Here we are and here we'll stay," she told her husband. And they did, through the birth of their seventh child the following year and for seven generations on.

# Stone Diaries

My longtime neighbour, Walter Tovell, of the Royal Ontario Museum and University of Toronto was the acknowledged geological expert. He lived in the Granger schoolhouse across from us before he retired to Orangeville and died and his *Guide to the Geology of the Niagara Escarpment*, loved by walkers and amateur scientists, corrected many of my ignorant assumptions about geology.

One day I brought him a perfectly circular stone from our field that I was sure had to be a meteorite. Ever indulgent, spitting as he spoke, his large eyes gleaming, he explained local erosion patterns. The stone rolled over and over in his hand as if he were water itself. Without pausing to breathe, stuttering all the while, he would whizz through Paleozoic tales, geological clocks, glaciations and meltwater paths until I felt I should register for his undergraduate course just so we could have chats.

When his wife Ruth died, I would see Walter, binoculars in hand, slowly walking his golden retriever and we would sometimes sit and ponder the returning wood ducks and their spring nesting rituals on Green Cow Pond and discuss the threats to this precious environment.

An avid birder, he was heartbroken when, one day as we walked, we came upon a goose dead in her bullrush nest on the back swale. How she died I don't know but we left her there for fear of disturbing the other egg sitters. Walter, forever an environmental crusader, wanted to limit the removal of aggregates from the moraines; he opposed paving roads and the relandscaping around new houses, anything that disturbed the natural order and impinged on the instincts of animals. He was virulent about pesticides, for birds constantly ingest toxins through feed and water as they migrate. He counted ganders and drakes, noting their markings and worried about what would be next on our list of things lost to unnatural extinction. Ice ages he could cope with but the foolish application of poisons he could not.

Whenever Claire found fossils, and there were many in our rock piles, Walter would correctly identify them and she would take them to her room and place them in an honoured space for ancient things. His understanding of the water table—the headwater sources that serve the needs of millions of people—should be carved into our foreheads. But there are many people who see a huge cash value in exploiting that resource.

When investors buy land they have their eye on future development; they do not see what is there at the present. One investment group wants to turn hundreds of acres in Mono into a golf course development that would destroy the environment immediately surrounding one of the highest points of the Niagara Escarpment biosphere. Against the wishes of everyone in the neighbourhood these developers have pressed ahead with designs to create a totally inappropriate faux hamlet of studio flats, townhouses, monster homes, commercial malls and a conference centre. Twenty minutes at the knee of Walter would have surely cured them.

Even rocks cannot withstand that sort of assault. There will be more than one poisoned goose, more ponds dead from chemical runoff and more nesting sites destroyed. I fear if this development, or others like it, goes ahead we will be sitting on one of the largest headstones ever to grace a place of death and the rocks we so treasure in this geography will appear gruesome indeed. If Walter Tovell has taught me anything it is to be extremely careful with what we have and remember that there is always someone downstream.

*The rock pile in the east field.*

# The Apprenticeship

There is little more exciting than arriving at an early morning equestrian competition: horses washed and braided, picnic and wine packed, loaded trailers gleaming, white jodhpurs, ties, jackets, polished boots, spurs and whips, riders focused, the warm smell of saddle leather, horses nickering in anticipation. For years before children, TH and I had been going to horse events: jumping, three-day competitions, thoroughbred races, low hunter, carriage racing, barrel racing, dressage. We followed the horses in the papers, in magazines, on television. The year was marked by the Kentucky Derby, Badminton, Cheltenham, the Preakness, Belmont Stakes, Breeder's Cup and the Woodbine yearling sales. We sat on the grass at the Palm Beach Polo Club and in the cheap seats at Goodwood. TH had been to every Royal Winter Fair in Toronto since he was twelve and I could count twenty-five under my belt. We rooted alternatively for horses from Britain, France, Italy, the United States and always Canada. The Canadian greats like Northern Dancer and all of his offspring appeared at every racetrack and we frantically tried to keep straight some of the Canadian lineages. That great jumper Big Ben, with his teammates Monopoly and Canadian Colours gave us many hours of throat-ripping, screaming pride. Some people like horses so that they can gamble or dress up and join a social club; neither of us ever had those vices and, dressed in our barn clothes stuffed with bits of apple and sugar, we looked like junkies on the prowl; horses for us were an aesthetic addiction.

We walked the British National Stud in Newmarket and drove south to Kentucky stud farms and saw the great Nijinsky, Secretariat, Seattle Slew, Spectacular Bid and their offspring in the barns. We visited the grave of Nashua and met his groom, Clem, who was waiting to die and be buried with his horse. We paid our respects to Man O' War and bet the only two dollars we ever wagered on Comtesse de Loire who came second in the Arc de Triomphe and second again at the Woodbine International. She just loved to come in second and that was fine with us.

We were as indiscriminate in our passion for breeds as we were for disciplines: Swedish and Dutch Warmbloods, Selles Française, Andalusians, Quarterhorses, Hanoverians, Holsteiners, Thoroughbreds, Canadian Sport horses. It was a love affair that got bigger and better every year, full of dreams, risk, grand successes and heartbreaking failures; it was a breeder's elusive game, enticing, thrilling, awe inspiring. The sport combined the best and the worst of human kind: cowboys, hucksters, frauds and royalty, from every socioeconomic group and every corner of the planet, people I admired and people I could do without; but I've never met a horse in any form, from any place, without some good in its being.

The horse has always been the epitome of grace, a source of kindness, strength in every muscle. Horses outperform any working machine, last longer than many marriages and are as companionable and honest as the most loyal dogs, without being subservient. Blowing into the open nostrils, exchanging breath, that universal equine greeting, dropping your eyes down and letting the horse prick its ears forward in anticipation of mutual understanding is the zenith of animal experience. Our lives were better for horses.

Mono was full of converted cattle barns, indoor arenas and like-minded horse enthusiasts. There were two international level three-day event courses with dressage arenas, show jumping facilities and cross-country courses; there were half a dozen private tracks for training pacers and trotters. The Ontario Trail

Riders' Association met close to the Mono Cliffs Provincial Park with their muscled quarter horses. Hacking paths were clearly marked and horses had the right of way over mountain bikes and snowmobiles. Endurance riders regularly beat past us on the road. It was a year-round sport and riders took advantage of the interlaced routes that ran from one end of the Township to the other. Many breeders, including The Park Stud and Turn for Home, were here: the International Carriage Driving Classic met one town south and hundreds of riders trailered in for the hunts through the park. From early spring to late fall there were schooling shows and provincial meets in all disciplines. Three Olympic riders came from here. The Canadian Dressage Owners' and Riders' Association competitions ran all summer. Of all the forms of the sport, dressage is the most athletically precise to perform for horse and rider, the most beautiful (if repetitious) to watch and takes years of practice to reach even the most basic level of testing. If a sport were invented just for risk-taking obsessive-compulsives this was it. We became rabid supporters.

A magnificently conformed, highly animated Canadian Sport horse stallion, Tamarack, lived just half an hour north of us and we went to see him. As the Royal Winter Fair Champion Hunter sire he was covering many local mares. A neighbour, Sharon (who owned the white quarter horse that raced against the Black Stallion in Carroll Ballard's film), also had an approved thorough-bred dam, Poly Chop Chop from Conn Smythe farms, who was in foal to Tamarack and we anxiously waited to see what the baby would look like. She called us on the day the filly was born, a bay with three white socks, a blaze down her nose and long, straight, heavily-boned legs. We bought her on the spot and when she was weaned, TH walked her the two miles home, jostling on a lead shank, to join Buddy and Fayden in the barn.

After puzzling over the names of all our favourite horses (Man O' War, Go Man Go, etc.) we came up with Mango and she settled right in, our first yearling in the barn. Hand-reared, she related better to humans than to other horses and responded well to Claire's constant attention and palm feeding.

One spring morning in 1983, after searching for months at Ontario stud farms for a good sire to cover Fayden, the Schickendanze trailer pulled into the driveway and the handler unloaded the snorting, Trakhener stallion, Merkur. We stood in awe as the beast pulled his great neck back, sucking in the air, pawing, stomping the ground. He was better than his picture in the studbook, more energetic, massively fleshed and heavily boned.

The handler waved, "Shouldn't take long. He knows what he's doing and he's already in a sweat."

Earlier that morning we had groomed Fayden, wrapped her tail and sponged down her winking vagina. Buddy pranced around the paddock, calling to her, knowing she was in season and enjoying the heat of the moment. Fayden flicked her tail, backed her rear into the fence where the pony was standing and returned the call.

Claire was nearing four and had seen the horses in all moods but she clung to me, aware that today was different. "Is Fayden going to be okay? Will he hurt her?"

"She'll be fine. Just relax. Daddy will take care of her. We'll watch Daddy." We settled on the house steps for the show.

My husband led the mare up the drive, leaving Buddy calling in desperation from the paddock. Merkur could smell her immediately and ferociously kicked at the ground in anticipation. His penis dropped out of the sheath, extending two feet from his groin. Claire screamed in horror. "Mommy, look at his dinky! He's twice as big as Buddy!"

TH settled the mare close to the fence line, stood in front of her chest and braced her shoulders as the handler led the stallion to mount her. Merkur landed his big hooves on her back, grasping sharply; the mare pushed back into his haunches, the handler slipping the engorged penis quickly into the ready mare. The stallion dropped his head, grunting, frothing, green spittle flying, bellowing hot breath into TH's face. In one minute it was over, and Fayden behaved passably well for a maiden mare: no kicking, no biting. Merkur was the old pro, covering 70 mares a season, often more than one a day. The stallion's composure returned; he walked calmly to his trailer, followed the hay bale in and fell immediately to eating. A few moments and a thousand dollars later the horse was gone, leaving Fayden to her grass and Buddy to his plaintive cuckolded calling.

Fayden had the perfect temperament to be a good dam; Merkur produced good foals, refined and strong. Trakheners had been winning medals at Olympic Dressage trials. In eleven months we would have our first foal. The champagne came out. We thought we were players.

# Welcoming Disaster

The spring when Fayden's foal was due was a wet and blowy one. The snow had melted and frozen several times and the paddock became a skating rink. We couldn't let the horses out for fear they would fall and break their legs. A neighbour's prize stallion had done just that, severing an artery when his shin-bone broke through above the knee. Most farmers have rifles for such eventualities and when people lose animals it is heart-breaking for all who knew the horse and the owners. Even the natural old age deaths of Northern Dancer and Big Ben affected many horse sport supporters. Anyone who has ever bred horses knows the statistical odds against unalloyed success. Many mares absorb their foals several months into their gestation. Some never manage to carry a foetus the eleven months to term. Many foals are stillborn. If there are twins, in all likelihood, both will die. Then there are genetic anomalies: crooked legs, deformed hooves, bacterial infections, and blindness. Foals so afflicted are always put down.

Three months before Fayden was due, TH spent weekends helping out a local large animal vet on his rounds. Often during birthing season it is good to have another set of hands on the hooves as the hundred pound baby makes its way through the birth canal. Most mares remain relatively calm throughout the ordeal but there are those who, in their confusion, misbehave. Sometimes the owners are in no state to help, being as nervous as new parents can often be. Several early morning births and late night watches under his belt, TH felt we could probably handle Fayden when her time came and he had developed a pretty good sense of when mares were ready to foal.

Buddy and Mango would defer the best position to Fayden when she was at the hay bale and they seemed to be aware of her changing condition and moods. Many mornings she refused to leave her stall, even for a brief walk, and we could feel the foal in the birthing position as we groomed her. Her belly was well swayed and every time she braced herself to pee we expected more. With both of us at work during the day we hoped she would labour early in the morning or on a weekend.

Our hopes were fulfilled when late on a Saturday night in April she began to circle her stall, stamping and nickering. We bundled Claire up in her stroller, tucked in a hot water bottle, and settled in on the straw bales for the evening. We called the vet, hoping he would be there when the time came but he was, of course, out on another emergency. Fayden circled a few more times as we watched and waited at her stall door, Claire refusing to stay asleep.

At first, a tip of the hoof appeared and Fayden lifted her tail and groaned. The embryonic sac, wrapped around the front fetlock, burst and a spurt of fluid soaked the straw. Quickly the foal's nose and shoulder followed and with one more push, the baby tumbled onto the stall floor. TH wiped her face, she was breathing, and within minutes the filly began to kick and struggle to her feet. The sac immediately followed and Fayden began to nuzzle and help the little one up as she licked the glossy liquid from the foal's nose and mouth. It was all over in an hour. Shortly after, the vet arrived and checked out the placenta to make sure it was all out of the mare. He waited until the foal found the teat and started nursing before he packed up his kit and left.

Amazing. A bay filly, four white socks, long star blaze, beautiful straight legs and good shoulders. She had the sire Merkur's head. We were as relieved as any new parents could be. Claire was ecstatic and sang every song she knew to the baby before passing out from exhaustion.

For the next six weeks the foal grew as she nursed. We were all in awe of the new life in the barn and Fayden developed fierce maternal skills, not letting Buddy or Mango close to the baby, always strategically placing herself between the foal and any of us. Claire insisted on calling her FlashDance, with an "F" from Fayden and 'Dance' from Northern Dancer and a movie for inspiration. She took to doing dances for all of us—dances in celebration of spring, dances in celebration of nursing baby horses, dances in celebration of green grass, running water and blue sky.

When the time was right, we opened up the pasture and let mother and foal out to graze for a couple of hours every day. Things were going well until one day we heard Fayden calling and saw FlashDance down in the field. We raced out to them but the foal was not getting up, she was in shock, shaking and sweating. TH stayed with her, checking her air passages, but it was not clear what had gone wrong. I got the other horses into their stalls, called the vet to bring his trailer and TH carried the foal on board, Fayden following in despair. We wrapped FlashDance in blankets; she couldn't stand, and we called the emergency surgery at the veterinary hospital in Guelph. The vet, TH, the mare and her sick foal were there in an hour and in surgery twenty minutes later.

It wasn't colic. Instead, her stomach had failed to develop fully, leaving an unusual tiny hole where the grass was falling through into her intestines and rotting. Her systems shut down and she was dead before they could do anything. My husband brought Fayden home and set her in the field where she frantically called and squealed in despair for three weeks, until her milk dried up enough not to cause her pain. Our suffering lasted much longer.

Fayden developed a cancer on her jowl the following spring and, at the age of eighteen, had to be put down.

# The Studhorse Man

As he slid the barn door across the rail and turned on the lights, TH played out the surgical procedure in his head and felt a twinge of nervous sympathy for the pony. Buddy pawed the sand in his stall calling to the mares out in the field. It wasn't the first castration TH had assisted at—it's a common practice—and the necessity is well understood. Unless a stallion is going to be used as a stud he should be gelded. Rarely, if ever, do uncut horses make good mounts for children. But each time, after a surgery that has a strong effect on the behaviour and personality of an animal, there is a residual sadness, knowing, as the owner does, that the animal is changed forever. Especially if you love a well conformed beast, you can't help imagining what his offspring would be like, what generations of breeding might have produced.

TH opened the stall door wide, spread some fresh shavings and kicked around the edges looking for manure, unclipped the water bucket, placed it in the aisle out of the way, picked the rubber curry comb out of the tack box and sorted the grooming brushes as he waited for the vet. He mimicked self control as best he could, knowing the animal would sense anxiety.

"Hiya."

He turned in the direction of the voice. "Can I help you carry anything?"

"No, just put Buddy in the big clean stall. I'm sorry I'm so late. There was a horse sick on plastic baling twine and a cow's prolapsed uterus this morning. One problem after another."

"Buddy's usually pretty good to handle."

"I can use your help. He's a bit late for cutting. It's normally easier before two, eh?" The vet unloaded the supplies.

TH approached the pony, snapped the lead shank to the halter and stroked the sweaty neck to the withers with his free hand. Leaving Buddy in the stall all morning, contrary to routine, had alerted the pony to a change. "I'll walk him a bit. He'll be alright."

"Horses always know what you're thinking. They react before you realize you've sent the signal."

The sweat from the young stallion now pervaded the air. "There's a boy." TH blew three hot breaths into the horse's muzzle and wiped the dampness from the animal's throat onto his jeans. He walked him, first to the left, and then circled around to the right, a repetitive training practice that Buddy knew well.

"Easy boy. What do you smell in the air? Springtime?" He circled again and the horse calmed a bit, his ears still forward, listening to the vet rummaging in the vehicle.

"Bring him in. He looks good." The vet snapped glass ampoules and filled syringes, laying them beside the disinfectants, scalpels, clamps and scissors. The glistening instruments were arranged on the tray, crude and simple.

TH led the horse into the stall and circled again, stroking him and keeping his head low.

"We'll drop him to the right." The vet ran his hand down the well defined neck, massaged the ear, felt the hot exhalations and deftly slid the syringe into the bulging neck vein, watching the blood briefly flood back before plunging the tranquilizer into the horse. They counted the rhythms of the respirations, circled around the pony and let him fall slack, first dropping on his knees and then fully, seven hundred pounds, onto his side.

"Hold him tight."

TH wrapped his arm over the pony's neck, grabbed the gritty tongue and held it clear of the air passage. He listened to the steady breath and noted the grass between the yellowing teeth.

The iodine hissed from the bottle, a steady stream and the vet wiped the testicles clean, the penis, limp, out of the way. A neat incision and blood trickled onto the yellow shavings, darkening a patch as a testicle was lifted from its sack. The clamp snapped on the veins and the connective tissue yielded under the knife. The vet prepared the other clamp, inserted the steel blade, gloved hands moving quickly. Buddy twitched as the second ball was slipped onto the steel dish.

"Wash him every day. I'm leaving the wound open to dry. I don't want any infection there. We'll give him an antibiotic and his chart says his tetanus is up to date."

The scalpel raced through the remaining pink, purple and graying sinews, the clamps firm until the bleeding stopped. The suture pricked and a fresh stream from the iodine bottle washed the blood away.

They were placed on the tray, like turkey eggs. The pony's tongue was getting dry in TH's hands. "I'm going to bury those under the apple tree."

"And waste such a delicacy? In some countries they fry them up and have a party."

"Not civilized." He spat into the palm of his hand and wetted the tongue. "He needs water."

"He'll be up in a minute. Keep him cool for the rest of the day, in his stall. He'll be groggy." The vet gave Buddy the antibiotic injection in the rump. "Just to make sure."

"He'll feel like he's been hit by a truck."

Buddy blinked and TH released the tongue. The pony hauled a deep breath of air into his lungs, lifted his head and dropped it again, before succeeding on his second try to struggle up on all four legs, wobbling on unsteady ground. When he was finally square, Buddy tossed his head, calling in confusion to the other horses.

TH and the vet stroked his chest and stood on either side for a few minutes in case the pony went down again, but the new gelding stood firm, occasional involuntary shudders rippling his muscles.

"I heard they thought of gelding Northern Dancer once. That would have been a tragedy. He was so short. He couldn't keep his weight on."

"Turned out to be the best stud in Canadian history. Lived a long life."

"You can never be certain about things like that. You have to do what you think is right at the time. I've watched too many stallions throwing lousy foals, wasting their years chewing down the alfalfa, living by themselves because they can't be around the mares."

"Testosterone isn't the chemical of choice for young riders."

TH stroked the horse again and left him to his stall as the vet packed up the equipment into the truck.

"No point in having him prancing around the barnyard scaring the shit out of everyone. They're all lather and energy if they're not breeding regularly."

"I appreciate your help."

"He's a good pony. My bill is in the mail."

*Claire and Mango.*

*Caitlin and Buddy.*

# The Biggest Modern Woman of the World

S ome people think there's not a lot to do in the country. People drive through and think it must be all about cows, horses, cold winters and plowing but it's not. It's about music as well. My name is Jane Simmons and I play the violin. Living here is about being the best you can be and listening to the tunes in your head, the tunes your dad sings, the tunes on the country radio station. I started fiddling so that I could one day enter the Shelburne Fiddle Contest. That's the biggest event in Dufferin and has been since I was born and probably will be until I die.

When I was barely old enough to hold the violin, before I could reach the frets with my fingers and hold the chin pad in place I played it on my lap. A waltz, a jig and a reel. My grandfather would teach me one a day after we finished milking, before bed, during lunch to the great anger of my grandmother who begged me "to keep the fiddlin' until after dinner, keep the fiddlin' outside on the porch, fiddle in the hayfield, but not at my table." But I couldn't; I just had to play at the table.

As I grew my hands got larger and larger, just like my father's and my mother's; they have the largest hands in the universe. When my mom waved me off at the school bus when I was a kid the last thing I could see of her six-foot frame was her large flat palm and doughy digits fanning the air. I inherited those fingers, along with a fair-sized frame. "Big hands is a blessing," she used to say.

It was good for the cows, my grandfather said and my dad agreed that I could calm them as I placed the milkers on their warm washed teats; I would run my hands down the udder, pulsing the warmth, and squirt the first few splashes on the floor before attaching the girls to the machine. Cows like to be milked, they like the hum of the pump and they get to chew their hay and grind their cud with the solace of that machine. There's great rhythm to that machine; I hear it in my head all the time: a jig and a waltz and a reel.

The farm is always busy and so when the cows are all hooked up and my father or grandfather is busy at the tanks I play to them to help the work get along. Waltzes are best. The cows relax and just let the music flow over them; dairy cattle are not as high strung as those destined after a short life for the slaughterhouse. I could never run a beef operation; I just couldn't. It's not in my veins but music and a dairy herd is my idea of heaven on earth.

The barn is always pristine clean and I never mind taking my violin out here. There's not a speck of dust and every stall is hosed as soon as the herd goes outside to pasture again. Winter, spring, summer and fall, I hose it down and there's no place safer for my music.

I never took my violin to school, except for once during the Christmas pageant and I played *Silent Night* and my mother said there wasn't a dry eye in the house. I'm not that keen on making people cry but sometimes I guess there's good crying and not just bad crying.

Bad crying was what I did when I lost at the fiddle contest.

Ever since I can remember, as I said, I've been going every August to the Shelburne Fiddle Festival. There's not a lot that goes on in Shelburne so when the contest is on I'm there for the whole week: 24/7. The contest itself is only three days, on the weekend, but the week leading up to the finals is what most of the fuss is all about. People from all over the continent and some from across the ocean come to Shelburne for Fiddleville. They plan their holidays with their families and they start driving from Wyoming,

Texas, Whitehorse and Halifax. All over the highways of Canada thousands of campers and trailers are headed for Shelburne. The police plan the highway route signs into my little town weeks in advance. And they all come in their SilverStream caravans and Winnebagos and RVs and pull into the big field behind the hockey arena and set up camp. There are thousands of families with barbecues and tents and lawn furniture and they settle in for the whole week leading up to the finals. They play every night and they play all kinds of instruments, not just violins. There's xylophones and portable pianos hooked up to electronic synthesizers. One gentleman, who came all the way from Utah, brought his harp and a stand and every day he spent three hours tuning that thing so that he could play a bit in the evening with the rest of the folks. I would go every evening and walk with my father and grandfather and our violins through the crowds. Sometimes we'd hit a small party and everyone in the circle, step dancin', would play the same reel over and over again until the children were falling about in the grass.

I entered my first final when I was nine in the children's division. Just because it's a Junior Division contest don't be misled into thinking that it's a walk in the park. It isn't. These kids had been playing *in utero* as far as I could tell and when I got up there to do my waltz and my jig and my reel I got a good hand from the audience as the big local girl but I didn't even place. I'm not sure if this was because I was a girl and most of the finalists were boys but I'll never know for sure. That was when my grandmother explained the difference between good crying and bad crying.

As I got older and taller and my hands got bigger I could really get a grip on that fiddle and my neck and shoulder muscles felt no pain even after playing for three or four hours. Leaning into heifers helped. Anyway, I got bigger and stronger and taller and faster and that was what it took to win third in 1980. By that time I had some repertoire in my head; I had heard so many different jigs and waltzes and reels from all over the south and the Appalachians and Oregon and northern Quebec I could pull any of them out of my hat whenever anyone whistled the first few notes. I learned to step dance better and tap dance and sing in French. I never had any use for French in school and I hoped the final exam would be on some song but it wasn't.

Tickets for the finals have to be bought early in the season or you can't get in nowadays. It's not just the fiddlers coming but tourists in buses from Toronto and Collingwood. The CBC is in the parking lot and they set up recording equipment while cameramen hog the lineup at the local hamburger place. There are TV celebrities and radio personalities and a whole row of trailers for the sound crews.

At first when all this happened I would get nervous in the finals but then I knew that nerves never helped anyone. My cows would tell you that. I just had to ignore all the faces and pretend that the crowd was here for milking. I had Elise at the fabric shop make my outfit for the finals so that the skirts were long enough and the new boots matched. She gave me three more inches in the sleeve from the size 22 pattern but it worked. I took to worrying about the costume when it became clear we were wearing what the director called "costumes for the television audience". Before that, as a kid, it had never mattered. I just wore what I wore.

I was eighteen when I won the first time. My mother cried the happiest tears. The hometown was ecstatic, whooping and hollering and waving Canadian flags. All my friends from school were there—the principal, the secretary, the bus driver, and the Co-op deliveryman. God I was proud: a waltz, a jig and a reel. Now whenever I'm away I'm happy to tell people I grew up in Shelburne, my name is on a plaque in the arena and I keep my trophy with the Royal Winter Fair prizes in the barn. People remember the year I won—the big, local, hometown girl.

# Night Classes

Walter Scott built a small post and beam outbuilding halfway to our barn, I suppose to house the horse tack and buggy, tools, seed, concrete, whatever he needed as he was clearing and building the farm. It is now my gardening and painting shed, reroofed and covered with charming pieces of barn board I couldn't throw away. It is also home to a colony of bats (*Chiroptera*) that have found the layers of wood conducive shelter. Through the cracks they can be seen hanging about, sleeping during the day, but at night they stream forth and begin their frantic sonar diving for mosquitoes—emerging like ants from a flooding hole—then spiraling into a vortex above the dark garden. The mosquitoes and other dinner bugs languishing in the evening trees are soon gone. Sometimes, by the light of a slim moon we watch the bats for hours, clearing the air.

From time to time one ends up in the house and we open all the doors and windows until the poor, terrified creature finds its way back to the shed. Bats winging through the summer night sky offer a first lesson in gentleness and teach us to be calm and learn to quiet unwarranted fears.

We have a few old sleeping bags that we drag out onto the lawn for night watch and bats often give way to star gazing. One night there was a total eclipse of the moon, sometimes the planets are brilliant, or there's a meteor shower, or a once-in-a-lifetime-or-longer comet. The airplane and satellite viewing gets interrupted by yips of coyotes or the howling of the wolves. Once, when the moon was full we saw our special wolf, Walks- With-a-Limp, who was with us for several years, also staring at the night sky.

He was a large, lone grey with a damaged left hind leg. The girls named him. He often prowled the south hay field for ground-hogs and mice. Max would pick up his scent every now and again and steer clear of the territory he marked. A few times, as I was chopping onions or rolling out pizza dough, I would see him out my kitchen window loping across the top of the ridge. The girls learned how not to be afraid of him at night, although Caitlin insisted for years that we draw the blinds in her room. He left scat along the trails and bits of rabbit fur over a darkened stain on the grass. Of the night creatures he was the most compelling, the one who yielded to our psychological needs.

Other night visitors are not so welcome. The raccoons that travel in strategic companies made me give up composting as they deconstructed an entire fortress around my vegetable peel-ings overnight. The porcupines got on our Most Wanted list when one of them chewed a perfect one-foot hole through the barn door in order to get at the feed tubs. Max got quilled more than once and we spent gruesome hours over many years with the clippers and pliers pulling spikes from his nose and cheeks. Skunks are a nuisance and we kept the animals in when we smelled that odour close by. I kept four gallons of tomato juice and frozen lemonade around at all times, foolishly believing that when the animals did get sprayed I would be able to wash away the stench. Nothing removes it but time. But, in spite of having to deal regularly with the unexpected and most often coming away *not* smelling like roses, we were all enraptured by night visitors. Nothing beats a summer night walk when the fireflies illuminate the pond and the owls dine on scurrying voles.

*Dark path through the forest.*

*Robin on the forest path.*

## Stone Angel

Of all the public walking tours throughout the Escarpment, the Bruce Trail remains the most popular but, for me, the cemeteries held a special charm all their own. I loved to walk past the old houses, figuring out who lived where, and then down to one of the local cemeteries to see the graves of these pioneer homeowners. Many of the Scotts were buried in Burns Cemetery. The Avisons, who bought our house when the Scotts moved in 1881, are buried in Relessey Cemetery along with their daughter Mary Elizabeth who died at 10 months, 17 days, perhaps in my bedroom. Samuel and Essie Thompson, who lived here in 1904 when they bought the farm from Avisons for $4,300, are both buried in St John's Cemetery. Their other friends and neighbours I found as I walked, my *Gravestone Inscriptions of Eleven Cemeteries of Mono Township, Dufferin County, Ontario* in hand. It amused me to ponder their lives and wonder what work they did on the fields, what apple trees they planted, which stone piles and fences they contributed to.

This was a preoccupation I shared with many people. When my husband and I lived in London we had a great friend, Nemone Lethbridge, who was responsible for organizing the cleaning up of many of the damaged gravestones in Abney Park Cemetery in Stoke Newington. We had wonderful picnics in her back garden, discussing the lives of those who were buried next door as well as the antics of several deranged people who insisted on sleeping in the cemetery and moving the bones around. Every gravesite has a story and more than just historians and archeologists are fascinated by the dead, occupying a piece of ground as bones do—as we all will some day. If the grave's inhabitants are related in any way to the curious visitor, more fiercely will the living hold the value of that story.

When the children were five and eleven we spent a sabbatical in France and we took our girls through Père Lachaise, Montparnasse and many other French cemeteries. At first, they thought it was creepy but we had a small animal cemetery on Sweetfield (TH's father's ashes are also buried under the pear tree) and the dead were not forbidden in our discussions. In fact, the memory of the dead enhanced my pleasure of this place. I do not believe in ghosts but that does not stop the locals from telling tales.

One of my favourite ghost stories was about a Mr Frame, a bonesetter, who lived on 15 Sideroad near the Blind Line. He died around 1892 after a lifetime of mending fractures, splinting broken legs, farming and running a lay veterinary practice. His son was a doctor and, after he moved out of the house, two subsequent families also left the old house because of the mysterious noises and unwelcome hauntings. Finally, some curious neighbour ventured into the attic and discovered several severed limbs and racks of bones that Mr. Frame had been using to learn anatomy. The bones were buried and the noises stopped, and another family moved into a new house on the property in greater peace and quiet. The original dwelling was burnt to the ground by persons unknown.

One of my neighbours claimed to have seen a mysterious figure slipping back and forth across the road between our houses. It was late at night and she was putting her children to bed when she looked out the window and saw a grey-coated man pacing back and forth across the road. She thought it might be Walter Tovell, out looking for his dog, and went downstairs to see if she could help. Her boys came with her and when they approached, the figure flew up into the air and disappeared. Confused, they walked back to the house, only to turn around and see the man pacing the road once more. Then they did what every good country person does in these circumstances: they got out the shotgun and called the police. Unable to fathom the mystery, the Shelburne Ontaio Provincial Police suggested she go back to bed, relax, take her medication, and turn the lights off. Our local ghost never returned.

Many of the houses have oral histories tagged onto them and walking with a long time resident elicits a story at every farm driveway: that house belonged to Low Church Irish, that house was where the Pentecostals lived, there the Dunker's house, the Black Stocking meetings were held there. Those people started the United Farmers' Party, that house is full of Mormons, that one full of Evangelical Lutherans. It seems there have been numerous sects, both political and religious, flourishing up and down the sideroads. Every dilapidated house and every gravestone, however disfigured by ice and erosion, had more to tell than just the short inscription about the time of death.

If the history of a place comes from the agreed upon fables, as Napoleon once said, it makes no difference whether or not the incidents which engendered those fables can be traced to a shred of supporting fact. What seemed to matter to the residents of Mono, like people anywhere who are attached to their landscape, was that if the spot on the globe where the tale started can be found and marked, then the story can unfold from that location and have a life of its own. Once a location has been verified as the exact spot where a cow was drowned or a murder committed or a hot air balloon crashed, the story begins to travel.

That was why I loved graveyards—they are the doorways to untold stories. It is why travellers go on vacation and search out historical fact: we like to stand where the Last Spike was driven, where the shot was fired, the exact turn in the road where the crash happened or where the water erupted from the ground. It is not morbid, not gruesome; it is simply the starting place of a story. What makes death in snow or death by drowning so uncanny is that the place of dying has disappeared—it is amorphous, it shifts, melts and disappears; yet it is compelling. The stone markers where Arctic explorers died—snowy freezing deaths—seem to haunt the northern edges of our maps, and by extension, the eerie peripheries of Canadian consciousness.

We like to be in the spots that give birth to stories because maybe our own story will become entwined with that place. Maybe this piece of earth will reveal something to us—about others—about ourselves.

Tom Thompson, perhaps the most famous of the Group of Seven painters, was one of those mythic Canadian figures whose disappearance and death gave rise to numerous conflicting stories. The most commonly accepted tale was that he died, drowned in Canoe Lake, and his body was later recovered. He was buried in Leith cemetery, north on the Escarpment, close to Owen Sound just down the road from where his parents farmed. However, there are those who believed the real body was never recovered, those who believed his remains were washed up on a more distant shore and disposed of to prevent a crime from being solved. His family was outraged by the gossip of criminality but when a mythic figure is involved there are those who will tell you the honest-to-God's-truth about what really happened and they do not doubt the veracity of their version because they "saw the place where it happened." The fact that someone also saw the body of Thomson laid out in Mrs McKean's parlour before the funeral is of little relevance.

There is folklore that brings justice to families who have been wronged—their ghosts haunt the places of the crimes as well as instilling fear in the perpetrators. Rapists, never charged or brought to justice, have had their testicles cut off by angry brothers and no one reports it, though several people will tell you the sideroad crossing where the castration took place. A house where a suicide lived loses its value. A brilliant blue spruce tree planted by a thieving lawyer is cut down for a Christmas tree. All of these stories add to the meaning we find in landscape.

Propriety over stories was tended with as much care as a lover's resting place. Tell a story incorrectly around here and you are liable to receive castigations, appropriate some relative's bones and you are no better than the thieving lawyer. Doubting someone's story was as obvious an insult as slapping. Everyone knows that their stories are the real ones, the true versions. Family feuds continued for generations if someone disputed a tale.

Now the local gossip is about who recently moved into our county: what musicians rented a house in the Hockley Valley, what actor owns a farm here, what director and which famous novelists. There are dotcom millionaires and industry captains, artists, sculptors, journalists and hockey personalities but that lust for local gossip, for memorializing places where incidents occur, especially when out walking, will never go away. Even Margaret Atwood used to live here: you can see her old house on the 4th line, and locals will tell you a lot of stories about what went on in that house.

*We all die one day.*

# Surfacing

The time has come to unburden myself—Miss Ethylwood Pinbottom at your service—of information that has come to me quite gratuitously over the past thirty years as a teacher of literature. I have been asked by my students, on more than one occasion, to discuss the work of Margaret Atwood, Canadian Cultural Icon. With only a few official biographies in print, and given that there is a rage in literary circles around the world for biographical information on even our most obscure *écrivants*, I thought it my public duty, as a retiring servant of the province of Ontario, to humbly pass on any tidbits which I possess which may illuminate the life of our Peggy.

Let me begin by admitting that I have never been introduced to the woman, though I have been in her presence on numerous occasions. Not knowing someone has not stopped most biographers from revealing much about the lives of their subjects so I count myself in good company.

My first encounter with Ms Atwood was in the early seventies in the Student Union Building at the University of British Columbia. Ms Atwood likes universities and, as a member of the Women's Studies group in the Department of English, we had invited her to read from *The Edible Woman*. I can confirm that she is a feminist, as we all were back then. In front of some seven hundred undergraduates she opined that there was something amiss in the way the world treated women. I point you now directly to her poetry to search out more references to women.

Women throughout the world are consoled by this information and a second reading of *Handmaid's Tale* can do no serious reader any harm. Interviewers and PhD candidates have no longer to inquire as to her radical views which, in public, she discusses quite openly and directly. She read, that early summer evening in Vancouver, in her pinched nasal voice that she continues to affect to this very day, although many listeners with musical ears may find it offensive. I have no idea what her real voice sounds like although some approximation of it may be found in the dialogue in her novels. In spite of that, she manages to put her audiences at ease and even elicits a chuckle or two from Canadians. Her readings are always accompanied by thunderous applause and a great deal of national pride.

Ms Atwood has continued to grace podia at a ferocious pace although I did not hear her again until she came to read in London, England, where again all my students were demanding more information about this incredible Canuck who must have carried a Canadian passport similar to my own. Many of my Hackney Technical College Plumbing Apprentices worked on papers delving into the mysteries of *Surfacing*. They concluded her images and themes were full of deep meaning. Her reading at Canada House, in Trafalgar Square, had matured into a more droll recitation than I had previously remembered and, what with the shawls and all, it was almost impossible to get past her smiling voice which seemed all nose, teeth and slit lips, to deal with the wealth of symbols below.

My Hackney students were all deeply moved and agreed they would apply to Canadian Universities and for Arts Council travel grants to study canoeing in the wilderness that Ms Atwood had so succinctly described. Many now grasped signed copies of *Survival* under their arms and badgered the poor bookstore owner in Stoke Newington to stock all the shelves with used back issues of Atwood classics.

On the basis of having read at least most of her work, I was granted a tenured position in Commonwealth Studies at the college. I will say that she has now totally taken London by storm with her win at the Booker and Canadian letters are elevated to a new level of respectability. Rumours of autographed copies of her books still float up and down Charing Cross Road and a whole new generation of readers and writers comb the shelves of Dillons and Hatchards seeking new paperback editions of her early works. Understanding of Canada is at a new *plâteau*. She is absolutely the most highly regarded international author we have (there are those who favour Ondaatje, to be sure, but is he really Canadian?) and the fine prose we read about her in newspaper columns is to be forever defended.

My next encounter with Ms Atwood was in more intimate circumstances where I came to see the softer side of her *visage*. I had decided to forgo the thirty pounds a week paid to academics in London and wished to try my hand at teaching back home. The onerous rents in Toronto had forced me to let the top floor of my house and who should apply but the authoress' sister! When I put the ad in the paper I had not expected the respondents to have literary relatives although that was, indeed, my preference. I was delighted when the young woman arrived with boxes of books and I was more than pleased to help her build brick and board bookcases to store her treasures, many of which I myself had read. We had a most animated discussion.

In addition, she was not at all perturbed by the various cockroaches that scoured the walls and floors. She never once complained about the noise during the drilling to rectify the termite damage and she was most understanding during the visits by the exterminator. I think Pater Atwood's entomological interests had a profound influence on both the sisters and traces of that insect passion can be found in Ms Atwood's work.

It was after her sister had been living upstairs for a few weeks that my doorbell rang and I answered. To my delight it was *the* Margaret Atwood and *the* Graeme Gibson. (Don't you love the way he spells his name? But why does he dress like that?). The pinnacle of my landlady career! Canada is blessed with many literary couples. They looked quite happy together, rather casual in jeans and T-shirts (I was not dressed for formal introductions myself). Much has been written about the weak and ineffectual men portrayed in her fiction but I think it wrong to assume these are all modeled on her husband. There are many fine men in literary circles. The fact that they pressed the wrong buzzer didn't distress me one iota and I happily led them up to the apartment. I know how grateful people can be for small kindnesses.

I believe I saw Ms Atwood another time, reading a book on the shores of Sunny Lake in Muskoka. The book she was reading, a rather large tome with the title embossed on the spine, was difficult to make out, try as I might with my birding binoculars. I think it is safe to say it was a political statement about the future of Canada. I am therefore sure she is opposed to free trade and is an avid nationalist.

The following summer I was invited to visit the family of some student who lived near Alliston. Here my sleuthing skills were put to the test. I knew she had lived on a farm close to the Niagara Escarpment and I was able to find the very line and the very house where *Bodily Harm* had been written. My student's mother, a delightful woman with many stories to tell, showed me a book about Bequia, a small Caribbean island off St. Vincent, resplendent with pictures of Ms Atwood and her family. As a lover of quiet places myself, I came to have a deep appreciation of the tranquil tone found in much of her later work. In Alliston's used bookstore it is possible to find dog-eared copies of *Life Before Man*, *Lady Oracle*, *Bluebeard's Egg* and *Dancing Girls*—a testament to the permanent effect her residency has on an area. She is a rock in the Canadian stone. Further to that I can highly recommend a walking tour of Leaside and a stroll along the Don Valley after having read *Cat's Eye*.

Much has been meted concerning who exactly the characters are in *Wilderness Tips* and *Robber Bride* and I think it is safe to say she has at times rushed into portrayals of notable Canadians; however, it will take an academic greater than I, with a specialty in *romans à cléf* to speculate as to who they might be.

In closing, I would like to say that I am sure Ms Atwood will be entertaining hundreds of thousands of people with her poetry and prose, at the very least one book a year, until the day she dies and for generations to come. I hope, for the sake of our students, that she will continue to provide us with bracing portraits of ourselves—readers can search out passages in *The Blind Assassin* and other more densely plotted tales—and I hope my few words here will serve to deepen, sweet reader, your love of our heritage.

*Teacher Drowns.*
*The body of Ethylwood Pinbottom of Beaver Pines surfaced this spring in Canoe Lake in Algonquin Park. It is believed she accidentally tipped out of her canoe while reading. She had been missing since November. This article was found in her knapsack left at her campsite on the shore. The coroner also revealed that she was a hermaphrodite.*

*The red canoe.*

# The Swing Era

The Italians have the perfect word for commuters: *pendolare*. The relentless push on the outward journey to work and the exhausted gravitational return. After many years of driving, working and raising a family one would think we would have had the schedule down to a manageable routine. But there was more than a little ambivalence in my life. The six o'clock mornings, one child off to school, baby in the car seat in the back, I was marking papers, and TH drove. Off to day care. The inevitable tears, then to drop TH at work, then to my work, then the tug of guilt as I thought of children left for hours in the care of others, no matter how competent. But we had to teach; we had no trust funds to fall back on.

It was particularly painful commuting while I was breast feeding Caitlin. My nipples leaked and I stuffed diapers into my 48D cups to stem the flow. In one late department meeting even the super diapers did not help and I excused myself on biological grounds as a pint of milk flooded down my dress. I felt a deep gut pull, back to my children, back to the farm. I was always just slightly off kilter when I was not there, aware that the farm was where I preferred to be. Being out of balance for two hundred days out of the year, well into our eighth year at the farm, seemed quite mad. However, the option of moving back to the city did not appeal to either of us. I preferred the stress of commuting than slow death by city life, an oxymoron as far as I was concerned.

In an earlier time I would have stayed home but mortgage payments being what they were, and me being who I am, there was no choice. I wanted to teach. It was what I had been nominally trained for, what I did, but not who I was. No one was making any money at farming—even the cattle people were taking part-time jobs as bus drivers to support their enterprises. In that way I was like most other working mothers of my generation: driven, exhausted, guilt ridden, trapped, ambivalent. The glass door had shut tight on my ticking mechanism: drive and release, teach and mother, cook and clean, eat and sleep.

Every semester, after a hedonistic summer in my garden, my conscience would rear up again and I would know that I had to leave my children and hit the classroom. I owed it to my grandmother, who could never speak a word of English, I owed it to my mother who never finished grade eight, I owed it to my children who, if they watched us, would grow up and work as hard as they could for the common good, and I believed, madly, that I owed it to Canada. (A Trudeau Liberal, I believed in his vision. I wept heartily, as did half the country, when he died.) Helping build Canada had been a great theme of my grandmother's that I shared.

So, for over twenty-five years I have bought this unqualified bill of goods that required piling 2½ lifetimes into one. I have taught over 5,000 students in Scarborough and the fact that I cannot detach my teaching from my other life is the source of my greatest internal struggle. Teaching is part delight and part one of the most stressful and exhausting careers imaginable. Teaching is subversive, not only to students but also to teachers; it is like a drug and most teachers have addictive disorders. We are activists, gamblers, lapsed churchgoers, train spotters, zealots, writers, painters, and drunks—outsiders all.

Some of my teaching friends, once they retire, come back to do guest lectures, fill in for someone who is sick. They need that fix, maybe today I can hit one out of the ball park; maybe today I can convince that kid to follow his own rainbow and not just go for the bucks; maybe today that punk in the back row will take the book

I offer him and go home and read it. Teachers are not in it for the vacations we are so roundly criticized for, or for the money. The pay is too meager to claim that. We all suffer from delusions of a perfect life.

But the world always gets in the way. Administrators are often shortsighted. Governments hit education budgets when the taxpayers revolt. Demographically unstable institutions are caught in the breach of constant change, marketplace whim, and political haymaking. It's having a bad waiter for a delicious dinner. A banquet ruled by Attila.

My students came from all over the world: 70% were second language speakers, 60% were in need of remedial instruction in both math and English. I performed mainly as a nurse in the trenches. From entrance writing samples we triaged the first-year students into may-pass-this-term, might-pass-in-two-terms and will-never-pass. Good democrats that we were, the department shared the wealth and every year we each got stuck with at least two sections of the final sort. It was a noble job, I told myself, and there were long-term rewards; however, I was not the first teacher to weep over sixty process analysis papers detailing "How I got to school". "How to change a tire". "How to open a CD shrink wrapper" and "How to feed a trutle" (I think he meant turtle). I taught narrative technique by having my auto tech students sing Bruce Springsteen songs, and helped them understand comparison by bringing in a bag of hats. Post-secondary liberal education is not, as some of the neo-con journalists would have us believe, all tax-wasting ivory tower musing. It introduces the idea of thinking; it is the bare minimum.

The height of my pleasure came when I got to teach my second term literature class and we read out loud. We argued about passages, we mispronounced names, we recited poetry, we consulted our atlases and our dictionaries. Some students developed a passion for Canadian writers, others responded as if being tortured. Authors dropped in to read to us. Paul Quarrington came to test out hilarious passages from a new book and my students all wanted to know the types of drugs the protagonist in *Whale Music* used. They wanted to talk about turning books into movies. Authors will talk about anything if they think students have gotten to the end of the reading assignment.

And then I watched as the brightest students downloaded reviews from the web, chopped them together, changed the title and handed in the resulting mosaic. That was a good solid pass where I came from and I distrusted any college teacher who claimed she taught a class of ethical writers. Some students ached for the written word; some were just dying to talk about their own lives. Getting them to spend thirty hours on a research paper was another story.

I read their writing. "We have a totally wired collage, (college?) or is that ceiling? And I can't find anything here to write about," one student wrote, *à propos* of absolutely nothing but totally indicative of the task. With spellcheck on every machine and rushed students handing in perfectly clean and perfectly unintelligible assignments I picked my way through paragraphs plagiarized from *The Toronto Star* hoping for a student's response. If I had my way everyone would be forced to forgo the technology and write by hand. We have fill-in-the-blank essay templates that allow students to click through a database and a thesaurus and—*presto!*—an essay titled "What People Say about Mordecai Richler". Every class on thesis statements had gone the way of the dodo.

I tried to find novels that would be of particular interest to specific students, started them reading where they could, and wanted, to begin. Any bookstore has a hundred good Canadian books; they have inspired my life. There are novels for Iranians, Indians east and west, Caribbeans, Scots and Vietnamese. From lists I found books for single mothers, second generation Chinese, and female students who had suffered genital mutilation in Somalia. I found out where they were and gave them one book at a time. It didn't always work; I knew that I'd been at teaching too long, but I wouldn't give up.

No matter how perfect *Jade Peony* or *Lives of the Saints* was for that student, if it came from a teacher and it was on a test then it was suspect. I remember handing out bibliography outline forms and watching as their eyes glazed over. But if I gave them something that helped them survive, earn more money, or find a lover, they just might have been willing to read it. Sometimes I think all literature classes should take place in desperate smoky bars with armed guards at the door. "Read this and you might get out alive." Thank heaven the universities were graduating more PhDs with subversive enthusiasms than the world could accommodate and they all wanted to bicker over the low-paying sessional jobs in the suburbs. Others were willing to take over. But (I kicked myself) teachers are famous for that. It was the three students out of every class that I was really there for.

S came from Sri Lanka at the age of thirteen, a refugee whose parents had been killed for leaving food for the Tamil Tigers. Her goal was to become a nurse so, as she so eloquently wrote, "I will learn how to stop the bleeding, apply pressure where the wounds are greatest." She is now a nurse at a Scarborough hospital. Or there was B who had a friend write the entrance exam for her and managed to stay in school three months before anyone realized she could only read at a grade two level. She now reads well in her job as a social worker.

I had hundreds of these students. I went to their weddings, saw pictures of their children, and wept as they became Canadian citizens. I had them up to my farm for spring sugaring off as they, in utter amazement, ate globs of delicious maple goop off the snow. I celebrated Chinese New Year and received boxes of exotic sweets in return. Pongol, Ramadan and Moon festivals had all become a part of each semester.

My tech boys taught me how to change the oil in my tractor and how to rewire a socket. A drafting student showed me how to use a mitre board and skill saw. I had my neck "released" by a Korean physiotherapist studying English and my palms read by a Chilean travel agent. I had henna tattoos painted on my hands and was presented with rings from Senegal. Three Jamaican girls braided my hair as part of an oral report demonstration and a student, in complete purdah, looked me in the eyes and told me she wanted to be a travel agent.

I took students to the Art Gallery of Ontario and the Royal Ontario Museum (places where they thought they did not belong) and stood by as they recognized parts of their own heritage glorified in what they thought of as a foreign place. I was the recipient of books of poetry from Iran, haiku from Japan, pictographs from China. I learned about Somalian warlords and poets, life dragged out in internment camps, voyages on the Pacific that lasted for months. I was retold Polish history and had epics read and translated from Hungarian.

One gay student from Delhi appeared in my office one day in tears. We talked about leaving friends and family behind, of cold winters and severe depression. He was on medication and slept more than he should; essays were hard to complete. He hadn't done the reading. I gave him *Funny Boy* to read and he came back a few weeks later to return it. In the bag, neatly wrapped in a scroll, were his family curry recipes, translated and copied by hand from his grandmother's cooking notes. We talked about being gay and how to blend spices and he handed in his essay late and passed the term. Whenever we met in the hall the following semester he would flick a lock of hair at me and say, "Funny boy, really funny boy, but a good cook."

The riding home rule that my husband and I first wrote in blood was that we had to leave the fearsomeness of our jobs behind when we hit Highway 9. It was a clause in our marriage contract. We were never allowed to talk about the overloaded classes, the failures to find adequately sized rooms, the strikes, the bitch of a chair who deleted faculty emails, and the lousy administrator who was being investigated by the fraud squad. No complaining about the teacher who sexually harassed students and continued to get away with it—in spite of written complaints. No discussion of the death threats and assaults, or the weapons charges. But we were always allowed to tell the funny stories, the howlers that occurred in papers, the sociology professor with the props and the magic tricks, and the students who made it through, got jobs, earned four times our salaries, started companies, owned restaurants, became pilots, went on to university, took to the law after being legal clerks. There was release in those stories, a sense of reprieve at the end of a conflicted day, some grace after all that working and driving, a certain temporary calm. And, by comparison, my family was downright boring, my childhood, uneventful.

*The road out of and in to sanctuary.*

# The Ice Fields

"W hen will Daddy get home?" Claire stared out the window, her nose pressed to the glass. "I can't even see the driveway. All I see is white. And cold." The wind was horizontal, slashing against the side of the house, making the bricks groan and the wood stove shudder.

"I'll put more wood on. Don't worry, Daddy will be home soon. I'll get your quilt. Do you want to listen to the radio? There's batteries in the Walkman."

"No. I want to wait for Daddy. Are you sure the horses are okay? Are they warm enough?"

"Daddy checked before he left. They're fine. They've got their blankets on. Don't worry."

Damn that husband of mine. Always playing the Good Samaritan, helping out people when they call. Being noble made him feel good. Damn the vet who couldn't make it back from Caledon. Damn the OPP for closing the highways north of the city. Everything was nailed down by the storm.

"Of course I'll go," he said. "I'll go and put the horses in and throw them some hay and water and be back in no time." That was four hours ago. Since then the storm had gotten worse, the power was out because the ice had pulled down lines; the emergency Hydro vehicles couldn't get out for at least eight hours. The weatherman on the radio had said twelve more hours. Twelve more hours! I will be mad by then, completely raving mad.

If he were held back at the barn he would be safe. The barn was warm because of the horses; there was water and straw. That would be manageable. But the danger was that he was on the road. The roads were officially closed. Not possible to clear. No plows could make it out, not even the Champions that could handle almost any weather. There was nothing to do but wait it out.

The drifts were higher now, well over the car rooftops and roadway signs. Everything was blown in. The heavy ice of the day before had encased the trees like glass mummies and every blast took down more limbs. It was one vast crystal plain, broken by shards of flying branches. Every animal was hunkered down, every bird under bush and every dog indoors. Except my husband who was out making sure the horses of a neighbour were settled— leaving me and the children totally unsettled.

"Horses die in weather like this," he had said as he stood layering and bundling himself at the door. "They have to be in the barn. Out of the wind."

"They're not our horses. You'll never make it there and if you do you'll never make it back. It's pitch black now."

"Don't worry." He had loaded the 4Runner the day before with blankets and flashlights and candles and chocolate bars but this was the kind of weather that buried even trucks.

"Don't worry," I repeated to the child as she plugged the earphones into her ears. Still the emergency crews couldn't get out, the airport was closed, schools wouldn't run for the rest of the week, hospitals were on emergency alert. The storm would blow over northern and central Ontario for three more days with only slight lulls. It was unlikely all the roads would open for a week.

How long before the child would go to sleep like the baby had? The little one I had tucked in and left to dreamland but the nine-year-old was not going to leave that window seat until her father was home. Could she stay awake twenty-four hours? Thirty-six?

The cupboards always had enough food for at least a week. There was juice and water and bread and eggs. There was pasta, olives, radicchio, chicken. There were containers of water in the basement. There were cookies and crackers and soups to heat up on the wood stove and a box of candles and a face cord of wood stacked in the mudroom. I could do without the power but I couldn't do without a husband.

"Where's Daddy? Where's Daddy?!"

"If Daddy doesn't come home tonight it means he's with the horses. He'll be okay."

"In the barn? Sleeping with the horses?"

"Yes, you know how warm the horses are. They're just hay burners. He'll be safe with the horses. You know that."

"Yes, but what will he eat?"

"There are chocolate bars in the truck. Water in the barn. He'll be fine, I promise. He won't starve to death in a day." Shit! That word came out of my mouth. How stupid could I be?

"Could Daddy die in the storm? People die in storms."

"Not your father. Not your father. He knows about storms."

"Let's make some sandwiches. Peanut butter and jam, or grilled cheese on the stove?"

"No food until Daddy gets home!"

"Just a juice then. We'll have some juice."

"Everything outside is frozen. It just breaks out there. It just breaks."

I sat with Claire as a deeper darkness descended and the howling continued. We sat cuddled on the couch for what seemed like days, late into the night. Every once in a while I would get up and put more wood on the fire, check on the sleeping baby, and the battery clock in the kitchen. Still Claire would not sleep. Time stopped.

"There's a light! Mommy, I see a light!"

"Can't be sweetie. The power is out."

"No, no! I see some lights. Two, three, four, five. Six lights! Come and see!"

Then I heard them, that throaty roar I hated so much as they whizzed over the trails, spooking the horses; those damn snowmobilers and their damn Skidoos.

"It's Daddy. It's Daddy! The skidooers found him. The damn skidooers found him! It's Daddy!"

It took all my reserves to keep calm as he strolled in the door.

"Promise me you will never do that again. Promise me you will never go out in the middle of the worst fucking storm of the century to feed some horses."

"You know I can't promise that. I can't promise that."

*Winter sun over the ice.*

# A Fine Balance

Almost every Saturday and Sunday from the time she was two, Claire would ride: first, on the front pommel of Fayden's saddle with her father and then, alone, on Buddy. Those first few attempts often left her on the ground, once slipping into a snow bank up to her thighs, on another occasion hard into a fence that left her bruised and shaken. But she was nothing if not determined. She would give up sleeping before she gave up riding.

In the eighties there were few coaches in our area but we managed to find a severe Dutch woman who lasted only a few weeks as she was in the habit of whipping the legs of her students until they learned to flex and grip. The next coach, somewhat more into the thrill of riding, was a low hunter fanatic who wanted even her most juvenile of riders to face four-foot fences at every turn.

Finally, we found Marsha, a second generation German coach who had all the necessary toughness tempered by a compassion for horse and rider. She took on Claire and then Caitlin, patiently turning them both into horsewomen—giving them confidence, developing their stamina, perfecting the well-balanced seat. Riders, in deep focus, have to imagine the dead centre of the ride in their seat. The body must be relaxed; the hips have to move with the horse, sinking into the saddle (a custom Barnsby Crown fits like a ball joint into a socket). The arms and hands must be loose and elastic, only an extension of the rein. The elbow and shoulders and seat belong to the rider, but the hands belong to the horse. The rider's head looks up and the eyes glance down but it is mainly all body proprioception. If the hips are relaxed and deep then the weight can come through to the heel (but not rest there) to be in line with the shoulders—an invisible thread connecting them all. Toes are up. All turning, suppling and control of movement comes through the hips and waist and legs. The upper body simply carries through the movement in the hips. Never hold tension in the hands, never jerk, never pull, never drop, never let the horse lean on the reins. It's really deceptively simple. Or at least that is what I learned from taking my children to Marsha.

I've watched the best riders in Canada adjust themselves when they first warm up: after a lifetime of riding the body remembers, every breath is an indication of the rider's position on the horse. They cover the landscape as one. Every horse that has been trained knows what to do whether the rider knows it or not. No one can fake it. Every horse will test an inexperienced learner. You can buy the $40,000 horse, the $5,000 saddle, the $2,000 boots and gear but without ten years of seatwork you're a fool in the ring.

All that commitment to training, however, does not guarantee a tension-free flawless ride. Maybe the mare is in heat, maybe the wind is in her eyes, or maybe she's cantankerous that day. Maybe there's a flapping umbrella, a terrier you want to kick, an inexperienced rider in the arena. I have watched 1200 pound Mango trip on a mound of sawdust and flip head over haunches onto Claire. The mare didn't move a muscle. For a moment we thought one of them was injured, but no. The horse waited till Claire was clear before she moved a leg that could injure her rider and then she got up. Dressage mothers always carry first aid kits, clothes brushes, boot cleaners and a hundredweight of panic protection.

And rain gear. One junior provincial championship Caitlin entered in September proved to be the wettest one on record. The arena was ankle deep in muck. The judges, from their booth at the end of the fence could hardly see the far corners. The wind whipped the rain under our umbrellas and we folded them away.

Rainwear was virtually useless. The horses were slicked and we carried towels in plastic bags to dry the slipping saddles and stirrups. Tight fitted boots were filled to the brim with rainwater and stock ties hung limp under sodden jackets. Mango, lifting her hooves high to avoid the puddles, lost her fluidity, ending a respectable, but disappointing, sixth.

That mare was more human than horse and would pin her ears back when other horses entered the ring. Another mare, even bitchier than she, once bit her on the ass and Mango couldn't resist a kick and a buck. Really bad form for dressage but perfectly in character. Most horses want to please their riders; most of them enjoy the work, and enjoy the grooming and the attention. Mango was not an easy horse, not an automatic transmission; she demanded constant commitment. Good riders found her a challenge. Caitlin once spent an entire summer doing ten-meter canter circles, first to the left, then to the right, for an hour each day. Months had been spent on trot/canter transitions, on dead centre stops, on serpentines, only to end up at competition repeating a tiny mistake of six months ago.

It is a small miracle that teams get to international competition with riders intact, horses in good health, finances in the black. The massive effort, the constant training, the thousand variables make the pursuit a logistical nightmare but there we were, twenty years on, dressed and fed, faithfully heading into the arena, Mango's ears down, green slather on the bit, and a well-balanced seat.

# Two Solitudes

When the girls were in elementary school the questions of religious and ethical beliefs came up with predictable regularity. Some of the teachers were members of the local churches: Baptists, Catholics, United, Pentecostal, Jehovah's Witness and Dutch Reform; they often referred to their convictions in class. Some of the students took it upon themselves to proselytize to those who did not follow their church doctrine. References to God and his Kingdom, the sinners and the saved, heathens and heretics, were common and when a child in their school died in an all-terrain-vehicle accident prayer—not discussion—was the answer. Both of my girls had some difficulty with this and were mercilessly hounded by other students who told them they would rot in hell for eternity if they didn't submit to the will of God. When asked what congregation we belonged to Claire learned to answer back, "We're secular humanists."

Most of the kids thought that was some weird church in Toronto and left them alone; however, there were the few who persisted in persecuting them for being "godless". Caitlin took to celebrating every multicultural holiday as they arrived on the calendar, painting her face and dressing up whenever she could, and Claire, regretfully, once told her teacher that her great grandmother was Jewish and she was taking the day off for Yom Kippur. She was going riding. At the age of eight, however historically and socially remote she was from that great grandmother, she was made to feel personally responsible for the crucifixion by both the teacher and her fellow classmates. There were few even vaguely foreign folk in town and in the 80s there were no "outsiders" willing to confront such issues with the Principal. Tolerance and respect for other belief systems are just making their way into the schools of Dufferin County and we took every opportunity to discuss this with the children and their teachers.

Parochial Ontario was not quite ready for our girls and so they were singled out as different. Too often they were told to be "seen and not heard" (a phrase I've hated since childhood)—to pretend the world was not the way it was. When our friends and colleagues brought their families and when the girls started having friends in Toronto and bringing them to the farm, they would later speculate that this was the first time a black, a Chinese, a Korean, anyone gay or lesbian had been in the township. Some things they hid from their classmates and then, probably quite naturally, they became perversely proud of things that could shock their teachers— Caitlin's gay godfather, Claire's pop-up book of the human body, penis included—but they were often made uncomfortable facing the narrow experience of some of their peers. Not getting invited to classmates' birthday parties could be a big social problem.

The rural distrust of difference is so entrenched that even educated, but otiose, city folk adopt these ideas when they move here, finding it easier to succumb to pressure and ignore the obvious rather than push for social change. In that way Dufferin was no different from rural backwaters anywhere; it is an attitude in local culture more oppressive than comforting.

Things are getting somewhat easier now; the teachers in the schools have become more sensitive (and younger); children are no longer told, like Claire was, to show up in frocks instead of track pants or jeans. We had an East Indian family move to the neighbourhood and Cait spotted a couple of women holding hands while shopping at Loblaws. Orangeville has stopped playing out old confusing feuds in Irish marching season, and Shelburne got an Italian restaurant. But we're not clearly out in the open yet.

The sheer idiocy of narrow attitudes and the vicious, damaging persistence of local gossip showed itself when one of the best chefs in Canada, Michael Statdlander and his equally talented wife, Nobyo, bought a farm north of Shelburne in the early nineties. The two of them opened the most exquisite dining experience imaginable: *amuse bouches* with preserved Japanese seaweed and ginger salads, farm raised suckling pigs turned into head-cheese with rosti potatoes, parsnip, or celeriac and lobster soups, roasted splake trout (a hybrid of speckled and lake), grilled quails with *foie gras*, roast caribou, caramelized pears and curried lentils, ducks with cauliflower mushrooms and wild rice and fleshy local fruit. All adjectives forgiven, these four-hour dinners were the most creative, innovative plates on the continent.

TH and I became their biggest fans but many of the locals were outraged by the increased traffic and weird visitors the restaurant attracted. Rave reviews in *The Wine Spectator, Gourmet* and *The New York Times* had well-travelled palates booking six months in advance, flying to Pearson International, renting cars and driving through god-forsaken back roads, past Singhampton in search of the Vatican of hip cuisine. There was no sign, except an inukshuk in the driveway pointing to a garden littered with ducks and geese and children's toys. It is not dining for the faint of heart; these people are artists and it was not long before they ended up being raided by the police.

Everything they did was locally suspect. It was discussed in church and at the feedlot. "Where do they get their caribou?" "Are they shooting deer?" "I hear they eat porcupine." "Why do so many people live there?" "What is a sous chef?" The police charged them with alcohol infractions never before enforced. (There are still little Temperance pockets in Ontario). People complained about how many fancy cars drove up the gravel roads. The fast food joints complained the renegades were taking away business from Collingwood, as if people had been previously flying from Chicago for the burgers and fries served on Georgian Bay. The kind of European country dining people saved all their lives to experience seemed unbelievable to some. It was months before the charges were dropped and the Statdlanders were able to continue their courageous culinary enterprise. The bed-and-breakfast businesses blossomed and loved the newfound clients but the neighbours still complained, jealous of what they saw as international success in the backwoods. Recently voted one of the ten best restaurants in the world, Stadtlanders has nothing to be forgiven and I'd like to slap a few small-town people for giving them a hard time.

But suspicion now works in both directions. Newer residents, concerned about the quality of their water, complained about the farmers' cattle after an outbreak of *E. coli* killed several residents of Walkerton in southern Ontario. Moving to the country means learning to live with the smell of pig shit, and sometimes stockbrokers won't go that far. The recent women who have moved into the neighbourhood would rather form book groups and cook fusion than join the old Women's Institutes and knit sweaters or design samplers. As lives change the established institutions have difficulty rejigging to new realities, and new residents are shocked by the ignorance and disrespect for laws of some of the old farmers.

The kids in school now learn ecological thinking as naturally as breathing and drinking water, but there are still those who continue to defend their right to spread untreated human and animal waste directly on fields if the price is right. Many do not see how it is possible to farm without vast amounts of chemicals, pesticides and fertilizers sprayed every year on every inch of farmland. The "right to farm" often rules over common sense. Social and political change is slow; some attitudes will only die with their holders, or with fierce legislation.

One farmer decided that to earn a little extra money he would adapt new marketing strategies, whereupon ugly ads sprang up on billboards along Highway 89. Recently, a movie company working on a highway scene on Airport Road erected some more billboards in a farmer's field as part of their set and alarm bells went off all over the county. Claire, Caitlin and I planned acts of political reprisal and sabotage; the billboards had to be removed. The town office got so many calls about the offending eyesores they couldn't get the message out fast enough that the billboards were coming down as soon as the filming was over. It was already on the agenda for the local citizen's coalition meeting and we were ready to boycott a couple of imaginary companies for scarring the visual environment of everyone who drove down that beautiful road.

Fistfights still break out in Dufferin but now it is between the developers and the greens, not between the Catholics and the Protestants. Golf courses drive out the wild animals and they have to be fought like religious wars. New bylaws enforcing quiet have been enacted and people with dozens of barking dogs and dirt bikes have become pariahs. Every moraine on the Escarpment is a beachhead to be defended against encroaching development. Gravel companies promise jobs for a lifetime if then can open-mine the moraines. Letters and pamphlets clog the mailboxes soliciting support for one side or the other.

We often sit on the porch and read the local papers, full of these stories of good and evil fighting it out in the countryside. The girls watch and read about families they know adapting to new realities. The court reporter lists the names of every person convicted of drunk driving, assault, or theft, some of whom were schoolmates. Announcements of Power of Sale and auctions attest to the economic plight of farmers. Childhood friends move further north. Photos of those who give to charity, local political wannabes and Olympic hopefuls are spread on every cover as with any small town paper. Jobs are scarce except, in the new tourism economy or home businesses, and graduating students wonder what they will do to survive. The local artists and artisans run their biannual shows with some success and locals and tourists alike flock to the sideroads to browse for creative gifts. The Horticultural Society's exhibitions, brilliantly photographed in black and white, show off the prizewinners every season and invite those new to the community to its meetings. Natural deaths, like the farmer in Dufferin

Oaks Retirement home who marked his one-hundredth birthday, and the birth of triplets are all respectfully announced. Headlines are rarely more serious than SPEAKERS SWIPED or MEDIEVAL FAIRE COMES TO TOWN but reading the local papers makes it clear to residents that Mono is not the same place they were born into. Many women find their lives in the country in turmoil and see the only viable futures for their daughters in further education or city jobs. Dubious enterprises in the modern economy cannot survive and even farmers need degrees these days.

The lives of all young people in the country are scrutinized more than they were fifty years ago. For most parents "the road not taken" is not the one they want their children to pursue in these chaotic times. Normal life passages are accepted and acknowledged, like the landscape, but the "unnatural" ones, which occur on a daily basis in the city, seem out of place in small communities. To become an art historian or a jazz musician is an aberration. Life is no longer predictable: girls go off to the Himalayas and boys don't grow up to be farmers like their fathers, and this makes people anxious. A young man, unable to cope with the modern world, was recently arrested driving around with the head of his former girlfriend wrapped in a box strapped to the back of his motorcycle. She had been at my daughter's high school. In spite of TV news, long-time residents still feel confounded by inexplicable behaviour—accidents happen that should not occur. Horrors are more accepted in the city; tragedies are things that most people who have moved to the country feel they have left behind. It is a terrible shock to hear of suicides in Shelburne, heroin at the local high school.

Somehow, by some miracle of location, modern atrocities should not touch one in the country. Two young boys found dead by misadventure at the bottom of the cliffs was almost more than anyone could handle. No one could understand how it could have happened but perhaps it is not so great a mystery in an area where city folk/country folk wars still continue into the next generation and modern anxieties are felt by all.

*Athena and her owl.*

# Fall On Your Knees

**P**hillip was depressed for most of the winter term and could hardly wait the three weeks until spring break. His parents' insistence that he go to Upper Canada College for grade ten so that he could be close to his father's associates' children was, to him, more of the cruel humiliation his parents heaped on him. He had wanted to attend the local school like his friends but that was not to be discussed.

At the age of six he had been sent, for his own good, to England, to Harrow Junior School to board and now he would go to Upper Canada, as the local Lord Dufferin High School was not appropriate. He only had his summers and brief vacations left to be free, to play as he did in childhood, to remind him of the time his parents were together, walking and talking through their problems in the park.

His memories were fragmentary. He had mostly been "away". Away from his parents, away from his friends and "away" for Phillip, this dark late winter in Toronto, was no longer good enough.

Being away had rid him of his Ontario nasal drawl and erased most of the local slang. Of this his mother had been proud when she came to visit. He had tried, on his own, to moderate the triple-syllabled words in his vocabulary and replace them with expletives but the boys he used to know now either teased or ignored him. They jeered at his pronunciation of "Lord" and "government" and "predicament", called him "Slimey Limey!"

The last vacation he was alone except for Oswald Hand, who came to the country house to help his father, the neighbourhood contractor, when work was to be done on Hawk's Ridge Farm. When Oswald came, Phillip almost forgot to think about what he was saying. They farted about in the park, kicked a soccer ball and searched for salamanders by the pond. They would do that again this spring when the snow melted and the park was muddy and dank.

But this afternoon he would have to go through another ritual, playing the role of Sir John A. Macdonald in his Canadian history project. His teacher chose him because he was able to precisely mimic the Scottish-Canadian tones, understand the text in the tangled tongue of the Prime Minister. Billy McDougall, his friend from Edinburgh at Harrow, who had tutored him through six semesters of Chaucer, Shakespeare, Milton, Scott, Tudor Kings and Queens, World War One and the Indian Mutiny, had also taught him to wrap his lips around the competing accents of colonial power and the colonized. They had watched Monty Python videos late at night and played the British schoolboy games that made mock of their imprisonment. Phillip was good at it.

"Come on, Sperling." He turned as Mr Mayhew came striding into the classroom. "Ready to perform?" He held his hand high above his head, gesturing like Olivier.

That evening, over dinner at Scaramouche with his mother, she had been persistent. "Tell me how it went, darling. Tell me how it went!" She shuffled the breadbasket towards him.

"Fine. Okay, I guess."

"Will you be doing it for the open house? So all the parents can see you?"

"I don't know yet. I don't know." But Phillip did know his mother's new boyfriend would be coming. Surely she would bring him along, if only to notify his father that she was no longer alone in their house in Toronto?

"I can go to Malabar's and get you a costume. I told Mr Mayhew I would pay for the real thing. The real costume."

For Halloween when he was nine she had rented the real *Phantom of the Opera* costume; before that it was the real *Cats* costume. She had forced him to go with her to every theatre series in town. Some of the plays had been on for so long in Toronto they ended up seeing things twice. He was disgusted when his mother expressed renewed shock at the helicopter coming down in *Saigon*, even though they had seen it in New York. Her appetite for the theatre was endless and, even though he had tried to please her, she never kept quiet about what part he should play next.

"It's not necessary. I don't care. I don't want to do this anymore."

"Of course you care! You're so good at these things—so good at history and drama. That would be fun. We want to have fun, don't we?" She was always wanting to make things fun: school was to be fun, dinner out was to be fun, dressing was to be fun, everything was to be fun when it was really all dull and lonely and boring.

"Suppose so. I have to study. I have to get back to school. I've got forty pages to do for a test in the morning."

His mother paid the bill, tipping more than was usual, and stuffing the receipt in her purse to show that, in fact, she needed the twelve thousand a month in alimony to pay for her son's activities.

On his way back up to his residence, Phillip took off his navy sweater, folded it under his arm and searched for his key in the jumble of his pockets. He didn't want to be here, convinced as he was that his was not the best education in Canada, and he didn't want to spend the next several hours poring over his history texts. He hated reading now as much as he hated long distance running. Others, it seemed, watched television, played video games, went to McDonald's, and they passed. Hamburgers were against nutritional laws his mother knew about but the common folk did not. Yet none of his schoolmates seemed to suffer from cholesterol problems or fat congealing in their teenage arteries, or faulty thought patterns, learning disabilities and the long list of physical problems stemming from MSG at the Chinese takeaway. He stood there a long time, holding on to the banister in his residence.

Phillip placed the sweater into his drawer and gently pushed it shut, turning on the reading lamp over his desk and arranging his textbooks, notepads, markers and pencils across the leather pad. He set his alarm for 6:30 so that he could read a few chapters of *A Tale of Two Cities* before breakfast. He was three hundred pages behind Nick Tommelty in the Dickens race and he should, by virtue of his English schooling, have finished the entire collection.

He stared at the headings in his history book and thumbed the margins. What really happened at the Battle of Batoche? Who was Louis Riel? What was the battle plan on the Fields of Abraham? When did the Inuit move to Davis Inlet and why? Was he, Phillip Sperling, supposed to be able to guess the truth about the histories of people he had never met or cared about when he couldn't answer simple questions about his own? Who was going to explain Louis Riel to him? Who was going to explain his life?

He stared at his pencils, at the boring order of his room, at his calendar and scratched off another day until his father would pick him up and he would go to Hawk's Ridge for the holidays. He looked at the pictures of Louis Riel and the maps of Canada and wrote lists and dates and began memorizing them all. After twenty minutes he reviewed the list again, recited the litany, chanted the names and added up the dates, sometimes into a single digit and then divided it up again to recall the proper sequence of events. No one had taught him these tricks; he had figured them out himself. These were ways to aid his memory, restructure things, and so in the end he had his version of how things went for Louis Riel and the rest of Canada.

As he pulled back the quilt, to his horror he saw a stain in the centre of his sheets. He pulled them off and walked with the bundle to the laundry chute at the end of the hall. Some other boys were up, giggling in another room. He thought he heard the repetitive click of a Nintendo with the sound turned down. He grabbed fresh linens from the closet and remade his bed. He fluffed up the pillow and put on the blue pajamas from his bottom drawer. He tried to be neat, do his homework, eat his proper meals and yet he could not control his dreams, control his body and the spasms that tore through it in the night. He would try.

He turned to the mnemonic in his head again, sorting through the letters and the numbers for order as it should be. He tucked his legs up and curled his toes in order to avoid the chill. At one o'clock he squeezed his eyes shut, pressing the lids together, feeling the red glow of the exertion behind his eyeballs, the letters and dates imprinted, reflecting into the darkness of his brain as he waited for sleep to come.

Three weeks later, at the cliffs, Oswald teased him about his part in the play. That sissy stuff was too much for him and he hoped they never got to that part of the curriculum. Phillip tried to laugh it off as just something they did at boys' schools but Oswald was relentless, partly because he felt that Phillip looked down on him for not knowing the same dates and place names that he did.

"How important can that be?" Oswald joked. "Not as important as who won the hockey game, that's for sure."

"The game means nothing! Games change every season, hockey players come and go. No one remembers their names and positions." Phillip kicked some stones over the edge of the cliff and they clattered down near the caves below.

"I remember them all! I remember what *time* the goals were scored. Not that sissy ass stuff you care about." Oswald pushed him.

Phillip grabbed him and pushed back.

*Shelburne Free Press*
*Boys Fall from Cliff*

*A fifteen-year-old Toronto boy, Phillip Sperling, and his fourteen-year-old friend, Oswald Hand of Shelburne, plunged to their deaths on Sunday afternoon in the Mono Cliffs Provincial Park. They had been hiking near the entrance to the caves when they apparently lost their footing and fell 60 meters to the rocks below. Both were pronounced dead at Orangeville Area Hospital. An inquiry will be held.*

# People You'd Trust Your Life To

What held some communities together was not common faith or common goals but landscape, narratives, shared history and, in our case, tumultuous, unpredictable weather: shattering ice storms in winter or drought in summer, road closing blizzards and overripe hay fields late for swathing.

"Most folks don't notice the daily weather no more," the snowplow man told me one day. "All they talk about is global warmin'. It's as if they forgot it's constantly changin' or can't see it. They only talk about it when they panic 'cause of the flooding or fires or ice. Can't always predict what Mother Nature is going to do. I think it's too much television. You know there's a whole channel for weather so people don't have to go outside and figure it out for themselves."

There is little in the shifting wind to warn of freezing rain. One moment, walking in a fog, the muffled ground can be wet with patchy snow and the next moment the cloud will drop lower, full of moisture, the opaque sun will set and within minutes everything is frozen, a thick glass sheet reflecting the world. All the birds go to bush, the coyotes to den. A silence. Broad wet boots become skates and one can only slide, not walk. It is possible to push the car as if it were a puck on a rink. Any slope becomes a chute and a dead branch the sword of Damocles, mortal danger should wind arise. Every branch, pinecone, sumac spear and fence post becomes a form for delicate silver cupping. Sumac seedpods form red candelabra. The down pipes from the eaves sprout frozen forms, rivulets dancing over rocks in the garden congeal in black ice. It is dangerous to move, even on foot, and nature warns that all is a precarious, fragile, glory.

Stranded travellers struggle for the nearest farmhouse. "No fool should be out on a night like this." Beds are made up, towels brought from cupboard drawers and tinned soups in large mugs are passed around, phone calls are made.

In the morning, with the temperature's rise, the ground is littered with silver casings, hollowed shards, mounds of ice dropped from the roof and eaves. Streamers hang under rail and wire fences, wasted wrappings, like the remains of a ghostly party they click and chink underfoot reflecting the warm sun. The horses in the barn whinny for release, the roads reopen, cars are pulled from ditches, there are grateful "Thank yous" and guests can get home.

"They should've offered to help with next spring's hayin'."

It was not just winter weather, it was also emergencies in summer that tied us together: hay to be baled and stacked, cows on the loose, horses foaling, and children suddenly ill. When a neighbour, Rudy, had to go to Waterloo for a funeral my husband volunteered to feed his pigs for a couple of days, to make sure the water was on and the liquid manure disposer was functioning. This farmer had two thousand hogs and I will never forget TH's smell when he returned from his promised duty. Like Bellow's *Henderson the Rain King*, he wondered what it was people were thinking when they took up pig farming. The acrid ammonia stayed on my husband's flesh for days and the sweat pants had to be burned. It was as if he had wallowed in it. Poor hog farmers, now no one wants to live next door. Twelve pigs are fine but thousands are another story. Most of the pig farmers went bankrupt in the 70s and 80s and hog farming moved to less expensive real estate in agribusiness factories. It's just not like *Charlotte's Web*.

"Pigs is like that."

One farmer nearby had two hundred and fifty head of Charolais and it seemed we were continually helping him round them up back into the barnyard. There is something about cows, greener pastures and poor fencing. One May, when calving started, his eldest son was left in charge but ran into trouble with a particularly difficult small cow that had a breached calf. TH went over late at night with the block and tackle and he managed to get an arm up her backside, wrap a rope around the ankles, and pull the babe out the right way. Calf Qr27 got nicknamed TH2.

Another morning, a cow with a half-disgorged uterus was down in the field. There were two other neighbours driving by who stopped to help; we managed to push the uterus back in and walk the wobbly old girl home. Her calf died but she went on to breed another season.

"Can't leave a farm in calving season. Can't shut your eyes for a minute."

Our neighbour to the east brought us a deer one spring that he had to shoot after it was caught in our mutual fence line. His wife didn't like venison and so we took the dead beast, removed the scent sacs, gutted, skinned and washed it with vinegar, and wrapped it in cheesecloth to hang in the barn for two weeks. My grandmother and father had been slaughtering and hanging reindeer and moose and I had helped out more than I cared to as a child, so butchering this small deer did not seem such a problem. I saved the roasts, steaks and tenderloin for freezing and ground a lot of the scraps for what Claire and Caitlin called "Bambi burgers." Needless to say, the kids wouldn't touch the meat but marinated in red plonk with black pepper corns and juniper berries and roasted with a sweet mustard glaze it was divine for adults.

"City folk eat anything nowadays—road kill and swamp grass."

We had a couple of homesick Italian hunters from Toronto who took it upon themselves to "help out the farmers" and they used to show up and ask if they could shoot pigeons and rabbits on our property. They always carried two fabulous Berretta shotguns and for the only time in my life (I abhor guns) I coveted one. If there were too many pigeons we let the hunters clear them as birds make a mess of the upstairs of barns once the hay gets inside to cure. On one of these visits and after a successful hunt, the two, with broken English and great pride, offered me a bloody brace of pigeon from their dozen birds. I smiled and took the two birds gracefully; they assured me that pigeon was good for my "bambini", good for the digestive system and wonderful for lactating mothers. Having no intention of nursing Caitlin now that she was three, I confess to burying the gruesome pair in my garden as it was one of those days when I had no patience for picking out buckshot and plucking feathers late into the evening.

"Why pay supermarket prices for birds? There's flocks of good eating out here for free."

Part of the farming community used to get together at the livestock sales barn on Highway 10, before it was razed by fire. It was as amusing a place as any to spend a Tuesday evening. We rarely went to buy, other than a few chicks and ducks to raise for the table, but more to watch as farmers herded in broken-down infertile cows, stolen sheep and horses destined for the slaughterhouse in Owen Sound. I once bought half a dozen goslings, hoping for good fall livers and roasts, but instead ended up being followed all summer by what had become annoying guard geese that refused to let me be. They hit the oven when they started opening up the screen door and crapping on my 1930 Peterborough wool carpets. It's not good to get too sentimental about some beasts and one has to draw the line at the door.

"Bloody fool people, think they're pets rather than livestock. Once heard of a guy who looked after a raccoon with a broken leg for six years. Nice trick if you're a raccoon."

As well as the sales barn, the garage at Violet Hill was a great place for local gossip: who was going bankrupt, whose wife had left him for a city guy. One of the most gruesome stories was of the pig farmer who slipped on the oily manure of his concrete barn floor and collapsed into the slimy sty of his prize boar. The poor man was knocked unconscious and consumed by the ravenous animal. Bones and rubber boots and a few scraps of cloth were all that were recovered from the pen. Until then I had no idea pigs were omnivorous.

"Pigs is like that. Some big appetite."

Another tale from several years back had a wealthy stockbroker, not a permanent resident of the community but a landowner nonetheless, importing a herd of prize Charolais from France to be used as breeding stock to improve the local beef. This was a wise tax position but, of course, the city guy couldn't tell a Charolais from a Simmental and eventually his hired farm hand sold off, at great profit, the well-bred French animals and replaced them with vaguely similar beef stock picked up at the sales barn for a few hundred dollars. It is endless class warfare if you don't know who your friends are, don't have someone to trust.

"Couldn't tell a windmill from a windrow. Always paid the top price to have his manure removed and then we sold it."

After over twenty years and a huge influx of new city folk, we passed for locals and there were those old-timers who called the farm "Sweetfield-where-the-teachers-live," recognized us at the Shelburne Co-op, phoned us if there was a fight to launch at city council or to find out who had the best horse hay that season. That was a good enough definition of community for me but it never stopped the gossip.

"Those college teachers mow trails in their woods so the wolves have a tidy place to walk. What a waste of gasoline!"

"It's the wife who does it—she's the weird one. Knows nothin' from farmin'. Still gives away her vegetables."

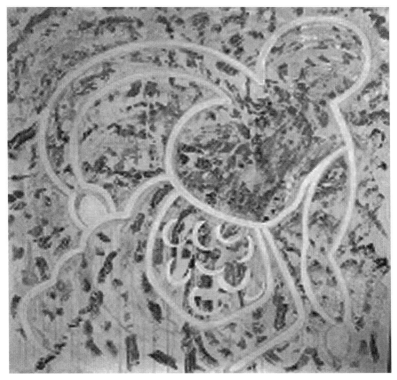

*Potato picking.*

# The Field

O ut my kitchen window I could see an expanse of well-tilled earth—a testament to many lifetimes of hard labour. For over a hundred and fifty years in Mono, long before country living was considered a respite from stressful city careers, generations of United Kingdom immigrants and their descendants had been busy, through ferocious winters, hand-cutting the beech, maple and pine forests and horse-hauling the lumber to build houses and barns. Countless springs were spent blasting the stumps, clearing the debris, burning the scrub, dragging out the stones, stacking them, splitting cedar rails, fencing the perimeters; then, plowing, harrowing, seeding and fertilizing in the summers. Generations more continued the repetitive swathing and thrashing of grain, the baling and stacking of hay and straw until late every fall. I had those hard-working people to thank for this view of fertile fields which extends to the forests and pond and marshes beyond, which put me in touch with the natural horizon, the history of where I lived, the food I prepared for my family table, and the satisfying memories I had stored from living on this farm.

Every field was a birthing and a burial ground. Some years the sun shone and the harvest was good. Others, with no rain, meant all the money and labour of a withered crop were plowed back into the earth in the hope of better luck the following year. Most people can barely imagine the long hours, the heart- and back-breaking strain of getting a crop to the barn or market with modern machinery, let alone with only horsepower. Fields evolve over generations, the soils improve or are depleted depending on the skill of the farmer. Cut the hay crop before it was ready, and you'd get a lesser yield; cut it too late, it would have gone to seed and lost half the nutrition; cut in damp weather, it was lost to mould. There's not a farmer in Ontario who can't talk for hours about his fields, describe the preferred soils, reminisce or weep about good years and bad, give advice to the novice. Emotions rise and fall with the whims of the weather. The spring wind, if there had not been enough snow, could steal the topsoil; a sudden rain could flood and wash away that year's planting.

At a school meeting in Primrose, a Mulmur woman recalls seeding down a sloping field twice over the last wet spring. She shakes her head and smiles, "We expected that," she admitted, "but it was the drought that followed that hurt us more." Dufferin County fields are relatively small by Canadian standards, and for most of these rural residents bread on the table was not solely dependent on cash crops, but for those farmers whose livelihoods come completely from their fields, whose success with a grain crop meant feed for the cattle or scarce money spent at the Co-op, every season was a feast or famine struggle. A field was full of promise and betrayal no matter what the size.

In winter, under cover, the field was a glistening lake, stretching to the horizon, ribbed with harrowed waves, alive with the choreography of white birds over snow, or dotted with occasional black crows, or a meandering flock of wild turkeys. Even in the dead of winter, with only a sliver of moon, the field would be criss-crossed by coyotes with exceptional skill at finding mice burrowing through drifts. Early mornings I saw northern shrikes and goshawks feeding on sparrows and chickadees flocking low around the bushes hugging the fence lines. The field was never quiet.

Every spring the forty acres of our farm under cultivation brought new discussions, choices and decisions to be made. With the neighbour farmers who helped us out, we decided on the crops, fertilizer, and rotation. We decided what we needed for our horses—what they needed for their cows. But there was nothing like standing in the middle of an open field, the horizon unfolding around, to bring out the amateur philosopher in every rural soul. We took the time to discuss the vicissitudes of raising children, what should be done to revamp the tax system, how to reorganize education in Ontario, how to put an end to world hunger, rid the world of war. Once while standing in the middle of the field, enjoying the earliest spring rain in memory, we contemplated the value of long marriages, celebrating birthdays and honouring losses. Before the hard work began, ankle deep in comforting muck, many of the world's problems were solved as the last of winter scurried away.

When the spring plowing started in earnest the rocks, heaved up by the winter frost, rose out of the muck like nightmares from the unconscious. We all wondered at the growth of such enormous boulders. "We should sell these stones abroad, they're so perfect. Surely someone would pay for these original stones?" The beasts were lifted aside with the forklift or rolled into the garden, where they stood, reconfigured into inukshuks, pointing the way down some invisible path. Each year the rock pile grew, awaiting a building project or barn repair. Each spring more rose to the surface, as if beckoned by our yearning for something to grow.

When our two girls were young and their book-fed imaginations were running rampant, they would tell their friends stories about the Roman aqueducts and Greek ruins on the farm, about the Sweetfield Stonehenge and the mysterious sun worship structures left by natives and secret encampment markings protected by bands of wandering gypsies who camped in our fields. Amongst these rocks they would find small animal dens, where French Resistance fighters hid caches of food from the Nazis.

Claire and Caitlin would go out, a couple of hammers and a picnic in a cloth bag, and spend the day at the rock pile chipping away to get the stones to reveal the fossils inside. Each cephalopod that yielded to the hammer had a story attached to it—an historical occasion invented to mark the discovery. The geologist across the road would praise them for each fossil found and correctly named. They would scour the rows, like seagulls after the plow, to find new treasures, to tell outrageous tales, to confirm their evolutionary link with ancient sea animals and kinship with noble heroines on the run.

Walking the freshly plowed field many summers ago we found well-rusted horseshoes from Clydesdales of Walter Scott, the farmer who broke this ground in 1884. There were forks and bits of old cracked pottery in a high corner overlooking the marsh, left perhaps from some party where too much drinking and carousing occurred. There are dozens of thumb-sized blue bottles near the perimeter of apple trees, perhaps laudanum or a herbal alcohol mixture designed to alleviate "women's problems" bought from some itinerant snake-oil salesman before the great Depression.

On the north end of the barn adjacent to the field I discovered, hidden in a cranny, a painted metal box dated 1929, which once held condoms. There was a yellowed note inside. *Intended to prevent pregnancy. Always insist on fresh stock. All condoms deteriorate with age.* This particular box of condoms had belonged to John Scott (a great grandson of Walter) who had dutifully pierced his initials into the tin cover using a small nail. All kinds of questions pop to mind: What was this doing in the barn? With whom was he having secret sex? Why the initials on the box? Were the condoms damaged by the nail pricks? The box was empty but why keep and hide the box? I'm glad he did, for several amusing hours were spent reconstructing the scenarios offered by this little bit of field-find. Later the same week a small femur led the girls to the complete skeleton of a fox. On another walk I stooped to pick up a round mottled object and a snapping turtle developed legs and scampered back to the pond to avoid me.

The field was an exciting and sensuous place to walk. The soil, a clay and humus mix, sent out different olfactory messages in different locations—a skunk was here, that horse manure needed turning, the leftover mash was composting. The soil was rich, black in places, heavy when wet, the rusty teeth of an old plow turned a few sods orange. A broken leather harness hooked over a fence line sixty years ago bore witness to the seasons of work and I could not bring myself to throw it away. A license plate, fallen from a vehicle, 1930, I tacked on the side of my gardening shed, a memento to work well done, a fertile field.

I looked forward to summers after the plowing, to another find in those perfect fields, to more lost friends, old bones, stones and memories released after a cold winter.

*Hay bales in the north field.*

# Going to Town

Unlike fields, most northern cities in deep winter are places of abjection: imposing sterile grey skyscrapers reflecting each other against a howling vacant horizon. Toronto is no different. There is no greenery apart from a few dead or struggling grasses, hearty cabbage or wilted flowering kale in desperate pots; there are no songbirds, only a scattering of pathetic pigeons, scraping in Glenn Gould parkette, or one of the few other parks, for leftover summer bread crumbs under the snow. A few geese stay by the lake, braving the winter, allowing themselves to be harassed by dogs. But, even in winter, books have to be found, operas enjoyed, toothaches have to be alleviated, provisions have to be bought and somehow we have to survive.

As one drives from the farm along the Queen Elizabeth Way the Skydome sits like a giant half-buried unhatched egg beside a spindle, beckoning visitors to warm hotels and restaurants. Post cards of the CN Tower look like a scene out of some 50s futuristic Martian movie. I wish people wouldn't buy them and send them around the world. They give the wrong impression.

My uncle in Stockholm (and Swedes should not throw winter stones) was shocked when he saw these pictures, amongst others in a magazine I had sent him about Canada. He read about Toronto's underground PATH system: miles of underground walkways, replete with lawyers, dentists, restaurants and boutiques attached to the subway system. He wanted to visit but was not sure he could cope.

"It's not human—it's not right! You have to be out of doors—even in the winter—walking—getting what little light there is," his arms, hands and fingers rich with approbation. "You cannot be mole people."

I assured him that most Torontonians lived above ground, in spite of movies and urban legends about people who stay below for years. But the image stuck with him till our next discussion. I assured him again that what he had read was not true, only the journalistic hook of a travel writer. But he had read more about Canadian winters. "They are globally famous," he warned me severely. "Do not become an underground person!" I assured him that in the country we lived above ground.

To seek supplies and diversion we bundled up: three layers, gloves, hats, down coats and our faces wrapped in muffler masks. We headed to art galleries with exhibitions of summer light and colour and to the movies, flickering briefly before we headed out again into the brittle, uncompromising cold. We spent hours in bookstores reading the fiction lists alphabetically to see who had something new, checking the foreign writers for thoughts of other, perhaps warmer, places. TH at Z, me at A, we'd meet at M with stacks of the usual suspects under our arms and new writers we'd never heard of. Our credit cards almost maxed, we headed briskly into the wind. Later, at the enclosed St Lawrence Market, we joined other shoppers foraging for cheeses, fresh breads, fish. We moved quickly, and ran out with our purchases back to the car. Winter keeps one moving at a pace.

Most Canadians leave for at least two weeks in the most dismal period, the darkest weeks between December 1st and February 15th, if only to keep themselves from having to medicate for Seasonal Affective Disorder. Outdoor storefront promenading in winter can be done in San Miguel De Allende where winter, it seems, never comes.

Inhabitants, more resilient than I, could be found cross-country skiing in High Park, winter camping, shopping in Yorkville, walking at Harbourfront, but they must have been a younger, bolder species, unaffected by darkness, wind, snow and concrete, or perhaps they hadn't read enough to know their lives were in jeopardy.

Our literature is full of stories of early immigrants who died their first winter here: pneumonia, frostbite, flu, scurvy, smallpox, whooping cough and diphtheria. In spite of the improved modern medical arsenal, dozens of homeless die huddled over subway grates or wrapped in cardboard boxes in bus shelters, their stories untold. A man jumped from the Bloor-Danforth Viaduct, a preferred suicide spot, but survived by landing in a snow bank and rolling to the bottom. Finally, he froze to death. A horrible exit, only possible here.

Many years ago several desperate Chinese illegal immigrants, stowed in a freight car, managed to get out and begin their walk to freedom outside of town. Barely clad in sports jackets and running shoes, they lost their fingers and toes, unaware what a four-mile walk to town, in Canada in the winter, entails. Their fate was not unknown to thousands of others; but desperate lives lead to desperate measures.

For many, that first glimpse of clean, open winter snow can be exciting and liberating, but to be bearable, winter in the country in Canada demands food, shelter, good books and warm fires. In my family, and we were accustomed to Scandinavian winters, that adaptation took three generations to accomplish. For the less fortunate, the city was still a dangerous place and going to town in winter required perseverance and preparation. Only those with fierce desires ventured forth when the weather was bad.

# This Is Not For You

Vanessa Ridgeway really cared very little that the neighbours despised her. She cared little that they complained to the Nottawasaga Valley Conservation Authority when she diverted the river to fill her fourteen-acre pond. She just ordered her lawyers on them and had the river partially rerouted after her pond had filled. It took months in the courts and she ignored the reprimand from the Niagara Escarpment Commission just as she always ignored the censure of others. She expected these kinds of things to happen in small towns and counted heavily on her city connections to swamp minor protests.

When the work began on the four buildings that existed on her hundred acres, she filled in the application forms calling the excavations and construction "restoration and renovation" when she knew the old out buildings were coming down to make way for the guest house, the stable and the pool cabana. What did these farmers and townspeople know? What did they care about how she spent her money? How dare they pronounce what was appropriate development and what was undesirable?

She knew what desirable was and had traveled extensively to the American eastern seaboard from Washington to Maine, admiring the estates and developments. Had these people never seen Martha's Vineyard? Do they read *Architectural Digest*? Had they ever played tennis in Rockport? She was doubtful. She knew exactly what she was doing and had no intention of abiding by their petty codes. She instructed her landscaper and architect as to the rebuilding of the farm.

After all, her family owned over five hundred acres along the river for as long as she could remember. Her grandfather had bought it sixty years ago because he enjoyed fishing. He had a small bridge built over the Nottawasaga so that he could stand there and cast his line into the middle of the rushing stream. In those days it was full of speckled trout and she could remember stories he would tell about catching hundreds of fish and holding vast fry-ups, the bulk of which ended up back in the river as fertilizer. Downstream was downstream.

From time to time when she and her husband, then only in their twenties, started coming up for the weekends she would sometimes catch the local farmers fishing from that little bridge and so she had it torn down to deny them access to her side of the water. Her grandfather was dead and she and her husband no longer enjoyed the non-competitive aspects of fishing when tennis was at hand.

Her husband had nurtured a Walden fantasy in his youth and spoke lyrically about the trees and the river and the fresh air and had not wanted to change the old brick farmhouse. It had been painted and insulated but he had insisted on tacky Victorian settees and bric-a-brac. Now that he was remarried and living in Ottawa she wanted to rid the property of any of that Gothic tightness and make it more Colorado in feel—cedar board and batten, pools, jacuzzis and large outdoor terraces. Had their marriage lasted into their forties she would certainly have been asphyxiated by his smug Ontario dreams.

She fought bitterly with her gardener who had sprayed with weed killer as ordered but the smell of the poison had stuck to the cedar in the sauna. She was forced to fire him. The landscaper had assured her he would bring in truckloads of sterile topsoil after the houses were finished and not one weed would get through the newly imported growth. This summer she would have the hedges thinned, after the construction was finished, so that she could see the cars entering from the road.

The demolition work had started in early April and, as soon as the frost was out of the ground, the new foundations were poured. She came up from the city once a week to supervise and by May she was able to see the frames of the new houses outlined against the pines and rocks.

And then something happened that she never expected. The town imposed a stop work order. The architect quit, claiming interference, misinformation and damage to his professional reputation. The contractor and his crew left for another job and her lawyers suggested she conform to the building codes. By the end of June she had no recourse but to hire another architect and contractor to handle the fiasco.

Vanessa blamed her meddling neighbours and kept her eye open until one day she had the satisfaction of calling the fire department and reporting the farmer next door for burning scrub without a permit. It cost him $900 he didn't have and she felt vindicated.

It meant however, that she would have to go to Lake Joseph in Muskoka for the summer and wait until the following spring for a restart. The permits would take three to six months and approvals from her neighbours would have to be paid for. According to her lawyers, each and every one of them had the right to make comments on her plans. Finally, to Vanessa, it didn't seem worth it and she listed the property in its unfinished and exposed state and left the problem to her realtors.

*Another Far Shore.*

# Dear Bruce Springsteen

When spring finally arrived we began to live outdoors with the animals again. Most evenings after dinner we walked and rediscovered some corner of the farm. Much work had been done around the barns, gardens and trees but we were always aware of wanting to leave some spaces totally untouched: places where the bush should never be cleared, where no raking or trimming or planting should ever take place, some-place completely wild. We didn't leave our scent there. That under-growth, free from human touch, was Eden for ground nesters, omnivorous chickadees, snakes that wished to shed their skins, rabbits, foxes, unknown insects, wild orchids and mosses.

Most of our farm was accessible all year round; however, the untouchable region behind the swale with its nesting herons, wild turkeys and ruffed grouse was sacred ground. Occasionally, we would see one of these creatures rise from its private nest and transform the air. As well as the massive Canadian wilderness that astounds first-time visitors these small areas of wild, that have not been protected, are miracles. And that is one of the rea-sons the country is so magnificent. I cannot imagine the day when the tipping point is reached and we lose that link to the wild.

One evening before walking, I heard Caitlin scream as she was out mowing on the lawn tractor and I ran outside to see a stone-grey six-foot snake, as fat as my thigh, glide slowly across the open roadway. I didn't recognize it as anything I'd seen before except in the Tarzan movies of my childhood or described in tales out of Africa. I later called the herpetologist associated with the conservation area and she could not identify the monster we had seen— obviously not indigenous. The final consensus was that it was a banned snake someone had been keeping as a house pet that had outgrown its enclosure and escaped, or been freed, the minute the snow melted in the park. Where it finally ended up we had no idea but it surely would not survive into the next Ontario winter.

The several species of Niagara Escarpment snakes, the garters, the milks and the rat snakes, seemed to be particularly evident as I went tooting around some bend on the tractor. They liked the paths and often stretched out to sunbathe across my route. I slowed down at known snake corners for fear of sending them through my blades. There were many wild animals I learned to love and take special care not to harm with my machinery.

The coyotes and their young howled and yipped late at night as food was brought to the den. We had been listening to them for so long, and watching as they prowled in packs across the back fields, that we were undisturbed by their eerie wails. Foxes have good and bad years and there had been talk at our local pub at the Mono Cliffs about the many healthy vixen and their young. Foxes had reappeared in the ravines in Toronto and seemed to be thriving in spite of the change around them. I don't worry for their survival but more for the larger wolves who are not so adaptive and require sanctuary to breed. Without these areas of deep privacy these animals would not survive and keeping the spaces where the wild things are was becoming more and more important.

Another requirement of cultivating the wild was darkness. I heard people support the idea of lit boulevards joining up all the golf courses and parks. Surely those people can move to Las Vegas? When we first moved there were few commuters and the farmers (long preservers of electricity) often left no lights, or only one, burning. North of us in Mulmur Township we had a wealthy gynecologist who felt it was necessary to floodlight three hundred acres of pine forest. Thankfully, the township passed a bylaw forbidding such nonsense and his *son et lumière* fantasies were dimmed. Night creatures like darkness; darkness makes the shy visible planets glow as they should and, on full moon nights, we often ate outdoors without so much as a candle, listening only to our knives and forks and the rustling of the insomniac wind in the maples.

When the kids were small they got flashlights in their Christmas stockings and they learned to light the ground in front of their feet as we walked at night. Until they were in school we had convinced them that the fireflies around the pond were fairies and we had to keep silent and dark in order to see the magic in the night. For years, they thought Bruce Springsteen must have lived near a pond to write songs about *Darkness on the Edge of Town.* He knew about screen doors and porches and "ridin' in the back seat". It became habit to settle back and drink tea and listen to the Bruce album of the moment after night walks. The girls were convinced the Bruce Trail was named after The Boss, not some long-dead Scot. When we finally started to go to all his concerts as a family the girls were surprised to hear him sing *Back Streets* instead of "back seats" but they were always happy to heed his advice and turn the lights down low.

*Place of the snake crossing.*

# For Those Who Hunt the Wounded Down

"**I** want you to do something about it, Mommy. I just can't stand it anymore! Those horses down the hill are dying and I know they are."

"Did you go there again after school?"

"On my bike." Claire looked guilty, as I had told her several times not to go down the cliff hill on her bike. "But I had to go. I brought the horses some carrots and I got really close this time. Every one of them has burdock in their manes. Every one has pus in their eyes and their coats have never been brushed, never been cleaned!"

"They're a wild herd."

"They aren't wild. They are just not cared for. Not one of them is healthy. They are all skin and bone. Why can't you call the SPCA? Call the animal shelter!"

"The town knows about the horses. They are not taken care of, I know, but they have pasture and water."

"But that farmer never worms them, never clips their hooves. I saw one horse with a hoof cracked right up the middle. He was lame. The ends of their feet are like broken dinner plates! I think that farmer should have his herd taken away. What does he keep them for anyway? He obviously hates them."

"He doesn't hate them. He keeps them as trotters and pacers. He brings them in as two-year-olds and they get some training."

"Then they get dumped at some track until they break down."

"I suppose that is what happens."

"Then they go for meat or just get hauled off by the dead animal man."

"I'm sorry."

"How can this happen?"

"What he does is not against the law."

"When Daddy and I went by his farm one day, there was a mother who had given birth by herself. No one to help her. And another time a horse was caught up in the wire that's all over the place. It looks like a dump over there. He is responsible for his farm."

"There's no law that says he has to keep his farm clean. No law that says his fencing has to be safe for horses."

"Then there should be that law. There should be and that man should be charged and sent to prison for cruelty to animals."

"There is nothing we can do."

"I'm going there again tomorrow and the day after that and the day after that."

"We're not going to take to feeding his horses. It's hard enough to feed our own."

"They should be cared for. I can't believe you're not going to do anything about it. I'm going to talk to Daddy. I'm going to call the newspapers. Someone should go out there and take pictures of those broken-down horses and that guy should be shamed into doing something."

"I'm afraid some people have no shame. He has no conscience."

"The newspaper. I'm going to call the newspaper."

"Maybe that will help."

"And I'm going to put it in my paper at school. Maybe that will help. Does this he have children? Are they alive?"

"I don't know."

"If he had children they would have died. They would have died. I hate people like that. I absolutely hate them. Someone should throw him outside in the winter to grow worms in his stomach. I hate him."

"I'm sorry."

"Don't say you're sorry! Don't say that anymore. Where does kindness come in this world?"

"There's not that much. We make it ourselves. We make it ourselves."

"There is not one drop of kindness in that farmer. He is evil. Evil itself."

"Yes, he is evil. There is evil. But there is also goodness, some happiness in this world."

"I don't see it today."

"Not today, but you will."

"My Dad is good, he would never hurt a horse."

"Your Dad is good."

The horses in that field never got better, never were cared for and their purpose, in our family, proved to be to help the girls understand something about our relationship with animals and something about human nature in the rough. There are those in this very wealthy part of the world who give no second thought to the lives of animals, who actively profit from suffering. For twenty-five years we drove by that field and never once saw anyone caring for those horses. Every mother who has ever tried to explain this to her young children will fail. They will become eco-warriors all on their own. By watching their world.

*Diptych: Athena's owl on patrol.*

## The Energy of Slaves

My husband, in his mature natural state, was amongst the laziest people I had ever met. In his thirties, when compelled, he loved to work hard on the farm, in his forties and fifties, out of necessity, all his energy went into his work at the college. His kindness toward horses had never been in doubt but his natural instinct for indolence was unerring; however, his sloth life had been slow to evolve and remained largely unrealized because of the necessities of survival. But he was working on it—a life without housework.

A good day, according to my husband, should start around 10:30 after ten hours of sleep. The day, like an egg, should start smoothly on top with breakfast, a leisurely read of the papers, progress into something fuller, like horseriding with the girls, a photography exhibition, a little travel, a movie, a peruse of thick shelves and wind its way down with food preparation, wine, dinner, sex and a few hours of page turning. A day should be a smooth thing, no rough edges, no stress: a big sunny yolk blissfully floating in clear viscous pleasure. There are maybe a dozen days like this in a lifetime.

More often days take the shape of the Titanic or the stricken Hubble telescope. You launch out into the day and wait for something to go wrong and then try like hell to fix it. And then you are never really able to totally fix things; instead, you get the job half done and then lurch on to the next pressing project. But you are free from what TH called a "false sense of completion" that could leave you smugly content and perhaps complacent in the face of the next insurmountable task. Nothing can ever be perfectly done; nothing in this world is ever complete. TH's notion of a false sense of completion came from a childhood of travelling on ships with his parents whose lives were full of unfinished business and reneged responsibility. And partially, I must confess, his flaws are magnified as a result of conflicts with me.

I like to get things finished and cleared out of the way. I some-times like to work deep into the evening and start early in the morning in order to complete tasks. I understand the chaos of chores—work and family; indeed, I build and create it—but I also understand completion. He thinks this is my obsessive-compul-sive Lutheran side taking control of my creative side. He sees no need for that sense of control in our personal lives—it was there in spades in our professional careers and so who, in their right mind, would want to have this false sense of completion thrust on projects at the farm? It was delusional. My need for a sense of con-trol, he says, is masquerading as completion in a world of constant process. He wants all projects to be managed as part of a life plan: the constant voyage at sea, a saga of complication.

TH could live quite well with the basement not being finished, the eavestroughs leaking and the windows being dirty. Why rush into those projects? They would have to be done again next year. Why bother to put another electrical outlet by the bookshelf when you can just run an extension cord across the living room carpet? Why bother to put the weights away after working out because you just have to bring them out of the mudroom the next time you want to work out? Every living room should have a bench press and a five-hundred-pound set of weights in the centre of the floor. It's very practical. Modern.

When company comes the women can go do books and birds and brunch and the guys can do books, brawn and beer. We've compromised. When it's winter the weights stay in the basement and TH goes to the gym. When it's summer, I set up my dining table on the patio so we can sit outside in comfort without tripping over the barbells. The weights go back into the living room so, for at least the duration of his holidays, he can pretend to work out every day without putting anything away. Even if he only worked out once a week it was good to keep the weights around just in case. Without the money to put an extension on the house just for his sweaty activities this was the best we could do. He got to leave his junk out for six months of the year and I got to tidy up for six months of the year.

Just when I thought we'd gotten this renovating/working/housework thing figured out and we were both happy with how smoothly things were running, TH decided he was going to take on some of my characteristics and learn to cook. It was a change I welcomed with trepidation. This happens when people are married for a long time; they begin to take on various manifestations of the other's character.

I think control issues got exacerbated when either of us walked into the domain of the other's greatest competencies. This was just another pathetic attempt to understand how to make the world run smoothly, but it is the only explanation I can think of for his needing to get obsessive about food preparation.

Cooking was a major chore, a necessity we tried to balance in our lives. I am the cook with the forty-year history and small talent and he the sous chef; however, he was master of the cookbook shelf and had some mysterious vision for creating culinary events I knew were far beyond his ability. Disaster was just around the corner. Cooking was creative simplicity for me. I read a recipe, adjusted it to our taste and then never read the book again. TH had every cookbook open comparing strategies for chicken stock from every chef from Singapore to Mississippi to New Delhi. I saw serendipity in food preparation, logic at the whim of markets, weather, curious palettes. He envisioned a machine. I never measured; he liked to check things in both metric and imperial. It was an illusion I was happy to let him live with. Cooking for TH, because he had no confidence in what he was creating, was an exact science that took forever—to me, an art to be finished in half an hour.

He tried to learn the ephemeral nature of kitchen activities but then proceeded, after demanding that things be measured and contained and timers be set, to leave some things out of the meal altogether or just "unfinished". As with washing the dishes, he would leave out key parts of a meal—like the vegetables. "If you cook meat *and* vegetables that's too much to deal with, easier to cook just a lot of meat and onions. Besides, I forgot to turn on the potatoes." Sadly, one does not feel like one has had a meal with just lamb chops. Young girls at the best of times are quasi-vegetarian.

When dinner was ready the rest of the kitchen looked as if it had been hit by a meteorite. "Don't get attached to the notion of process and clean and tidy!"

How, I ask, can one half of the project require the mathematical precision of landing a space craft on Mars and the other half be strewn across the planetary system? It is an infuriating contradiction in his personality that he refused to address. The few dinners he prepared were never ready at mealtime and the girls often preferred Kraft Dinner to rare hunks of grilled beef. Cooking for children is rarely learned from the gatronomic musings of wannabe three-starred chefs. TH's cooking career was over in a matter of weeks. He just didn't get it.

"It just is—that's all. It just is who I am. You do the cooking. I do the eating."

It was the same thing with clothing. If clothes got put away into the closet and he didn't see shirts and pants hanging over chairs in the dining room there was the chance he would forget he had them. Why, he might walk out one day without his pants on if he didn't see them slung across the dining room sideboard and the tie thrown over the lampshade. TH's idea of decorating was to drape a pair of gonchees on the piano.

The same rule, of course, is applied to books and magazines, papers, dry cleaning receipts and pens. All of these things have to be visible or he might forget what he had been thinking and reading. My husband wrote textbooks and every few years when another edition was due, galley proofs and amendments got flung across the open plan of our house. If he could see it all, he could organize it. If he couldn't see it all, it couldn't be done.

I had taught school long enough to recognize a visual learner when I met one and so I indulged this rather weird sense of productivity in spite of the fact that it was antithetical to my own. I can see a whole meal for forty without spreading the entire contents of all the cupboards over the counter. Not so for my husband. Some people are pilers and some people are filers. Plates came together quite naturally in my head just before they appeared on the table.

TH saw this as some sort of sleight of hand, some sort of trickery, and on one memorable occasion, when he took over the kitchen to prepare lasagne, he made sure that every cupboard door was open, every spice (even the ones not being used) was there to be seen; every detail of the meal was spread out across the counter like the entrails of a chicken for auguring.

Now back to the lazy part. Because we all need to dress every day and cook every day and read every day there is no reason in the world why these things, all of the necessary implements of living, shouldn't be constantly in sight. Nothing should ever be put away.

One of my mother's irritating aphorisms that had stuck with me was "a place for everything and everything in its place". This was way beyond my husband, way out of his comprehension. In the barn and his office, areas of his absolute domain, if you thought of it you could see it. Everything was visible: vet wrap, hoof picks, worming paste, shovels, pitchforks, buckets, hammers and rope.

His office was infamous around the college: thirty years of paperwork, reports on general education from 1976 to this semester's budget—all were visible. Every liberal arts model route from Harvard to Hong Kong was on his desk. He worked like a medieval monk trapped by mountains of paper. The closed drawers of his filing cabinets were full of old running shoes he couldn't bear to throw away, and not one active file.

Now it was true that when people wanted something they went to TH. I have to give him that. For all our technology, most things from the past seem to be locked in some never-never-land rabbit hole of impossible recovery and we are forced to fruitlessly reinvent the wheel. For this, TH was amazing. The first draft of the 1988 text? Right here. Faculty lists from 1992? Right here. Ten-year-old telephone directories for New York? Over there. I'm sure he could put his finger on every old losing hospital lottery ticket. (Why? In case they decide to run that lottery again, of course.)

The vast upside to all this clutter was that it tied him immediately to the day's work and the world at hand. One could never get lost in a completely visual world; the next task as well as the last one was staring him in the face. One was never lost because there was no room to get lost, no empty space. And no false sense of completion, no ending till death. TH would assure me it had nothing to do with laziness.

But I like a clean, well-lighted place—an empty space in the house precisely because I can get lost there. Outdoors, except for the patch of wild, the farm and garden are cultivated and cared for. The forest in the back was actually planned. Those paths that people get lost on are actually bound by logic in their execution—any small airplane can see that from 3,000 feet.

It discomfited me to entertain in a room where six projects were spread out, like crimes ready for the confessing. I couldn't relax and discuss the state of the world if the state of my kitchen was like a war zone. I couldn't write a sentence unless the birds were fed and the kitchen coffee pot was washed. My grandmother's copper coffee pots were always polished. I liked to create on my worktable in the basement—take the lamps there to be fixed; my mother's old buttons there to be glued into landscapes with the kids; my wool there for mending old sweaters. No clutter, nothing from last year. I liked the books on the shelves; I knew they were there. I liked clothes in the closets. When I opened the door I knew my clothes were going to be there. I liked my kitchen tidy, all the pots and pans put away, not left out for tomorrow. I bought very little, threw out useless junk and stored seasonal things in the basement. Who knew if I would cook tomorrow? Or what I would cook? I liked projects neatly tucked away on the hard drive.

It was a miracle we learned to accommodate each other for as long as we did; we often teased that we would switch roles for the next thirty years just to understand what the other had had to put up with for so long. Jack Spratt and his wife, I supposed. Our children told us that we were a match made in heaven because more than anything else, more than our warring space needs, more than his need to see all things visible and accessible and my need to be tidy, finished, pristine and private, we needed each other.

*The chicken and the egg.*

## Autobiography of Red

"**I** am going to die."

"You are not going to die."

"Yes I am."

"No, you're not. It happens to everyone."

"Not to Daddy."

"No. Not to Daddy but men have their own set of problems. Really, the list is just as long for them."

"But this is ridiculous."

"Take an Advil. I'll get you a hot water bottle."

"I'm going out to freeze to death in a snow bank."

"It's too cold out there."

"I don't believe I have to go through this to have children."

"So they say."

"And did Claire go through this?"

"The very same thing."

"That's why she's decided not to have children."

"She only says that when she's bleeding. The rest of the month you almost forget it."

"Almost? Hah! Never. Two weeks of PMS. One week of bleeding. One week of recovery."

"I know it seems that way."

"Not for you any more. You've got the merry pause."

"That's menopause and happy it is not."

"So, how long do I have to wait for that?"

"Don't wish your life away. Don't wish away forty years. You don't bleed when you're pregnant."

"That's why the lady next door had seven children."

"Learn to deal with it."

"I don't know if I can."

"There's no choice."

"I can't use tampons."

"You'll learn when its time."

"I feel like I'm wearing a pillow. My saddle fits better."

"I know. I'm sorry."

"I think I'll kill myself."

"I brought you three movies in my bag: girl flicks. Claire will be back with the car soon. Plug in the heating pad. I'll make pasta and grilled chicken."

"I hate chicken. I want popcorn."

"Fine. Tonight you'll have pasta and popcorn."

"There's Claire. Thank god she's home. She said she'd bring chocolate."

"Good. Popcorn and chocolate."

"Hi Mom. Hi Cait. I'm sorry I'm late."

"Claire! Did you bring chocolate?"

"Yes. I brought chocolate but I feel really shitty."

"What's the matter?"

"I've got my period."

"Me too! Me too!"

"Oh, dear. I'll boil the pasta water. Here's the Advil."

"Let's watch movies."

"I want to watch *Thelma and Louise* again."

"*Thelma and Louise* it is. There are parts I haven't memorized yet."

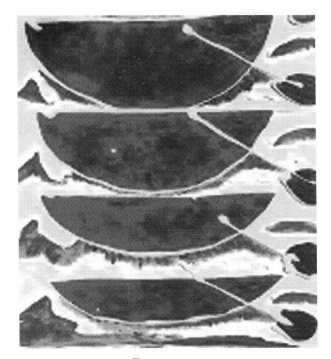

*Four canoes.*

## Wilderness Tips

I confess to having had a monthly year-round birdseed account of $200 at the Farmer's Co-op in Shelburne. I bought sunflower and mixed grains in 44 kilogram sacks for most of the feeders. One farmer complained to me that he spent all summer trying to keep the birds off his sunflower crop only to sell the seed to the feed mill who then sold it to twitchers like me to feed to the very birds he's been chasing off all summer.

For my wild turkeys I bought whole corn that wouldn't blow away in the winter wind. There were suet balls rolled in seed for other birds and pinecones covered with peanut butter. My nyger seed came from India at $70 a sack. Bushes had been planted in hedgerows dedicated to summer bobolinks and indigo buntings: if you plant it they will come. Two or three times a week I spread seed in bird boxes around the house and on the grass for ground feeders. I filled the oriole and hummingbird feeders with glucose (honey makes them sick). Every year I planted blooming annuals and, after the perennials had recovered from winter, they provided nectar for dozens of hummingbirds.

There was a cartoon in the *New Yorker* showing an attractive woman eyeing a rather weedy dinner companion around whose head swarmed half-a-dozen hummingbirds. The caption read, "If I'd known you attracted ruby-throated hummingbirds I would have married you." I clipped it and stuck it on my office wall and when department meetings demanded my attention I remember those hummingbirds, magic creatures that they are, able to transform the worst of days. Worth marrying a guy for.

For over a decade I had been feeding ruby throats (*Archilochus colubris*) and every year I indulged in large hanging baskets over our table on the front porch to entice the birds to dinner. Guests soon learned not to bob and weave fearfully as the birds zoomed in, hovered with needle beaks in flowers, drank their fill and bulleted away. At times there were half-a-dozen zipping over feeders and flowers as pasta and grilled swordfish were devoured below. Maybe it was because they are so tiny, so iridescent or travel so far down to the Gulf of Mexico, Florida and California that they are so fascinating.

My amateur ornithological habit had expanded to include a love of large birds like raptors and wild turkeys but such birds need more coaxing to stay around and nest than their smaller brethren and there was little I could do except ensure the habitat was available. Occasionally, from my window, I watched as a sharp-shinned hawk dropped from a thousand feet and carried off a chipmunk for dinner; the high-pitched screams and calls from goshawks, harriers, osprey, kestrels and broad-winged and Cooper's hawks were constant companions while I was gardening or walking. The plentiful sparrows, chickadees, voles, mice, frogs and other tasty nibbles ensured a broad spectrum of nutrition in the food chain. Red gobbled vultures made good work of road kill in under a day. Owls of all sizes and shapes, though hard to spot, were abundant year-round. Wild turkeys with necks like emus pranced along the cleared paths in front of me.

After a few years of winter watching, a birder can easily distinguish tracks in snow. Following a short, mouse-scurry-marked distance from my woodpile, a hawk had left her fantail and double wing-beats imprinted on the powder where the mouse trail ended. A pack of heavy feet around my empty low feeder one morning attested to another raid by the flock of wild turkeys that lived in our forest. The ice around the scalloped rim had been pecked clean by hard beaks desperate for seeds trapped within. I scraped out a handful of frozen turkey turds—yellow-grey squiggly tubes—before I emptied another half bag into the bowl. TH thought, now that my turkeys numbered in the dozens, I should have bought commercial loads of feed but I feared that would have made them too dependent on the Co-op truck arriving. There were many sumac bushes and clumps of milkweed seedpods poking through the snow around the pond and they liked to feed there. I only gave them enough so that they'd make my station a part of their regular circuit of scavenging. The wolves and coyotes may have kept the number of fat birds in check, but there had been a marked increase in the past few years since the Ministry of Natural Resources Wildlife Branch brought in the first breeding pairs. That these wary birds are caught at all is a testament to the cunning and hunger of predators. A few years ago one flock of thirteen came by intermittently and another flock of eight visited quite regularly. Finally, I had over sixty in a flock, a robust crowd.

In order to watch wild turkeys I learned to be absolutely silent. When they were approaching my kitchen feeder (I saw them marching in a line, a hundred yards away, over the frozen snow) I unplugged the phone, turned off the dishwasher and sat in the shadow behind the sliding glass doors—moving only to breathe, focus my binoculars, and write notes. A turkey could hear me place a glass on the table indoors with the outside wind howling at sixty miles an hour and they would scatter back to the safety of the trees.

The flock I had been watching all winter regularly sauntered up to the corn and sunflower seed. They weighed in at 12 to 20 pounds, and stood 2 ½ feet off the ground. Their tail feathers, layered gold and tan, were striped with glistening blacks and blues, and spread out a foot and a half behind their bodies. In fierce wind they dropped their fantails to the ice to steady themselves and spread their four-foot wingspan above the feed to brace against the wind. To identify the individuals I named them after poets.

The big old jake, Irving Layton, I identified by the partially balding feathery white scalp and warty horn protruding from his forehead; he also bullied the young hens from the centre of the feeder. He always jumped in and stabbed at the corn with his scalloped neck, like a bushed man who hadn't eaten for days. One slightly younger male, Leonard Cohen, with a sleek blue face was always around the younger hens. Michael Ondaatje had striations around his neck and a pronounced three-sack gobble beard. One of the tribe, the old hen with the broken tail feather, PK Page, was constantly alert, listening for crow calls warning of predators. Another young hen, Gwendolyn, with wobbly legs, a weak chin, and tiny ear holes was always twitching on her periscope head. Anne Carson, classically inclined with a rusty red cape, circled around the edges. Silent for as long as they were there, I let them feed without moving a muscle. I sketched and named them all but as the flock grew larger at a steady rate I ran out of poets and had to start including non-Canadians. My reading could hardly keep up with their numbers.

Turkeys are always anxious; they would stamp and strut at the blue jays and red squirrels in the vicinity. There was a hierarchy and a timetable at feeders and the turkey troop was nervously aware of those waiting turns. Even the dumb, slow doves seem to distract them whenever the wind died down. When the feeder was almost empty, I would put my pen down and the birds would all scatter, racing away, skating, falling, sliding down the ice on the driveway until, like the corps de ballet in Swan Lake, they would take to flight and head gracefully past the barn on slow wings, satiated for the moment.

One wintry morning, leaving before dawn to teach an 8:30 class, my high beams caught a snowy owl, a full two-foot mound of white feathers and two tiny black eyes, roused from his sleep on a fence post. I dimmed my lights; he blinked at me, and with a six-foot stretch of wing lifted off to a quieter post. I was in a state of grace for the rest of day in spite of a ferocious storm. Another December morning we watched as a murder of a thousand crows headed south, leap-frogging in flocks of a hundred from field to orchard to forest, over fence lines and ponds. The sky was black with them, ominous, like a scene from Hitchcock and they took an hour to clear away.

Over one summer a large horned owl took up residence on Green Cow Pond, swooping to pick up ducklings and feast beside the water. The crows screamed at him for days, dive-bombing in battalions of three and four as the larger ducks quacked and gabbled below, but there was too much good food here for him to move on and he remained, unperturbed. One day I watched him climb up a tree, almost like a cat, rather than lift his bulk with his wings. He slept in the arms of the branches until a hapless duckling, paddling through the lily pads, came too close. In one breath the owl dropped, his large talons plucking the meal. A silent heron, all blue grayness and legs more length than substance, camouflaged as a Giacometti sculpture, witnessed the kill with me.

Of such days heaven was made.

*Turkeys on the winter snow.*

*Hawk over the bird feeder.*

## Away

In the fall of 1989, burned out after fifteen years of teaching, we decided to take our sabbaticals and headed for rural France, like thousands of others lured by the well-documented friendly natives, warm weather, food, wine and lifestyle less stressful than the North American norm. We left the horses in the care of the girls' coach and rented out the farm to another family of horse lovers. TH had a colleague at work who had inherited a small goat herder's cottage in a tiny village in the Cévennes, west of the Rhône, which he was willing to rent to us. Without too much preparation and second guessing our desires, we dropped our children into a French school and spent the year tasting wines and cheeses while contemplating the course of our lives. Sabbaticals should be mandatory in all fields of endeavour and, before TH could be certain of his decision to move from a faculty position to a more demanding administrative role in education, he needed the time off.

I have a photograph of him walking down a small path in the Cévennes with Joseph Barrial, an old *paysan* resistance fighter who, during the war, blew up the bridge into Joyeuse to prevent the German tanks from crossing. Joseph is hunched over his cane, his bowed legs jutting up at awkward angles. They are following two slow cows, Sylvie and Blanchette, taking them to higher pasture. TH and Joseph are laughing.

My husband's French was poor and Joseph's English was non-existent but, for six months, while our children were in the local school, he stopped at the little stone house in the mountains of the Ardèche and called out to us. "Bonjour, les Canadiens. Vous voulez boire quelque chose?" The answer was always yes—it had to be—and Joseph would sit at our table drinking his harsh *vin du pays* as we sipped tea if it was before noon, and wine with him if it wasn't.

He pronounced us "vrais copains, vrais ardèchois" and taught us how to crack walnuts by cupping them under our index finger and smashing the knuckle with the other fist. At first, it hurt but once we got the knack of it we took to carrying pockets of fresh local walnuts, cracking them with our fingers on rocks as we paused in our walks. I'm sure this did my arthritis no good, but it was worth the risk if we could be "vrais ardèchois". Joseph took us to the local wine Co-op, a *cave*, down the hill from Sanilhac where we filled our five-litre plastic jugs in the trunk of our car from a gas pump nozzle before we headed off to the markets.

Every day of the week a convoy of caravans would set up in different town squares, selling the best local cheeses, rich sausages, fresh breads, fruits, jams. We could drive to Sète for fresh oysters and to Montélimar for nougat. It was always worth the drive along some rickety terraced ledge to get a perfectly smoked pork shoulder or truffles from the man with the smartest pig. We went to the raspberry lady in the valley, the *lasagnerie* in Joyeuse and the strawberry lady near Vernon, a few miles away.

When we got there, she welcomed us, "Ah! Les Canadiens! Finally, you come to my farm. Joseph has spoken about you." And she insisted we walk further over the ridge to see one of the most spectacular views of the river gorge below, a ribbon of the Beaume twisting through cliffs and forests. We are overwhelmed by the vistas, the succulence of the fresh berries, the *chaleur* of the local residents.

"No! You cannot pay for the jam. It is a gift. You must come back next week when the other varieties are ready." She pressed another apricot jam into my already-full arms as we left. "Stay for the apricot season," she insists. "Stay for the apricots!" We assure her we will not go back to Toronto until each fruit in the valley has reached its peak. Joseph's pride at the tales of our delightful prizes, found by his direction, deepened our friendship with him.

With TH's EU passport and a donation through the mayor's office we arranged to enrol the girls in the local one-room communal school with a dozen other children. They would do what lessons they could; Claire in grade five, Caitlin in kindergarten. We had bought a run-down Fiat in England for £600, caterpillar green, right hand drive, and the children would scream and laugh and point at us in excitement as we arrived to drop off the girls. "Les blondes Canadiennes, les blondes!" And, in their most disdainful accents, "What ugly car!"

Claire and Caitlin would go to class, at first wordlessly, and then repeating every phrase; finally, at the end of the first week, they were playing footie and skipping and laughing. The language, as with TH and Joseph, developed as the friendships did.

Near the market in Vals-les-Bains I found a bookstore where we picked up our English papers and I bought a dozen French/English translating dictionaries and gave them to the children at Sanhilac School. Before long, they were all translating words for toilets and body parts and I offered to teach English on Saturday mornings as they had so generously welcomed our children and helped us acclimatize. After some moments of terror and tears from both the girls, some learning took place for all parties involved. At the end of the first month math, geography, history and art seemed second nature in French, and shopping, family and field hockey in English were no longer foreign to their friends.

It is surprising how much language acquisition can be built on a few verbs, a handful of nouns and grateful loving patience. We soon met the children's parents who stopped by and brought us gifts of sublime *framboise*, wild strawberries and *marron purée* for helping their kids learn a smattering of what was fast becoming the predominant language of business in Europe. I was overwhelmed by the generosity and rather sad because I knew, had the reverse been the case, had these mothers and fathers moved to Shelburne, no such welcome would have awaited them.

We walked every day, around the Renaissance fortress where the *médecin* lived, through the cherry orchards, along the winding rivers, up to the Tour de Bresson at the top of the hill close to us. From there one could see for miles—on the east to the Rhône, on the west to the Massif Central. The Romans would have watched troop movements and campfires from that tower as far south as Avignon and north to Le Puy.

We stayed in that little house six months, long enough to fall in love all over again, and for the children to develop a French space in their heads. On the first week, I had rashly invited our nearest neighbours, Michel and Marie, and their children to dinner. There were a few pots and pans, a Butagaz two-burner stove and a small fridge, but the market was open and I rushed down the hill to load up what I could find. Later that evening, after lentil salad, *coq au vin* and lemon tart I discovered our guests were chefs and owned one of the prize local restaurants.

We acquitted ourselves not too poorly and Michel and Marie later admitted to having guided their children, as they had been walking to our house for dinner, through the possible scenario of hamburgers and chips. They explained the horrors of the North American palette to their shocked children and instructed them to say nothing until the meal was done. The greatest compliment I have received as a cook was from that family. "Ah, we are so relieved that Canadians eat as we do, not as Americans." I assured them that there were even Americans who ate well and that the best French restaurant of the moment was in New York, but they were having none of our Canadian humour. Some things were just *pas possible.*

Over subsequent dinner parties we were required to tell stories of winter, igloos we had never built, of the grizzlies in the Rockies, ships on the St Lawrence and storms on the Great Lakes. They were disappointed we had never been to the real Hudson's Bay, though I had shopped in the store, or canoed the *voyageur* routes to the North West Territories. Their disappointment could only be assuaged by a rendition of Leonard Cohen's "Suzanne" and a discussion of forty-pound salmon fresh out of the Pacific.

José and Chantal, neighbours and parents of one of Claire's classmates, insisted we learn to jazz dance and Grand Philippe, (so named for being 6 foot 4) brought arm-loads of mimosa and fresh lavender to my door—if I would correct and let him practice his English poetry in the form of Bob Dylan lyrics. "Please translate for me if you would, please. 'the ghosts of electricity howl in the bowls of her face'." I tried to explain to him it only made the vaguest metaphoric sense in English but he was certain I was keeping some rare insight into American beauty from him and so I stabbed at several more possibilities before moving back to "Sad-Eyed Lady of the Lowlands". Not all things work in all languages.

One night, too tired to dance, I turned down an invitation from Grand Philippe for a quick run to the bar in Largentière and missed an impromptu jam session with Ry Cooder, one of my favourite musicians. Life lesson: never say no when a Frenchman asks you to dance.

Most of the friends we made there had moved to the Ardèche after the May riots in Paris—*soixante-huitards*, who developed careers as restauranteurs, math teachers, sociologists and musicians. Chantel worked with the Maghrebin women from North Africa, many of whom were shunned by the French bourgeoisie. Chantal, her family, and the rest of the people we met in that circle were embarrassed by the racist slogans painted by Le Pen's National Front supporters on the bridges going into town and as a community they worked to remove them. The graffiti, as well as the desecration of the Jewish cemetery that summer in Carpentras, became a source of national shame, and dinner conversations never avoided heated discussion of the problems of the French psyche.

We were called on more than once to justify why Canada had not declared Quebec a distinct society within the nation. It was such an obvious wrong and they could not imagine the logic. We listened to their disgust and anger at the raiding mentality of American culture and toasts were given when, at the end of its first year, Euro Disney was posting heavy losses. We argued for the European Union; they argued against. Comparisons between French civilization and bland consumerism were drawn; the tenacity of the British was applauded and disdained in the same toast, glasses clinking. Envy of the Italian Renaissance was kept alive at those dinner tables as if it were five hundred years earlier. We drank and danced and argued until three in the morning when we would pack our sleeping children on our shoulders and struggle home.

We came across Canada, the image and metaphor, on almost a daily basis. In the market, "Ah! Les Canadiens. Tell us about winter." And with Joseph's friends it was a big hug and "Thank you for your help in the war." And in forest fire season as the Canadian-built water bombers flew overhead the locals would look up, "Ah, the Canadian bird." One of the neighbours had perfected the Calgary cowboy gait, including the hat and the riding style. The locals called him "Canadian Cowboy" although he had never visited Alberta. He invited us for dinner and showed us his albums and books (all of Jack London, all of Farley Mowat, every Ian Tyson record) and boxes of memorabilia. He was more Canadian than we were. Many people dither about moving but he had already "gone west" in his head.

That experience of rural France took us back a few Christmases later and our village friends greeted us like prodigals returned. Thomas, a boy in Claire's class, confessed to his heartbreak when she had left; and all the children — Lisa, Julia, Nadia, Clara — promised that one day they would find their way to Canada. Memory takes us back there as often as we eat cheese and drink wine. It was a landscape, dramatic like the Niagara Escarpment, with a familiar comfort that seemed to breed like-minded souls. The *souffle* of the wind over the hills was not foreign to us, as our home would not be to them. To some, the door is always open.

At the end of our sabbatical we returned to the farm. Being away had intensified my appreciation (if it needed intensifying) and I saw it again as exotic, fresh, clean. Unfortunately, a year off absolutely ruins one as far as teaching work is concerned. Who, in their right mind, would want to give up that time? Those lingering days—mornings of sex on the warm verandah, reading all afternoon, marketing, dancing, dining, hearing our children laugh with French intonation—will always stay with me.

Life for most farmers in rural Ontario is a far cry from the joyousness of Joseph Barrial or the romantic peasant we meet in W.S. Merwin's *The Lost Upland* or in John Berger's *Into Their Labours*. The land is young and we have no rock terraces, ancient fruit groves, no sacred familial places to forage, no *caved* cheeses to nourish and remind us how our ancestors survived.

We all order from the local Co-op and depend on the grocery chains for most of our provisions. No one has time to go out shooting wild birds or searching for leeks and dandelions. Few farmers store their own grains for replanting; everyone is tied into the economy, utterly dependent on market forces. There is no romance at tax time. It is almost impossible to earn a decent wage at any kind of traditional farming in southern Ontario. Rarely do Canadian farmers stay up till 3 am arguing over cheese. The plight of farmers, their core role in the economy, seems mere background to the everyday discussion of business practice in Canada. The crucial role of the farmer needs to be appreciated and nurtured in order for the culture to change and I am sure this cannot happen in North America.

When we travel we learn to love foreign places for our own reasons and when we return we appreciate and love our own land with new eyes. Living with other families forces us to re-examine our own—for better and for worse.

*Love each other wildly.*

## No Great Mischief

Lists of small town crimes reported in local newspapers like the *Shelburne Free Press and Economist* seem familiar the world over: petty theft, fraud, assault, drunk driving, public mischief, tenants burning down houses, but every now and again things happen which reverberate in a different part of the mind: the pathetic acts of old people, the unexplained, the out of place, the bizarre follies of the greedy.

As days shift into months and months into years we often forget events and passions that seemed large in our youth. Rethinking in times of fullness and selectively remembering the world makes old hurts disappear, wounds heal and daily living finds forgiveness nearer at hand than revenge. But there is something about a constant landscape, something that holds a memory in the world longer than it should normally stay. Perhaps a tree or a stone or a bend in the river can trigger events of sixty years ago. The same air courses again through the lungs and the pain is relived as if, in that instant, a teenage betrayal is alive again.

That is the only explanation I can find for a recent gruesome murder of a husband and a childhood friend by a seventy-nine-year-old woman. In a fit of jealousy she took an axe, handy on the snowy cord of wood outside her kitchen door, and bludgeoned her husband of sixty years to death. She then took the ten steps next door and neatly, over the kitchen sink, cracked in the skull of her lifelong best friend. How long this hatred had been festering we'll never know. Maybe it was rekindled by a slant of light through the window, maybe an embroidered pattern on a Christmas cushion, maybe the woodshed. Lives like loaded guns, as Dickinson would say. Maybe friendship didn't matter any more—she had been nice for too long. Holidays do not bring out the best in us. Maybe, like another neighbour, she had seen enough of marriage.

John and Bonnie had been together for seventy years—through the war, through the worst of winters, through two children, through good times and bad—until the time of broken hips and night wandering came and their children had to move them out of an unmanageable house and into a nursing home. Visits were made to the local care facilities, appointments booked, the house listed and ancient furnishings dispersed to the grandchildren. The best of nursing care was found and, on the day of the move, a photographer came to secure the memory of the house and gardens into a silver frame. Bonnie was happy to go but John decided, there on the steps, that the good times were over and he was going to stay in a nursing home in Ottawa. There was no way he was going to "spend another minute with that woman." From his pension he paid for the divorce proceedings "so they wouldn't bury her anywhere round my corpse" and the decree absolute came three months before he died. Passions fade.

Small quiet towns and grand city places go in and out of fashion and some characters need the city heat and then retreat from the fire to rural communities. So it is with our local drug dealers. We have had two or three sets (they don't come in singles); traffickers who flit in and out and the locals instantly figure out where the money is coming from. Some of them parade as consultants, some import-export specialists. It is easy to spot the coke dealers—they seem to revel in their secret identities; but there isn't a hard-working farmer anywhere in the world that doesn't, by instinct, follow the money. The entertainment promoter who bought the big Victorian house with the pond stuck out like a sore thumb at parent's night at the local elementary school. His wife claimed they had moved to the country to keep their son in hockey and "out of the troubles" he could find in Toronto. After we met them a second time and heard his fiery-tempered stories at a local gathering to stop an aggregate company from tearing up farmland, TH whispered in my ear, "Cocaine". They desperately wanted to be part of the community and out of their past lives but there was a certain amount of *schadenfreude* at the Co-op when he was arrested in one of the largest drug busts of the decade.

Interesting crimes are not always committed by interesting people but this is a case that breaks the rule. The carpenter who was replacing my hundred-year-old windows told me about another house he was working on just past the Dufferin Forest Main Tract. It was a stunning 1837 stone farmhouse with expansive gardens, barns and fields. The owner, a Vice President at one of the biggest securities investment firms in Canada, had bought the property with his young handsome lover and the two of them took to renovating full time and buying staggering amounts of Canadian and contemporary American art: A.Y. Jacksons hung between the Mapplethorpes, Danbys and Michael Snows. A magnificent wrought iron and glass greenhouse had been imported from London. There were tales of great parties with painters from New York and the city's best caterers lost on the roads outside of Orangeville with truckloads of foie gras and champagne. Garden designers worked to fit large outdoor installation pieces between the ornamental grasses and the reflecting pools. Curiosity got the better of me and, when the collector and his companion were away at a memorial reunion for Canadian vets in France (perhaps the VP's father), I couldn't resist visiting the carpenter at the wonderful house. (He had a small workshop there: I needed a piece of wood cut. It was an emergency. I just had to go.)

I had driven by many times and admired the Andalusian horses, their grey manes flowing, bought to decorate the fields. The barns had been redone with oak doors and brass fittings (word gets around with the horse crews). The tack room had a stained glass window and the horses lounged in twelve-foot square stalls with automatic watering troughs and winter heat.

The house was chock full of wonderful paintings and sculptures; the kitchen and bathrooms had murals and suspended hangings. I had to shimmy between the marble busts and the wrought iron pieces. Each item of furniture had been carefully chosen; the bookcases were laden with first editions of Wilde, Auden and White. There was ubiquitous evidence of charm and wit. They ate, entertained and relaxed like nobility. Brokers, a conservative time-deprived lot, don't normally develop exquisite taste like this; few flaunt it so radically.

A few months after my visit the scandal hit the papers and we all read the details of fraud and embezzlement. A great charmer, he controlled the accounts of several wealthy widows and invested their money freely in art, travel and real estate. Unfortunately, none of ladies knew about this and the figure soon grew to over seven million dollars in absconded funds. The art lover packed up his wing collars and spent some time in prison; the contents of the house were seized by the police. Overnight the contemporary art market in Toronto dropped twenty percent. The horses were turned over to a dealer; the lawn quickly overgrew the sculptures that could not be moved. It was a stupid folly and the firm repaid the widows, but every time I drive by the house I silently applaud the chutzpah and fine taste.

*In the dark forest.*

# The Needs of Strangers

Contrasting value systems are often seen very clearly in the rural home. My mother wanted to have her own work, to bank her own money, to control her own time but that was not done in immigrant families like mine. Indeed, those were complicated issues for many women and huge issues for most rural farmers. The women's movement, less embraced by these groups than by working women in the cities, had little impact and little support from those who could not see any way out of the demanding needs of farming and feeding the family. Survival takes precedence over everything else. The fragile agricultural economy ripped the soul out of century farms and left families penniless. The fallout of all this was, of course, alcoholism, child abuse and battery.

In the first twenty years on the farm I read stories about farmers who hospitalized their wives with gunshot wounds and got away with it, farmers who electrocuted their cattle for insurance money and then committed suicide. We've had mothers chase their children down the road with hammers and drugged teenagers found hanged under the bridge over the Boyne River. We've had fathers murder their children, then wait for their wives to return to finish off the job. Mothers have drowned their newborn babies in feed sacks along with feral cats in the local lake. All of this is too close to home for me to ignore. It's a personal issue.

My father once tried to push my mother out of a car on the highway to collect on an insurance policy; she hung on to the door and stayed with him another ten years. When my brother confronted him with his criminal behaviour, his only answer was that she could never prove it in court. Of course, she had no interest in taking my father to court. She had no interest in even discussing "the accidents". He broke her finger, twisted her wrists and bruised her shoulders and *he* left *her* in the end. There is no explaining attraction/repulsion except in metaphorical or psychoanalytic terms and sometimes the emotions are too complicated to even begin to untangle. Certainly I cannot do it for my mother but I felt a strong urge, all my life, to do what I could to confront that sort of abuse and educate young women to a healthier way of survival. All teachers are teachers for a reason. That is mine.

In truth, this battery will go on as long as men and women continue to breed, which makes women's shelters a necessity in this ugly world, the domain of love and death. And yet, these buildings are often not wanted in towns where residents would like to deny the problem exists and, even when it is abundantly clear that a woman has been murdered by her husband, it is often difficult to recognize such behaviour early enough to stop it. Rural folk don't like to interfere. "Surely families or churches or friends can help women deal with their problems?" one neighbour asked me. "I wouldn't want any of my taxes going to a place like that."

Our shelter in Orangeville was an old house on Mill Street, constantly full and in need of repairs. Women and children had to be turned away when beds were not available. Kids in Claire's school would be absent for days living in the shelter and then have to move schools to avoid their fathers. Often women in these circumstances do not want to go to other family members. They do not want to go to neighbours who are quick to judge. We needed a shelter in Dufferin County and, having been asked on more than one occasion to help out, I joined a committee in 1998 to see if we could raise some funds for a proper building.

Many professionals and successful entrepreneurs had moved to Mono, seeking the sanctuary of country life, but getting them to part with their money required more than just asking. Often newcomers did not see themselves as part of the blue-collar world of Orangeville and Shelburne and showed little solidarity with the often troubled farming community. My friend Ricci, mother of four, cooking school manager, chef extraordinaire and organizer *sans pareil*, thought a huge dinner would entice the people we needed. I thought about a literary festival, discussion and drinks. Some people would open their chequebooks for a black-tie affair. We would charge for a community reading at the Mono Cliffs Outdoor Education Centre, entice a few writers and donors with a goodwill dinner, and we'd at least be able to put something in the women's shelter kitty. Ricci prepared a menu, a committee was launched to sell tickets, and I began calling every writer I knew.

I had organized readings for my college through the Canada Council and knew whom to contact but writers were being asked every day for their free time. Irene and Winston at Writers and Company, the greatest little bookstore that ever was and sadly is no more, agreed to set up a table and sell books. But a hundred book sales for some writers was not sufficient payoff for days of lost writing. Publishers gave us dozens of recent best sellers for door prizes. Our local brewer, Creemore Springs, gave kegs of beer, the Mono Cliffs pub put on free *hors d'oeuvres*. Still that wasn't enough. We'd offer more. We'd offer cottages and converted pigeon cots, carriage houses and barn lofts. We'd offer lakes with bass and rivers with trout, views of Hockley Valley, the smell of horses and chickens in the backyard. We'd offer duck pâté on plates in the garden and geese honking overhead, wine and wild raspberries, arugula salad and ragged vistas. Bird watching, I was certain, would bring them.

Dozens of women offered to give up space in their homes and studios for writers and their families to come and spend the weekend. They took kids and dogs and grannies in wheelchairs. In the end, it was not a hard sell and, as any writer knows, a glorious family weekend in the country, great food, free booze, companionship, adoring listeners and book sales are not to be sniffed at. It sure beats the normal book-flogging circuit of middling hotels, empty bookstores and takeout restaurants.

Carole Corbeil, Marian Fowler, Matthew Hart, Rohinton Mistry, Michael Ondaatje, Paul Quarrington, Sarah Sheard, Linda Spalding, Susan Swan and Lola Tostevin all agreed to come. *The English Patient* had a lot of buzz and Canadian Literature was rising in the firmament so every ticket sold within a couple of weeks. The writers loved the accommodations; the trout fishing was good, the birds and wolves showed themselves. The dinner was divine: fifty-two for a brilliant four-course sit-down, fine linens, fine wines, great conversation and money for the building fund. I fantasized that when I retired, it should become an annual charity event: Books, Birds and Brunch.

It was rewarding for the organizers and good for the community. Books were given away as door prizes. Many women who had been resident in the shelter came to the reading. Because most shame is silent and we all lie so easily, especially women in isolation, discussion is often hard to start. Sometimes the only way in is through reading about others in similar circumstances but *The Woman Who Walked into Doors* had not yet made it to the Co-op. Sometimes it helps to hear of other's suffering, sometimes just knowing that people write about lives that are lost, troubled, in need of repair, is enough to get one going. I wish my mother could have been there, my aunts, my grandmothers, my second cousins twice removed—all of those women who never seemed to get what they wanted out of life. We are brutalized by this world and it is necessary to pay close attention to our needs and our dreams and we must offer what comfort we can to others.

The distance between people's experiences of this tiny rural town staggers the imagination.

*Portrait of my father as a rooster.*

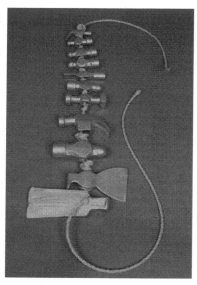

*A necklace of gilded hammers.*

# Lives of Girls and Women

I knew this woman once; she lived in the country. I met her while I was working on the volunteer committee trying to raise money for the women's shelter in Orangeville. I was there because as an English teacher I knew some writers, but privately I was there because my father had been abusive to my mother. Millicent was there to feel less guilty about her wealth and good fortune. "To share," she said. We were raising money from a literary event—writers were coming to read and she was going to offer her carriage house in the country as a place to stay. A good feminist cause, I thought.

I drove around the country looking at the places people offered, trying to figure out where to put all these messy writers, their partners and dogs—knowing they would perceive a ranking by the quality of their lodgings. The committee-women, for it was all women who were offering their homes, also perceived a ranking. The more exclusive her home the higher up the bestseller list should come "her writer." I was determined for it to be otherwise, determined to find some democratic method in what everyone else viewed as a chance to cherry-pick, a chance for bragging rights.

When I got to her house, following the beautifully printed map she normally mailed to her weekend guests, I was not disappointed. It was exactly as she had described it: set back from the road, just like the pictures in *Architectural Digest*, white board and batten, gables, gingerbread, leaded windows; the pond in front had a small wharf with a perfect red Tom Thompson canoe under the golden willow. The drive wound around the water, ending up in an English garden near the carriage house. There was a huge hanging clematis over an arbor, masses of tulips, crocuses, daffodils dotted throughout the perennials not quite ready to show their colour. Several forsythias were in full yellow bloom. I got out of my car, stung by the scent of spring flowers and marveled at the magic of her gardener, busy with his wheelbarrow in front of the greenhouse, who managed to perform such miracles so early in an Ontario spring.

"He is good, isn't he?" said Millicent coming up behind me.

"Fabulous. Spectacular. I'm still in mud and melting drifts at home."

"I've made tea and then I'll show you the place. Do you have a writer for me yet? Someone I've read, I mean?"

"We haven't heard back from them all and so we've not decided who goes where," I lied. Not one writer had turned down camaraderie, free wine and meals, great accommodation and a weekend in the countryside, all for a good cause. "I should know by next week and I'll call or email the list around if that's OK with you." I already knew this process was too open, too liable to exercises of 'compare and contrast'. Hair would fly.

"Sure, but let's have tea. I want you to see the house."

Millicent had told me, when I confessed a love of David Milne, that she too liked painting and, in fact, had a couple she would let me see. I could not feign lack of interest. "I'd love to see the paintings."

The interior of the home dwarfed the entrance. A vast amount of money had been spent, floor to ceiling: draperies, Persian rugs, marble sculptures, ceramics. Not only Milnes (an early still life and a later street scene) but also Milton Avery, Ben Nicholson, Lismer, A.Y. Jackson, Grandma Moses, an array of Canadian landscapes. I darted from one to the other like a hummingbird after a long migration.

"I like the Group of Seven but I really don't know much about the rest. My husband's dealer tells us what to buy that fits the decor. I think we've done well on the Milnes."

"I'm sure you have," I said, feeling my peasant roots and the pathetic paucity of a teacher's salary.

"Is Milne Group of Seven?"

"No," I said, mindlessly ogling an Emily Carr. "Thomson, Harris, Jackson, Varley, Casson..."

"That's five."

I always only remember five dwarfs, six deadly sins, four ways to skin a cat. Menopause was an ugly time. "Maybe Carmichael and McDonald. But there were others that followed. Seven is an arbitrary number."

"Oh, but that's what the catalogue says!"

"Yes, of course. I only mean there were many who went north to do landscapes and who followed in their footsteps. First there were seven. Later there were ten."

"Right." Clearly she had decided I was an idiot. Every Canadian knows the Group of Seven, not the Group of Ten. Who cares about the others? "Let's have tea and talk about who's coming here."

Over tea she let slip the news about her housekeeper doing breakfast for her guests, the gardener setting out fresh flowers, the canoe being available, the library always updated. "There's an internet connection and a laptop in the desk in case they want to write or do mail."

"I'm sure they're here to relax and not work," I said. "And it's only two days." This was far more luxury than most of these writers had seen in a lifetime. Most lived on meager grants.

"I'd like to tell my book club that Michael Ondaatje or Rohinton Mistry wrote something in my carriage house. Shortbread?"

I didn't know what to say. "Thank you. Well, whoever stays here I'm sure will sign your guest book—that's writing."

"So, who is it will be coming to me?"

"I don't know yet."

"Who else has given you their places?"

"I don't have the list. I have twelve more to see."

"Will you be done by tomorrow?"

"Not likely."

"You have to let me know."

"I will by the weekend. I'm a little behind as I'm still teaching till the end of semester. But I'll get at it on the weekend." All of a sudden I felt like one of her staff. One of those people she gave instructions to and paid out of her healthy monthly allowance from her investment banker husband. We weren't working on the same committee; we weren't sharing the same agenda; we didn't share a love of books or art; we weren't even having tea together. My failure to immediately submit an A-list author was perceived as intransigence. The tour through the carriage house was faster than sex with a two-bit whore.

As she showed me back to my car I felt guilty. I had alienated her. Made her worry. This trapped bird in her gilded cage was now so worried I would choose the wrong writer for her she doubted her accommodation offer. She might have to rescind it if I chose someone she had not read, as she didn't have time to read a bunch of second-rate books. What would her husband say? He had to know immediately whose name he could conjure with. She had promised him the top two. And, as there was no Atwood, Munro or Shields, she didn't want a woman writer. Only *some* sisterhoods were powerful. Not all. How far off the bestseller list would I let this woman slide? Was her house—her art investment—worth nothing? What was the *real* value of a David Milne? Her anxiety broke and she snapped off a daffodil clearly past its prime.

I thanked her and nodded goodbye.

My own concerns surfaced. Who would feel comfortable here? Should I tell the writers this is a lottery or should I tell them straight—you're going to the highest bidder: the broker with the most money, the lawyer with the most clout, the banker who's deciding the interest rate, the developer with the largest estate, the most horses, the grandest lake or garden, the woman I have to call up again for some other good cause? One rich wife spurned could drop the shelter fund several thousand dollars.

Guys look for notches on their headboards; some women look for names in their guest books. Millicent's monthly allowance was probably more than we would raise at this entire benefit. This was an event for the ladies of the country, not for the women's shelter, and my free work was useful. She saw me as a pawn. A good go-between. Expectations on both sides were so out of whack I wondered why I'd got involved in fund raising. What was I trying to prove to my mother? What ghosts was I trying to appease— expiate what pettiness? Who was I trying to teach and what was I hoping they would read? What benefit my misguided desire? I drove down the winding road fearing I would become one of those people who did nothing for the common cause because it left me with nausea, left me having to deal with people and their insecurities. People and their agendas. Nothing more. Teachers are idiots.

God! I hated it all.

*Contemplation near the back swale.*

# A Guide to Animal Behaviour

A lot of children who grow up in the country, in the company of horses, always have the dream of wanting to become a good rider. "I see that horse" soon becomes "I like that horse" and then becomes "I want to ride that horse." We didn't start out thinking that Claire and Caitlin would enter competitions and become fascinated by breeding and training; it just evolved over the course of the years. Every little town has a fall fair and by the age of six or seven, like all their friends, our girls were taking their pets to the local schooling shows. It is a long way from the Shelburne Fall Fair to the provincial finals and only love of horses and determination can get a rider there.

Before a horse and rider can perform graceful piaffes, pirouettes and passage there is the lifelong training; it requires the patience of Job, the creativity of Picasso, the musicality of Beethoven and the passion of St Teresa of Avila. A committed family and some financing also helps but even without much cash, riders who just have to do it, do it. Our girls fell into that category.

Trainers and instructors from the ancient Greeks to Monty Roberts have detailed the loving care necessary to get horse and rider from birth to the ring. Choosing the right mount means examining bloodlines back generations and comparing all varieties of European Warmbloods and Sport horses. Aspiring horsewomen begin this process as soon as they can recognize one breed from another. From the larger Hanoverians to the more graceful

Trakehner/Thoroughbred crosses, the rider takes to imagining that perfect ride and matching her genes and abilities to the inherent potential of the dream horse.

For our girls, Friday night movie rentals had to include videos of the Lipizzaners of the Spanish riding school in Vienna performing airs off the ground, the Cadre Noir of the cavalry school in Saumur, France, defining routines evolved from the French Military, or the Russian Cavalry School in Leningrad executing charges and syncopated battle manoeuvres. The classic methods started in the ancient Italian riding schools are still gospel around the world. National pride began the first time Claire and Cait sang the anthem and saw the Royal Canadian Mounted Police Musical ride. Olympic dressage competitions, training sessions and stallion-breeding tapes were a constant source of inspiration. Writers from the Duke of Newcastle's *New Methods to Dress Horses* (1667), to Diane Ackerman's 1998 *A Natural History of Love*, become mandatory reading. From *Black Beauty* to *The Legend of Sleepy Hollow* and the thousand other books on equine life on library shelves, the obsessive horse lover develops ruthless appetites.

Once bred and on the ground the conformation in a foal begins to prove itself; this includes good bone, defining muscle, temperament, alertness, graceful pace in all gaits, easy strides, good hock flexion, three beat canters, a light float off the ground. Mango had it in spades but Buddy didn't begin to calm himself into his gaits until much after his castration. Both took well to daily early training in accepting the halter, lead shank, tying up, grooming, and hoof cleaning. They quickly learned that we were the source of affection, food, cleanliness, turnout and amusement. As soon as the girls could walk to the barn they were involved in the daily rituals, noting and commenting on the development of the horses as they watched their father and me go through the paces of horse care.

When they were three and four respectively, Mango and Buddy made the trip to the Equine Studies program at TH's college where they were used as training horses for the students studying how to break a young horse. The process began with lunging circles using a snaffle bridle, lunge whip, surcingle and side reins. Under the tutelage of Elizabeth Ashton, Canadian Olympic medalist in show jumping—Claire directly out of day care, Caitlin a babe in arms, and TH and I after work—we watched as the students learned to achieve the proper contact with the young animal. Horses know that they are built to work and most like the routines and respond immediately to voice commands: walk, trot, canter, whoa, stand. We learned by watching them learn. It is a brief three weeks from introducing the saddle, then accepting weight across it, to finally having a rider mount. Riding the lunge line at a walk, trotting in both directions, and listening to the aids of seat, legs, hands and voice was, in the case of both Buddy and Mango, a pleasure.

This, of course, is not always the case. When most horses get to the artificial aids of whip, spur and martingale some resistance begins to develop. They realize their own power and won't take to being pushed. Sometimes there is an anatomical problem that needs to be corrected. Buddy had wolf teeth in his upper jaw in front of the molars that had to be removed, as he was uncomfortable with the bit and had a tendency to wave his head about. He has had more dental work than anyone else in the family.

After the horses came home from college the first stages of training were repeated in the paddock or in the grassy field; however, the next few stages required an arena.

All good riding schools have an arena of at least 40 x 20 metres, if not the International Equestrian Federation sized 60 x 20 arena. Grass is good footing for young horses, though I found myself constantly heeling the divots into the ground and prinking them up whenever one of the girls went off at a canter, scattering grass in her wake. As head groundskeeper I decided to call my neighbour Glen, he of the sewage tank episode, to level a full-sized sand arena with his bulldozer. That spring, we had to wait while a group of nesting killdeer moved out to a higher field and I paced out the necessary length and breadth. Glen leveled the area, creating a high berm on the east side that we referred to as the bleacher seats, where the rabbits have now dug a home. The ground was rocky and the clay hard and thick so it took a few turns with the harrow and some new sand to make the footing softer.

Laying out a small arena requires precise measurements to be taken as once the horse has learned the paces her hoof strikes within centimetres of the mark. The markers AKEHCMBF are laid out across the breadth starting at A and continuing left around the rectangle with C at the top. The standard British way of memorizing this arrangement is All King Edward's Horses Can Make Big Fences. However, at home, All Kids Eat Hamburgers Chips Milk But Fart seems to be more readily at hand as no one knows King Edward anymore.

With the proper training, weekly coaching sessions and daily practice, horse and rider can soon walk, trot, canter around the arena, displaying the rudiments of collection, suspension and impulsion. Working trot, collected trot, medium trot, extended trot, posting and sitting come along with half halts that shorten and heighten the step. Keeping the horse supple, entering serpentines with the proper flexion and a perfectly relaxed four-beat walk or composed three-beat canter with an arched neck, is ballet at its finest.

To get to the basic level of provincial competition in Ontario all this must be mastered and then on to transitions, counter canters with complete collection and extension. Days of turning on the forehand, getting the pony to complete a 360-degree turn using leg yielding develops spectacular leg muscles on both horse and rider. The arena is worn with ridges, and five- and ten-metre arcs inscribed in the sand attest to months of circling practice.

The trouble with dreaming of perfection is that nothing short of that will do and a lifetime seems too brief compared to the demands of executing the perfect canter circle or shoulder-in down the complete length of a dressage wall. And just when these things started to come into being so did the girls start into their teenage years and begin the demands of high school and university preparation.

One of the coaches who was a regular at all the competitions once told me that we had soon to decide whether our girls were to become serious riders, that is train five hours every day year-in year-out, and get ready for team training, or continue on in school. They were good enough, he said, to begin training and practicing for his three-day eventing team. For all of us, as a family, the love of horses would always be there but the idea of not going on to university was out of the question. Claire and Caitlin learned to make choices early and both, not without tears and anxiety, chose education over life in the horse world.

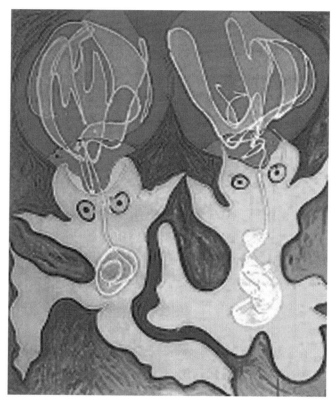

*Children in synchronicity.*

# Mad Shadows

When my father was angry he would stop speaking for several days. My childhood memories are full of these moments. "The silent treatment" my mother called it and all conversation was banned. The TV blared and, I swear, a psychosis descended upon the house. I never spoke until spoken to and I retreated to my grandmother or to my room. I often see that madness around me—people worked, distracted, silenced, and haunted to death. I see it sometimes in the local farmers. I see it at work: my college is an institution famous for its wounding psychic conflicts, some of which have gone on for twenty years, people desperately caught in the box, fighting the cardboard. Some Finns, perhaps more than other genetic groups, suffer from these maladies, compounded by months of depression from light deprivation, silence and alcohol. Numbness dulls the pain of depression. The Finns call depressives the Walkers of Darkness and research has found genetic as well as cultural causes. For a while I feared myself a member of this company of casualties.

There is a joke about two Finns, Pekka and Mattusi, who go into a bar in the middle of winter. The barman sets them up continuously for several hours. Finally, Pekka leans over and asks Mattusi what time it is. Pekka answers, "Did you come here to drink or to talk?" The first time I heard this joke I laughed for days. Clearly he felt the same about talking as my father did.

There is a documentary made about Finns and the tango. Improbably, these silent stony-faced, people walk into the middle of the dance floor and begin to ferociously pace and dip and whirl like the most passionate of Latin lovers. However, it doesn't get to their brains and they retreat immediately after the exertion to their separate seats. There is no carry over. I fear this is true of many entertainments and not just with Finns. There is a sameness to amusements, fleeting and insubstantial. There doesn't seem to be a permanent change, no melting into the space where happiness dwells which allows a feeling, an idea, to be nurtured over time.

Most North American cities don't hold a lot of happiness for me after a couple of weeks of visiting. I find the visual clutter depressing. In Toronto, a relatively innocuous offender as far as modern capitals is concerned, marketing and advertising are ubiquitous, and time is compressed by the many contenders for attention. The first thing—before the lousy air, before the noise, before the crowded spaces—that affected me as I drove to work were the billboards and ads, the Babel of language clutter. A reader, I find it hard to turn myself off and so I registered the brand names, the injunctions to attend religious talks, the insistent flashing of restaurants, gas stations, girlie shows, car dealers, fitness clubs. It destroys my internal space, my calm, my understanding. For the stoned, the drunk, the comatose, I suppose there is some jolt to being in an atmosphere like Times Square. For the hard to entice, dance floors, motor racing and three movies a day may be mild caffeine. But for me this is hell and breeds an anxiety and depression like no other.

When I feel that sadness well up in me, like some alien life force, I instantly retreat to my couch, to that view of the landscape, to my books, to my painting, the birds and my family. I completely cut out the extraneous world. I avoid television, stick to jazz, opera and classical music on CBC radio, watch only the few videos I really want to see, choose carefully whose company I keep. My toxic sensors are a survival mechanism and I trust my instincts. There is little healing, and only rare happiness in external city diversions; we are utterly responsible for our own psychic space.

In another northern story a dour, childless mathematics teacher, who taught all her life at the University of Uppsala, retired and became a widow in the same year. She sold her medieval house in Sweden and moved to a Greek island with only her books and a cat. She learned Greek, ate in the restaurants, spent the happiest ten years of her life reading Homer and then died. Her will stipulated that her books and ashes be thrown off the cliff into the Aegean and not returned to Sweden. I heard that story in Stockholm one dark March winter break when I took my mother, a few years before her death, to visit her last surviving relatives. When I told her this story her response was, "What happened to the cat?"

There was nothing unusual to my mother or my aunt in the story except for the cat. "But what about the previous sixty-five years?" I asked. "The point of the story is surely the first sixty-five years?"

"No," answered my mother, "we expect to suffer like that." My aunt sagely agreed that suffering was everything and there was little chance of happiness in this world.

"All the women in our family feel like that, except most of them never wasted their money on cats and they never got to Greece." My mother and aunt laughed about that story and my pathetic understanding. I wanted to talk about Queen Christina flying off to Italy to run a salon but they refused to accept that hairdressing was better than being a Queen in Stockholm and, rather than begin a pretentious academic explanation of literary and music salons, I put on my parka and begged my uncle to take me walking.

The rest of the afternoon, with the light at a steely horizontal across the water, I went with him sightseeing in Stockholm's old town. Thankfully, Gamla Stan, that northern Venice, is full of bookstores, churches, fine museums, galleries and sweater shops or I would have stayed with my mother and aunt musing on our inherited family depression, life's suffering, the abandoned cat and permanent waves.

The following day, wanting to see the illuminated manuscripts in the University of Uppsala library, I took the one-hour train ride north. After the manuscripts, after a glass of wine and lunch as a visiting academic in the faculty dining room, I went to rest my feet in the magnificent medieval church close by. After walking all day I briefly fell asleep. When I woke, grieving relatives and solemn clergy surrounded a casket. The civil servant whose body was in front of me had worked hard all his life and never strayed from the path. "There was some pleasure in the suffering," one of them said, "some pleasure in the suffering."

When I went outside to walk back to the train station I passed by Linnaeus' garden and pondered the nature of genetic mutation and constancy. On the late train back to Stockholm the starless sky was unrelenting as it barreled through the night. I wondered who I was and who I was not. I cannot truthfully become a Sàmi, a Lutheran, a Jew, or a Swede, or a Finn, or a Catholic as my brother has become, and find consolation in any of those places. I have to be that singular amalgam of all my history. But I have to live with some genetic material that spirals in a dark direction. I take no pleasure, no consolation, in the suffering around me—do not feel honoured to have witnessed the suffering of others or the decay of the world in the past fifty years. But there it is; survival is no small task.

TH and I regularly had meetings of the Niagara Escarpment Chapter of the John Banville/Ian McEwan Slow Dinner Book Society for just the two of us and accepted the state of the outside world and our own biological shortcomings. We lived the life we had built and chosen. We were not living at Sweetfield by accident. It was a necessity.

*Self portrait.*

## Fugitive Pieces

"What are these books about?" My mother pottered with her dust rag, reaching up from her wheelchair, more to see what was in each nook and cranny than to clean.

"Stories, mostly stories." I paused in my marking, watched as she pulled the books out, carefully wiped them and took audible breaths as she noted the prices.

"Are they all false? If they're lies I'd rather read the cookbooks."

"Well, they're fiction, if that is what you mean."

"I know this one. They made a movie about her." She held *Anna Karenina* in her hands. "This must be her biography."

"No. It's fiction, by Tolstoy. But there were many women like her." Her hands moved more quickly now, feeling she had made contact with something she understood.

"She seemed very Scandinavian in the movie on television. Killing herself like that. Under a train. Is it the same in the book as in the movie?"

"Yes. Russian, actually, but yes."

"What I really want," she said, "is a biography, or some science, or something about the mind."

"All fiction is about the mind."

"No, more about the *science of mind*. And about what happens to mind, not the brain, after death."

"If it's not written down in a book," I said to her, trying to avoid yet another discussion of parapsychology, time travel and astral projection, "not much is left behind."

"Well, I believe there is. A place where all the minds go after they've left their bodies and I don't mean just heaven. Do you have any books on bodies?"

"What do you mean? Like medical books or books on health?"

"Yes. And about freezing bodies and leaving them to science."

"Cryogenics?"

"More autopsy, I think. More autopsy."

"Well I do have a *Granta* which has things about autopsies." Where was this all going, I wondered? I knew that the dismemberment scene in *The Innocent* was not what she was looking for. What was she after here?

"I want to leave my body to science," she finally said. "I want them to figure out things about me. Not for myself, but for them. I mean, wouldn't it be interesting to see a piece of liver and a pancreas and a spleen that has been diabetic for fifty years? What about my kidneys?"

"Yes, I suppose so."

"Well, that's what I want to do. I want to leave my body, or at least some little pieces of it, to the medical students at UBC. If I die in Toronto my body could go the University of Toronto—that's a good medical school. I want them to figure out what rheumatoid arthritis does to the hands and feet. The bunions on my feet are interesting. I want them to look at my breasts and see why my implants got so hard. I want them to see the inside of my brain. And look at my heart. I think that would be interesting to them, to those young students. I think it would."

"I'm sure it would. I'm sure it would." There were times when it was best to just let my mother talk, just let her stroll through the alleyways of her mind and see what she found. It was always a surprise to me.

"I just think there must be something useful left. Maybe some part of my eyes they could transplant—I mean the parts without glaucoma—some skin they could use on a burn victim. What about all those expensive minerals I've been taking for my bones? Can they transplant bones? I'd like to be useful after I die."

"Did you sign your organ donation card on your driver's license?"

"Yes, I did that. But I'm afraid they may take one look at my corpse and decide there is nothing worth salvaging. Then no part of me would go on. I don't want my ashes to be just meal for the roses. I want something left over for someone else."

"Well, I can talk to the doctor. Maybe someone needs cadavers."

"When I'm dead you talk to the doctor. See if there is something to recycle. Something for science."

"I will." Just like *Margaret's Museum*, I thought. She put her dust cloth away; she had found what she was looking for on the shelves—a place for herself in history, a purpose—and headed to the kitchen.

"Is there any more flour? I feel like baking bread."

"Yes, in the bottom cupboard. Lots of flour. Make bread."

"I put the last of the crumbs in the bird feeder so you don't have to buy bird seed this week. Shouldn't spend money on birdseed. Shouldn't waste anything."

I turned back to my marking.

"And I took the big bag of bran from the barn. I don't know why you feed that to horses. Let them eat grass. I am going to make muffins."

# Dropped Threads

Nearing my fifties and certainly menopausal, I had my
fiercest year. It was one of those psychological passages I suppose I had put off for a long time but, as I got
more intent on dealing with teenagers, more certain I was going
to make all the mistakes that everyone makes, I began to confront my own demons. Why did I work so hard? What forced me
into making myself uncomfortably exhausted? Was it so pleasing
to others? Was I so desperate for approval? Was all of this making
me happy? Was it necessary to have vast dinner parties, seventy-
five acres of garden, horses, dogs, cats, flocks of feathered friends,
stacks of books and magazines, a full-time professorship, grand
community work projects and a husband and two kids?

Several times, starting in the fall until the end of the following
June, I suffered debilitating migraines. I dutifully went off and
read Oliver Sacks and all the recent research from the Migraine
Foundation every time I came out of a devastating crash, but I was
at a loss to explain all my triggers. I gave up chocolate, red wine,
coffee. I didn't smoke or do drugs. I could only sleep with the aid
of sleeping pills and I regularly suffered stress that I could not
deal with. Sometimes I would override my own breaking points,
I would be too nice about things that bothered me and I didn't
like that about myself. Sometimes I failed to respond when some
vicious sociopath sideswiped me at work. I never had road rage

or any other kind of rage. I would take all of my anger, all of my concerns and plant them in my garden, and yet sometimes roses were not coming up.

Instead of escaping to my farm and lawn tractor I would try to deal with problems head on. This might not make me a better or a happier person—it certainly made me less popular—but it would surely help me confront my anxieties. A hundred years ago I would have retired, or been retired, to the quiet of an attic with a barred door.

At the low end of some biorhythm, when the menopausal clock indicated, when my asthma was bad or I was bickering with TH over some household chore he yet again failed to complete, I would feel a migraine coming on. Maybe Claire would come home from high school with a horror story of being bullied by some creep. Maybe Caitlin was sick with an ear infection or up all night with a cold. Maybe Claire was having a jealous period when she felt she wasn't getting enough attention from her parents. Maybe a horse just died or a neighbour got arrested for child abuse. Maybe it was the second three-week strike of teachers and the subsequent loss, again, of two paychecks. Perhaps another box of remembered dead things from my mother or another round of abusive nastiness from my now bankrupt father. Whatever it was, or whatever combination of things it was, I would begin to feel that familiar nausea in the pit of my stomach, the hollowness in my head, the ringing in my ears, the loss of peripheral vision, followed by vomiting, blindness and brain axing that would drop me down for two days.

My doctor prescribed various drugs and from time to time I went to the hospital for a shot to kill the pain. There were no abortive drugs on the market and so I had to go through the full cycle of the seizure, ending up two days later feeling like I'd had electroshock therapy. For a few days after the migraine I would move around in a molasses state, unable to think terribly well, uncertain of my driving and parenting abilities.

I talked with the other women I knew who had migraines—there were several in my office, several in the country nearby—and examined all the options they had tried. It seemed everyone I knew had migraines, just as when I was pregnant everyone in the world seemed pregnant. Many suggested comparable drugs (some massively addictive), herbal remedies, acupuncture, massage, hypnotherapy, psychotherapy, group therapy, yoga and high colonics. Most of these did not appeal to me so I retreated again to making lists of triggers, the most obvious of which, for me, was a sense of psychic wounding.

I had to ask my mother before she died to stop sending me the detritus of other dead people and stop discussing how much more she loved my brother than me and what a finer human being he was. My mother became diabetic when she was pregnant with me and never failed to remind me every time she took a shot or tested her glucose levels that had I not been conceived she would not be insulin dependent. I told her more than once that I was not responsible for all the horror of her life and I would listen to her stories but I would not take the blame. It needed a few simple declarative statements, a letter or two, but—lo and behold—it sunk in and her later visits became less stressful for me.

I asked my father to stop telling my girls they were sexy young things and to stop asking them to prance about for his gratification. I confronted him about his gambling, told him we would no longer lend him money and we would no longer bail him out. For a wedding present my father had given us a piece of land in the Yellowhead that he then sold and pocketed the money when his gambling got out of hand. He had paid about $5,000 dollars for it and I maintained the taxes although he never "got around" to transferring it into my name. I asked him for the money I had paid in taxes and he began to bellow in his usual fashion. My father was one of those "my way or the highway" bullies who refused to acknowledge that anything he could have done could be even slightly construed as wrong. He had no idea of the notion of unacceptable behaviour. He was who he was and the world was better for it, he always said. Finally, for my girls' safety, for my family pocketbook and for my own psychic space I decided to have as little to do with him as possible.

These are ugly decisions but decisions that are demanded for health and sanity. When my mother was dying she said that I had been a better mother to her in the last few years than she had been to me. She said, for the first time in her life, that she loved me and my children. I think her capacity to love had been kicked out of her very young and instead she tried to "keep things tidy and work hard".

She taught me this quite well but I'm afraid I was never as good an actress as she was.

Mothers and daughters are like seaweed sponges in warm salt water, distinct entities but so totally immersed in the same swell it is impossible at times to tell us apart. Biology binds us as does a sense of rhythm and universal flow. Disentangling that is a difficult process.

My mother and I would talk on the phone each week and whenever I called she would say, "Oh, I knew it was you." or, worse yet, "Hello, Lyn, I've been expecting your call for twenty minutes. What were you doing?" It gave me the sense that perhaps no one else in the world called her (although I knew my brother did) and I felt I should do something more to help her in her loneliness. She, of course, put it down to her psychic abilities.

One day the secretary at work called me from a lecture with "an important phone call". I walked down the hall thinking someone had died, or had had a heart attack. I prepared myself for the worst. On the other end of the line was my mother. "Did you know that carrots are on sale this week at Safeway? Ten cents a pound. Bushel baskets!" In my relief I told her I would go out and buy some immediately after I finished teaching the class I was in the middle of, even though Safeway had no stores in Ontario.

"Thanks, Mom. What a great deal on carrots."

"I thought you should know," she said. "I know you're too busy teaching to read the flyers that come in the mail."

"You know that I'm teaching right now?"

"Yes," she answered. "But this is more important. Your students don't listen to you anyway. I'm making carrot muffins." Sideswiped again.

I think she preferred to be alone for much of the time; it meant she would not feel the compunction to get up and do something for someone else. The compulsion to bake bread or wash the floor one more time came more from the outside than from the inside. I am this person too.

Now I like to have my house in order so that I can do what I want to do. So that I can work in my garden, read and write, watch the horsewomen casually perform manoeuvres on weekends after their homework is done. I challenge women who have messy houses to tell me that they don't mind living in chaos. My husband, when he was on his own, lived like a pig and many teenage boys find it necessary to breathe moldy socks in order to develop testosterone. This is intolerable. My gay friends are of a mind with me. I now have a cleaner who helps me out regularly, but in order to stay sane and keep working I have to live in a clean house. Pathological.

To finally rid myself permanently of migraines I knew I had to have therapy. Biologically, migraines arrive with disorder. They come at times of emotional uncertainty and stress. When my boundaries have been crossed, when my good nature is taken advantage of, when I am the target of someone's gratuitous anger, all regular behaviour patterns in this world, I hit the pillow with a crunched skull.

Since menopause I have only had one or two migraines. The biology has changed and so has my ability to say no. Mind you, I now have rheumatoid- and osteo-arthritis, genes I inherited from both sides of my family, but that is not, as yet, as catastrophic for me as migraines. It's a different type of pain, a different set of circumstances beyond my control.

Bodies are funny things, parts of them are inside the skin and parts of them extend into the world, past and present. Emotional stability, strength and tenacity are hard to come by; you work at it every day and sometimes when all things are in balance, when you have drawn enough circles and you accept all that is within, the world hums and you do have time to do the things you want to do.

*Night on Green Cow Pond.*

# The Martyrology

F amily visits continue for lifetimes and I've had many discussions with my brother, Martin, about God. After my mother died these conversations obviously had some significance for him as maybe they replaced the ones he also had with my mother when she was living. I don't know why we keep having them but each time he visits we do what siblings do: we prod each other, poke to see who might move. It was like when we were children, playing Chinese checkers; it was the same thing, and we keep doing it. My brother had a great fondness for my family, especially my husband, and I enjoyed his visits even though I felt I did not quite live up to my brother's expectations of the spiritual life well lived.

"And when you go to church and listen to the Catholic version of what God is, do you believe it all?" I asked him one visit.

"Yes, every word of it." He stroked his thinning hair, nodding with an assurance somewhat like my father's.

"Really?"

"Yes. Why?"

"I just don't understand that. We had a similar childhood. I don't understand, when that is not there in your past at all, when no one in our family believed or, indeed, behaved in what you would really call a Christian way, why it is that you now believe?"

"Well, the story just seems right, well-presented, entrenched. I like the stability. So many people live their lives that way and have for two thousand years. When I read about a Catholic life, I think that is the way life should be lived. Your bookshelf is full of Catholics. I think we should do what the Catholic Church tells us to do."

"But I don't believe that. I don't believe in the doctrines, I don't see the stories as anything more than good literature; they have a function. They help us metaphorically to understand what it means to be human, feel certain spiritual needs, but I don't believe they are the literal truth."

"But you're wrong. They are true. 'There are more things...'"

"Don't quote Shakespeare to me. I'm the literature major."

"Well then, you should see it more clearly. You should see the truth of the story and the institution."

"That's the last thing I feel. I believe the Catholic Church has been absolutely wrong about so many things: the Jews, women, homosexuality, marriage, birth control, abortion, child sexual abuse, condoms."

"You're being distracted from the true message."

"I know. But I just don't accept rules. I don't see it."

"You will."

"Don't be patronizing. This is a silly argument. We can't have this fight. There's no point."

"Well, I'll wait for you to come around. One of the reasons I am sure you will is because of your husband, because he was trained by the Jesuits. He's a moral man. I think of the way he is and I am sure that he is still Catholic."

"He's not! He hated private school; it was a thoroughly repressive place. Not as bad perhaps as the native residential schools but the same bunch of bullies. He hated the Jesuit brother who chased him with a hockey stick all the way into the church. He hated the brother who would get erections every time he spoke of St Ignatius, every time he read a line from Milton. Those kids were brutalized there. He couldn't get out of that school fast enough."

"But he still behaves in a moral way."

"That is because of who he is, because he has a fiduciary responsibility to the students, to the taxpayers of Ontario, to his own sense of right and wrong. I can tell you for sure it has little to do with the Jesuit brothers."

"But they showed him the path. He'll be back."

"Stop it! I won't have a discussion with you about my husband and the Catholic Church. I'm willing to give them the fact that he can spell well, he knows the roots of words, and when we're traveling he can translate the Latin over doorways. Religious knowledge helps when looking at paintings of the crucifixion or St Sebastian. It helps when teaching some literature. But that's it. Don't assume because he spent a few semesters in a Catholic school he swallows that doctrine hook, line and sinker. Let's talk about something other than my sleeping husband. It will disturb his dreams. Have a glass of wine."

"The Catholics don't disapprove of wine."

"How could they? They don't disapprove of the Mafia either. Italians are famously capable of holding many diverse opinions on the same day. It's what I love about them. The more conflicting ideas the merrier."

"The church loves sinners."

"Yes, it does. Yes, it does."

"I think that mother would have liked the church. You know all of her searching, all of her wondering what the world was about could have been answered if she had only found her way to the right priest, to the right doorway."

"Mother found her way into many doorways. The last thing she needed was to have a priest tell her how to live her life. She needed to figure that out for herself."

"You're so angry."

"Not angry."

"Cynical."

"Perhaps a little. But it is hard not to be. We have more genetic reason to follow the well-trod Scandinavian path of droll cynicism than the teachings of the Pope."

"You need to be more forgiving, more spiritual."

"Me? I'm spiritual firsthand, sweetie, firsthand. I'm the one out planting the trees, communing like St Francis of Shelburne with the birds and the toads and the fishes. My atavistic tendencies are there. My blood comes straight from Aiti. Call me un-Catholic yes, but unspiritual? Perhaps I'm a little too pagan for your taste. A little too attached to the land and not so enamored of institutions to be sure. But don't even think I don't have street credibility in the spirit world."

"So maybe one day you'll find your way back to church?"

"That's unlikely. Considering I've never been there as anything more than a tourist, a student of art history, architecture and music. My religion is my home and family."

"Maybe your husband. He will come back to the church."

"Unlikelier still."

"There is always hope."

"Hope springs eternal."

*Easter egg hunt under the full moon.*

# A Good House

Books answer my deep desire to know the stories of others, to live in their houses. Stories that take the reader, entice her in, bring her to an experience and place she can understand and let her walk out of that house a changed woman are rewarding life experiences, more significant than a week in Prague or Madrid. A reader is a guest, the dining room before her, the candles lit, all the courses patiently delivered: amusement, something bitter, something sweet—and she has only to take the time to live through it. Endings bring a sadness, like all wonderful companions at a feast when you have to leave them, a little of death creeps in leaving a reader weeping, laughing, comforted, disturbed in varying doses. The job of the common reader, once you have chosen the book you want to read, is to be a patient guest, enjoy what you can of the meals and the rooms, leave behind what you don't want.

I like to watch people reading, nose to text: in the subways, in parks, on beaches, in classrooms. I assume they also read naked under sheets, in the bathtub, reheating the water with their toes on the hot tap: slow-finger readers, hundreds-of-words-a-minute readers. There is something voyeuristic about watching people read. I always try to peak at the covers, the paperbacks, the ragged old hardcover copies with torn dust jackets. I watch people dog-ear books, scribble marginalia, tear out pages. The absorbed are the most fascinating, missing their stops on the trains as they do;

making no eye contact with anyone, the traces of light and shadow over the brow. The mild expletives as they get off and return on the lost route home.

We have all become amateur psychoanalysts—reading houses, reading clothing, reading body language, reading hair—but nothing is so revealing as reading bookshelves; a host will often give tours of gardens, kitchens, hearth settings, kids' rooms, but nothing compares to scanning private shelves. The secret mystic reveals himself, the professor who stopped reading when he finished the PhD, the insecure mother, the cat fancier, the fetishist, the one who cannot love her gay son. I love to see stacks of poetry—Philip Larkin on top of Seamus Heaney. Discovering someone's deep love of Celtic folklore, Chinese music or Chilean history is one of the most socially satisfying occurrences.

I rarely feel book envy. My little library is over 5,000 strong, but when I hear of a home where collections are measured in miles, where, generation after generation, readers have collected volumes—15, 25, 50,000 books—I imagine an unlimited world and my envy gland starts to pulse. It must be like living in the Robarts Library or the Fisher Rare Book Room at the University of Toronto, with incunabula haunting your every step. TH wanted me committed.

I once stayed at a bed and breakfast in Edinburgh replete with rolling ladders, maps on folio stands, and magnifying glasses. It had one of the best personal libraries of travel writing I have ever seen: Africa for the last hundred years, India, Malaysia, Antarctica. I fantasized that the reader never left that room but he was broadly travelled; I deduced from the ages of the books and the titles on the spines of first editions that it was a man of about eighty-five, who hated war and loved foreign places. Perhaps he was wounded and walked with an uneasy gait but was close at hand with Clive of India, Lawrence of Arabia, Richard Burton and his wife, and the adventurer Gertrude Bell.

Claire, at fourteen, was asked to babysit at a neighbour's house and she went over to find the children's room bare of books. She called after the parents had left and I dutifully drove over with half-a-dozen picture books and stories about training tigers and runaway princesses. It seemed like a good two hours of evening fare. When the parents returned, a tearful Claire was dropped home having been corrected as to the error of our ways. The mother, full of disdain, handed me the offending bag of reading material.

"In my home we only read the Good Book," she intoned. "We do not allow the children to read this trash." Claire's babysitting career ended there, a pathetic seven dollars in her hand, and my suspicion of parochial reading habits was confirmed.

It is true, my children will tell you, that I am quite judgmental and deranged on the subject of houses and books, but I just can't help myself. It is hard to underestimate the value of reading to children, it is impossible to count the number of illnesses cured, families saved, wars averted by reading. Teachers cannot help themselves—occupational handicap.

*The little yellow farmhouse.*

# The Follow

O n one of the last Sundays of our foray into the competitive horse world we were up at five, loading the truck, getting the horses on the trailer, and listening to Caitlin humming in the back seat. This August morning was not to be the monotony of test after dressage test, but her final musical freestyle—a *kür*—before high school started again. I'd made *muffelettas*, wrapped prosciutto with melon, figs poached in port and threw in some grapes and pecorino for good measure. But lunch would not be till twelve, served off the tailgate of the 4Runner. First there was the ballet, the elegance and lightness of horse and rider, summed up in four minutes after a decade of work.

Caitlin knows how to persevere. The choreography from memory, the forty tapes for the perfect music: classical jazz to enter and salute, funky blues, Scott Joplin to loopy serpentines, the *Ride of the Valkyries* to extended trot. Discipline in sync with music. A minute from *The Planets* for the long walk. Mozart for canters, Strauss for the circles. She had tried them all, rewound the tapes, replayed the execution; but a foot wrong anywhere and the rest of the sequence would be out, the aligned world would fall apart.

She made three copies of the tape in case one was broken, the judge misplaced it, or the machine jammed. Mango's bathing and braiding had taken all of Saturday: hooves shone, silver stirrups sparkled. The white shirts and jodhpurs had been bleached, the black boots polished, and Caitlin hummed all day, but not too loudly, just so that the music syncopations pulsed, just so the visualization evoked the proper lift of finger, flex of buttock, dip of shoulder. Freestyle is a meditation, a capture of breath and line and blood, a delight for even the uninitiated to watch.

If, for the instant, the audience believes the horse is Pegasus, the rider a goddess, the moment a mythic one, the earthly job of horse and rider is done. The musical *kür* is on a par with opera and ballet and poetry, a brief victory if it works. It is sleight of hand and in that short time the horse and rider join with the forces of the universe to take my breath away. Everyone applauds the brilliance of the horse and the skilled athleticism of the relaxed rider managing to follow the music. For us, it was a magical day, a fitting end to all the training. We would not be doing this for the rest of our lives: our children would grow up, the horses would age and be retired, and we would also retire and join again the ranks of watchers. We would again be in the back row at the Royal Winter Fair, on the sidelines at Woodbine, cheering on the horses and riders while watching our own children go on to other parts of their lives.

# The Mother Zone

Natural instinct in mothers tells us to circle our children, to keep the world at bay. Horses, even in a long-standing herd, protect their young from others. We let them out to socialize in controlled circumstances and time frames. We keep them warm, fed, comforted by our nurturing. We love them unconditionally, one eye on the horizon for predators. We seek the best pastures, hoping they will grow strong. The natural instinct of children is to break away from the mother, find their own feet, and walk in the world on their own. These conflicting impulses, at the core of all relationships, the coming together and breaking away, motivates the species to keep reproducing, seeking out the best genes, securing the food source and some pleasure and happiness. There are obvious flaws in this formula.

Our influence and control ends relatively early in the scope of their lives; however, if memory serves well, they will always have the childhoods we gave them. They will have had their share of pain, sadness and death: pets, friends, grandparents and of course, someday, our own. They will have suffered the petty jealousies, angers and resentments along with their peers. We invent complex intellectual narratives most of which will not stand the light of modern day and they will accept or reject these as their histories dictate. They will not be free from their animal natures and will indulge in deadly sins. They will live their own lives.

There are no perfect nations, no perfect cultures, and no secure landing spots. We send our children out to a world of uncertainty, hostile conflict, relentless greed and moral vacuity. We hope that we have armed them well enough, given them, in those crucial early years, enough skill to manage the chaos they encounter. We cross our fingers and hope against all evidence that they will find deserving partners, that they will work in satisfying circumstances that bring out their best qualities, that they will find happiness at least to the degree it did or didn't happen for us. How can we expect the world to treat them any differently?

Demographers call North American baby boomers the most fortunate generation. Our children are indulged. Most from the middle classes grow up with the full complement of childhood acitivites: swimming, piano, ballet, art classes, technology, higher education, travel. We grew up without major wars, with economic certainty and opportunity. Canada is often cited by the United Nations as the most humane country: health care, education—one of the best places in the world to raise offspring. Our landscape is inspiring, our climate manageable. (Why don't foreigners know that?) We all have jobs. Is this as good as it gets? We have lost something but I'm not sure what. In our rush to improve things we've thrown out something we weren't sure we valued. The smug perfection we aimed for with the birth of our children and worked for most of our lives guaranteed nothing. We laboured to save our mutating genes for an uncertain unknown. We can only hope that we were good enough mothers, good enough fathers, and some happiness will be found.

The energy to persevere through the most difficult phases of child rearing came in the form of endless discussions, not only with TH, but with a circle of women friends whose ideas and presence are life sustaining to me.

"I had one child but my husband, a famous philanderer, left me for another woman when I was pregnant. I had little money but I worked and did the best I could. It wasn't the best thing for my boy but I had no choice. I had to take care of both of us. I love my son very much."

"I had two children; we both worked hard but there was always so much to be done. There wasn't much time and I was ill. I couldn't help myself. I also cared for my parents; they had to live with us until they died. My children are the most important people in the world to me. I love them very much."

"I had three children and worked hard to make this a better world; my husband had money and cared for them a great deal. I didn't deserve him. We had nannies but I couldn't spend enough time with the children. I couldn't help them enough. I love them very much."

"I had four children but two died: one was stillborn and my son died of AIDS at thirty-five. My husband and I loved them all very much. I tried to help him die easily but I failed. It was the worst pain in the world. He didn't deserve to die. Maybe it was my genes. Maybe I tried too hard to have children. The two who survived always live with the two who did not. Maybe I wanted too much."

"Mea culpa."

"Mea culpa."

"Mea culpa."

"Mea culpa."

When I hear people say that the women's movement hasn't done much to change the way we struggle with this world I stand up and rail at the falsehood of that statement. My mother never had a constant circle of friends to count on, she had a few sisters scattered across the country at a time when phone calls were out of their financial reach. They wrote barely literate letters to each other, with instructions on preserving moose meat. When they died they didn't pass on a wealth of knowledge about humanity, they passed on cottage cheese containers. They had little access to birth control, health information or professional jobs and, more than that, they raised their children in isolation.

In my generation we got right to the core as quickly as we could. We talked about the problems, we discussed our shortcomings and we shared our successes. There are a handful of women in this world who, I would say, have changed my life. There was only one man. Maybe you only need one man but you need a whole host of other women's voices to keep you from pulling your roots out and going starkers. Without those friends and the coffee *klatches* and without those books the world of motherhood would be light years behind where it is now. And motherhood, however much some women will disagree, was still my major task—the most important thing I have done in this world.

*One of my great grandmother's coffee pots from Finland.*
*(Photograph by April Hickox.)*

# The Wars

The only birds I have ever gone to war against are the starlings (*Sturnus vulgaris vulgaris*). They are ugly, short-tailed, speckled, nuisance birds with a rasping cackle they occasionally disguise to imitate other, more welcome birds; but I am never fooled. They were brought to Central Park in New York by a British ornithologist who wanted to contribute to a complete and correct version of a Shakespeare play. They quickly spread throughout North America, robbing nests, destroying eaves and jettisoning mail from rural boxes so they can nest comfortably. They breed ferociously from two to two hundred overnight, streaming white globules of crap along the roofline, and return with irritating regularity. They are the only birds I would shoot, had I a shotgun. I have plucked their nests from inside the attic, nailed up the soffits and changed mailboxes twice—now the post lady can't even get it open. I fear I shall have to live with them till my grave.

Further down my hate list are rats that grow to such size that I have occasionally mistaken them for rabbits. The unwelcome silent rats of the grain bins that startle me each spring are quickly downed with rat poison. For every one I see I irrationally count ten more in my mind. Friends who have a larger barn counted thirty dead one spring. Now I know these numbers are small compared to New York and London—even Toronto has rats in the subway—but, perversely, I accept them in cities more than at the farm.

One morning, up at six, I heard a scurrying in my kitchen, grabbed a mop and cornered a big rat by the door. I paused, not sure what I would do next and he bolted past my feet. I swatted again with my mop and he fled to the bathroom. I knew there was no way out for him, having personally caulked all around the tub, so I slammed the door shut while I planned how to catch the old geezer. He was very large. No little soapbox would work. I ran down to the barn in my slippers and found the raccoon trap and a short piece of two by six.

When I opened the bathroom door, there he was still, sitting behind the toilet, staring me down. I put the board on one side of the toilet and jammed the open cage between the toilet and the wall. Then I hit him with my mop. He turned and ran into the cage. Now I had him, what to do with him? Whenever we trapped raccoons or squirrels and chipmunks that were too numerous we dropped them at the Mono Cliffs Park (after they had invariably peed in my car trunk) but this rat would be back. I decided to kill him—drown him on the spot.

I put the plug in the bathtub and filled it, full blast, to the top. Then I picked up the cage and dropped it in the bath. Damn, if that rat didn't start swimming and held himself and the raccoon trap above the water line. I ran to the garden and grabbed two enormous bolders from the rockery, lugged them back to the tub and placed them on the cage. Finally, the cage submerged, a few moments later the rat was dead.

I sat on the toilet seat, my heart pounding, watching the matted grey hairiness twist and turn as the water spiraled down the drain. Even a lapsed Lutheran draws a line about rats in her house, I told him. I don't accept you in my house. He got no further eulogy as I buried him in the garden.

One summer when I was up in the Yellowhead of British Columbia watching bears, I had to shoot an old female who was rustling food from my kitchen and eating my butter, frozen in the river. The cabin windows were only plastic and she had no difficulty breaking through in the early morning on more than one occasion and smashing through the tins of tuna and gorging on dog food while the dog slept blissfully upstairs. After three days of cleaning the kitchen and nailing up the windows I lost my patience as she broke through first the screen and then the wooden door. I waited for her in the morning, banged some pots and pans when she appeared and fired off a warning round from my rifle into the air. She just looked at me in the way that old women can and proceeded to climb up the window frame.

One shot, between the eyes.

My closest neighbour, a native woman three miles away, came over with her tractor and took the carcass away. We split the liver and some of the meat (although bear needs a lot of marinating) and the pelt she sold in Prince George. I try to tell the rats this instructive story about my propriety over my kitchen but they don't listen.

Last summer I had two rats at my bird feeders and there is no catching a rat out of doors. Poison would kill all my birds. You have to be a pretty good shot with a rifle in order to dispatch a small moving target and both of these beasts proved beyond my skill. I really do abhor violence. My husband, however, never lets me down when a crack shot is needed and those two rats are now buried under the rose bushes. We have a man in Orangeville who makes his living getting rid of nuisance animals but that is a level of abrogation of personal responsibility I don't think should be tolerated in the country. You live here, you deal with the vermin.

The occasional skirmishes with groundhogs, skunks and porcupines are less taxing. I have always feared one of the horses breaking a leg because of groundhog holes but it was I, chasing the horses in before a storm, who stumbled into a hole and hobbled about on crutches for two weeks. Now the groundhogs have moved out of the paddocks and into areas of less traffic and I didn't mind the occasional mound around the swale or in a hay field.

I probably suffered from a petty dislike of rats and starlings, rather like D.H. Lawrence and his snake, and I will have to expiate this irrationality at some point but, before that, I would have to undo all my genetic material and go for much re-education. Until then, I keep them on notice. There were two types of animals on my farm—those I loved and lived with and those I could not abide.

*Voodoo doll keeping the world at bay.*

## Lives of the Saints

In the course of my gardening, running the farm and raising a family I came to understand things about myself and others that could not have been learned any other way. Our labours often define us. The landscape of Sweetfield: the sacred grove, the secret garden, the reflecting pond, the forest caves, the dark wood and the open fields, gave me access to many parts of my genetic and psychic self. It also gave me an awareness of a liminal, transitional—and very Canadian—world. My name comes from Finland, "*Suomi,*" which translates as land of lakes and marshes. I now know much of that marsh. Every summer for over twenty-five years I rode my lawn tractor around in repetitive circles, narrower and narrower until I ended up in the centre of some section and had to break out along another trail and repeat the process. I rode in loops from the back garden to the front, from the jumping arena to the driveway, from the pond paths to the maple forest. I raced through paths at rabbit speed and slowed down to turtle over bumps, to avoid shrubs and small animals, around maples, oaks and pines. I listened as pilots stalled their engines and started them again only a few hundred feet above my head, narrowly averting disaster. Hot air balloonists hissed in my ear and ultra-lights buzzed the grain field in front of me but this was my ground, my work. My world felt round and whole from horizon to horizon.

I once found a group of confused hikers from Berlin who had climbed up the Niagara Escarpment rock face and ended up lost in the maple forest, a mile from the Bruce Trail. They were about as surprised to see me tearing round on my tractor in mad reverie in my pajamas as I was to find them. I was disconcertingly at home in this world of unexpected narrative, myth and tale, the eternal verities that overwhelmed the perishable world. I mumbled at them in made-up German about being lost and found again on confusing paths. I guided them, as they shook their puzzled heads and apologized to the crazed woman in the nightgown, to the safety of the beaten trail. In the weekly repetition of my tractor meditation I revisited old ideas about my family, carved out new ideas about my partner and my friends, saw my house and family for the first time. I am not the person I was when we moved into Sweetfield in 1979.

I swooped under the pear tree where TH's father's ashes are buried and sneaked around the one where his mother's ashes will go. As I drove down the hill near the dressage arena I passed the graves of Max, the first brave hunter, and our cats, Alice and Lefty, and Tarzan (our last hunting poodle)—noble animals all. I passed the spot reserved for the horses, now that they had retired, and came round to where at some future date I imagine my ashes spread. In the old orchard section, one I only started tending in the past few years, I thought about my friends who are ageing, have become ill or recently died. It's called the Sweetfield Lawn and Zipper Club (no fees, no applications, please).

When I first started cutting that section of weeds, TH asked what project I was clearing the land for, and I thought lawn bowling was as good an answer as any. I called it the Zipper Club because the only people I know who would ever be interested in lawn bowling are those who have had major surgery so anything more strenuous would threaten the stitches. It was a field of dreams where riotous weekly dinner parties and outdoor dances came together as I mowed through the constant white pain of my arthritis. As I was now past having large parties it had become much easier to imagine them. The guest list in my head changed and people were added, as they need to be: hysterectomies, mastectomies, colostomies, ovarian cancer, hip replacements, lung lobectomies, scleroderma. I admitted the young who had impacted wisdom teeth, broken hearts and heavy periods. All the ladies from my physiotherapy class at the YMCA were honorary members. I included all depressives, widows, AIDS widowers and an indeterminate number of friends who had no time because they were too busy working themselves to death. I included the paranoid, the embittered, the isolated misanthropes who didn't get invited to more prestigious affairs and because we simply wouldn't have listened to them if we didn't want to. I whooshed around them all on my tractor and asked them how they liked the *mousse* and if there was sufficient Merlot.

I paid particular cerebral attention to family who have died: TH's father Henry; uncle Leo; my mother with her 18 inch leg scar from a metal pin replacing her shattered shin bone; my cousin, whose corpse revealed the violence of a bullet mark in his head to my ten-year-old eyes; my grandparents—Aiti, Isa, Bertha, Richard. To those who have suffered too much: Sandie, Carole, Pat, Loeween, Sheelagh, Val, Sherill, and those who will. To the children: my stillborn nephew, Caitlin's classmate, Claire's high school friend. To writers, living and dead, I loved to reread and who still lived here at the farm on my shelves; to the woodsman killed by a falling tree; to the farmer who died under his tractor and the one who got eaten by his pig; to the Scotts who built my house; the woman who left the shelter too early and was murdered along with her children by a deranged husband. Madness is easy to come by for some. Death is a certainty.

The still living, those mildly maimed and bruised, were expected to help out; being short one arm or one leg too few was no excuse. Trifling mental illnesses are a requirement: my friend Louise was checking all our astrological charts and we are a strange lot. Working mothers (that included all of my generation) were invited to read, and work less. We had parking for wheelchairs and napkins for those who flung their spittle when aroused by development issues and spittoons for stroke victims who could not finish what they chose to chew. The single and lonely in my head were required to sing out loud, the parsimonious ordered to bring the most expensive clarets, ports and cheeses. The healthy and wealthy were stripped of their arrogance at the door and left to clear the manure in the barns for half an hour before joining true hearts at dinner. The famous were required to put on funny noses and the too skinny were required to carry extra jockey horse-weights on their hips. Journalists were required to reread everything they had ever written and occasionally eat crow. Once a month there was an honorary Canadian: Pierre Trudeau, Grey Owl, and at least one crook, con artist or pompous professional with a shingle, and an old pedant or art historian who knew more than the rest of us to correct us all and then be teased.

Those with too many ideological convictions were led to the end of the table and not allowed back unless they brought along their nemesis. Psychiatrists could come but only if they did not practice what they preached. Too much polite sanity is boring. Writers were allowed as long as they did not talk about what they were not writing. Teachers had to be aware and reminded of the chalk in their anus. (I once dreamt that Salman Rushdie was hiding out in the barn and needed to be fed, but only if he could sit between Iris Murdoch and Conrad Black—perhaps that was my arthritis drugs.)

No one might presume to criticize the company or my food.

In our lives we build up complicated networks of relationships. I'm sure there must be some diagram in some sociology text of the circles of intimacy and trust, circles of acquaintance and acceptance, circles of rejection. In the course of developing that schema we define ourselves as best we can and ultimately we have to live with those boundaries. It is the hardest thing about being middle-aged. It shocks me now to remember my younger self, a self who thought that all things were possible; there was goodness in everyone. Oh, to be that naïve again.

It took me three full hours to finish my lawn cutting each week. (Many more hours in the flowerbeds.) It was the most productive, most amusing, most rewarding task in the universe and no place was better than the Lawn and Zipper Club to try to figure out what life was all about and play with my imaginary friends. I was always starving and ready to eat, write, read or fling paint around when I got inside.

*Diptych of the farm in full summer.*

# Open Secrets

I learned to read well because of Sweetfield. I learned to stay on my couch and finish a book; to listen to the writer, to pause at every comma and to endure what I thought I could not endure. Reading has taught me that suffering is not mine alone and that a weird childhood, family and inhospitable world, does not exclude one from beautiful things and a measure of happiness. Hope, beauty, time are mine to hold; not something reserved for other people, as my mother would admonish me. "Books are for the idle rich!" There have been times, no doubt, when I wanted to give up on books, stop my worse-than-birdseed habit of spending $100 every weekend to keep my sanity. It is a major addiction, as expensive as many a drug my mother would say, but as essential to me as breathing. Every chapter title of this book is the title of a Canadian book that has meant something to me. Teachers are subversive: this text is now a reading list. We all live *In The Skin of a Lion*. As Michael Ondaatje wrote, "Everyone has to scratch on walls somewhere or they go crazy."

As a child there was only the family Bible—in Finnish—on the bookshelf and the odd *Reader's Digest* in the bathroom that my mother had purloined from a doctor's office; "Increase Your Word Power" was my favourite part but I also pored over the true reports of war heroism and families overcoming tribulations. I am a horrible sentimentalist (but you know that by now); I weep for cats stuck up trees. Apart from the flyers that came in the post there was, of course, television that entered the family when I was five. My father turned it on and never turned it off. When we started to get American channels there were three televisions in the house, all on in different rooms on different programs. The subjects we talked about over dinner concerned Archie Bunker and Ed Sullivan. The family philosophy came from *Father Knows Best* and *Ozzie and Harriet*. One Halloween my parents went to a party dressed as that famous historical couple, Fred and Wilma Flintstone. After I learned to forgive my father it became a photo I could not throw away, but I could not treasure it either. It was a silent time for me, a time I did not enjoy but, in the 50s, that was what was available to children from immigrant families like mine. Maybe if my family had forced me into reading I would have loved it less, found it less of a sin, less of a hidden excitement. All books were to me like *samizdat*, more precious because they were forbidden.

In twenty years the rift healed with my mother and she took to some skimming and scanning herself when she visited me at the farm. Someone had once given her a copy of *The Egg and I* and she often asked me for books just like that one—a story about living on a farm in the backwoods. Here it is. She took some pleasure in going over the bookshelves with her duster asking me to summarize the plots. My father took no such interest. He seemed proud that I was able to marry a professor but unmoved by the fact that I was one. Reading had freed me but, by some implied criticism, left him out and chained him down to his television even more.

When my mother was dying she made me promise that I would make sure that all her grandchildren went to university, that all the books at the farm got read at least four times so they would be worth the expense. All of her money was to go to the kids, for their educations and their book needs. Even at the end she was turning over the books, reading past the bar codes and commenting on the exorbitant price of hard cover over paperback. When I told her the value of the first edition of *The Collected Works of Billy the Kid* she thought the return on investment quite good but couldn't resist noting that there was only one on the shelf. Every penny from the sale of her house, she said, had to go for tuition fees. All gifts had to be books that kept their value, coffee table books on Rembrandt that would become heirlooms. I had to help my brother's children as well as my own if they wanted to go to school in Toronto instead of Vancouver. Nothing was more important. I call that as close to reconciliation as one gets in this world.

Passages of poetry and prose, literary reviews and anecdotes float around in the back of my teacher's head like old shoes in a closet. I'm not sure I'll need them anymore but I hate to throw them out. Images, characters and plots, like old movie reels, live in a portion of my brain adjacent to the neurological cells reserved for worry. I have this notion that, like an overly-kind but greedy neighbour who likes to mow the lawn next door to look like his own, if I read enough I will see the world rewritten and reread so many time that fictions will overtake and delete some of the horror from the section of cranial hemisphere reserved for storing real life pain.

Salvation, or at least reprieve of sorts, was in books and in a mate who also loved books. Sanctuary, a reading place, was on this farm. Reading creates another whole set of needs: to see the places writers were talking about, to visit holy spots and graves. Maybe there were landscapes still overlooked.

Now that we are retiring we want that absolute wandering space again. The freedom of childhood should come twice in a lifetime and now that my children are adults themselves I'm ready, as I joke to them regularly, to take up the responsibilities of retirement. My knees aren't as good as they should be but, hell, I've never required them to read, and the halt and the lame still travel in Europe.

Teachers and literary types will tell you there are only a dozen or so plots in the world: boy meets girl, boy loses girl; girl meets girl, girl dies; girl meets boy, falls in love has family then dies in a car crash. All stories are a variation on these themes. The only plot I'm interested in now is that beloved by nineteenth century writers like Austen and Charlotte Brontë where the couple lives happily ever after. It has such a deceptive loveliness and squishes out so much of the reality of living that, even though I know it is not true and those books are really hard to find these days, it's the motivating fiction I'm going to run with in dark winters. The wonderful, inexplicable thing in this world is that writers emerge from nooks and crannies with yet more tales from the trenches and the spiritual supply is inexhaustible.

*Reading in the garden.*

# Last Seen

Physical exhaustion sets in too early and rather ungracefully. This year I have already been to three funerals. Even fiction is getting filled with aches and pains. Old age is all that greets us when we visit TH's demented mother; discussions of pathetic retirement funds recur over dinner. Friends in second marriages face untold terror with new children reaching the age of ten when they turn sixty-five. To keep the horror at bay I looked to young writers and more travel.

The bracing ice storms of winter, those days pulling the sleigh full of groceries from my car in February are over for me. One recent summer I visited my eldest daughter who was studying art history in Siena and nosed around for December rentals in the south of Italy. Madrid and the Balearic islands are beginning to spin round my head as I soak my sore feet in the tub. I go as regularly now to the doctor as I go to art galleries, movies and bookstores. I meet my women friends for lunch and we swap names of housekeepers, physiotherapists, foot doctors. Caitlin is afraid I'll become one of those weird old crones who endlessly talks about sciatica.

I fantasize about a cob studio out of straw. Our last crop is baled and ready to be turned into wall material. There's a man down the way who does post-and-beam construction and the forest we planted out the back when Claire was born has thousands of thirty-foot pines, just waiting to be cut into joists. There's an imaginary windmill erected and it's time to get off the hydro lines, time to get a hydrogen hybrid vehicle and encourage green grannies to lie down in front of the bull dozers brought in by men threatening to develop golf courses in the Niagara Escarpment Biosphere. But I don't really know if I can do that kind of work anymore. Perhaps some dreams are best left for the next generation.

There are a lot of new things to do and that life is short is abundantly clear. My Italian is improving and there are courses to take in Renaissance Art. TH is anxious to start travelling again. Old friends around the world call and entice me with tales of Rome and Puglia and Trieste. The University of Toronto has a Finnish Studies program and maybe I can go back and brush up my childish understanding of that language. I have relatives in Stockholm and my Aiti's village to visit in Finland. I have to help my brother get his boat in the water and help my girls finish university in whatever way I can. And, of course, there's the birds nesting at the swale, the garden, Green Cow Pond. If luck keeps shining, and this body holds together, I'll get to be a grandmother.

Running this farm has given me some perspective on the problems of this world and the work here has kept me away from too much psychiatry, providing, as it did, a rural form of daily introspection. What am I doing here? What had to be done today and why? I had to pull the dead green cow out of my own psyche, rebuild my architecture, tend to my garden as best I could without too much professional help. God knows we all need more than a little assistance to understand what gives us a modicum of joy on this planet, and this farm gave me that. No one can have any happiness without suffering some penury, family loss, defeat, humiliation, physical pain, for it is in knowing those states that one can begin to recognize that struggled happiness for what it is: a plant that has survived the winter, fawns camouflaged under bushes, laughing children, someone who was happy to be in your peasant company. Tolstoy said all happy families resemble one another but I think happy lives and happy families are not all the same, they are carved out of our genes and moulded by our labour, environment and culture. And happiness comes to each of us only in small amounts for some small part of our time on the planet.

The children have moved on to universities and careers in England, all the parents are now dead, the animals are buried in their graves. My health does not allow such a level of physical labour as once I enjoyed and it is time to move on to the last act of my life in sunnier climates.

Sweetfield Farm was sold in 2004.

*Hawk descending.*

# Acknowledgments

I wish to thank all of the women in my painting, reading and writing groups over the years—colleagues, sisters, mothers, daughters and wives, working women all. We shared more than books, more than reading and editing each other's work, we shared a way of becoming ourselves through a challenging and transitional time for women. Specifically, I would like to thank Allison, April, Bertha, Carol, Carolyn, Dianne, Elizabeth, Heather, Hilma, Laura, Linda, Liz, Lori, Louise, Marilyn, Marion, Marta, Mary, Nemone, Ricci, Sandie, Sarah, Sheelagh, Sherrill, Susan, and Val. I would also like to thank David, Jack, Johnny, Martin, Michael, Morton, Morty and Patrick. My invaluable editors, Gareth Vaughan and Richard Heller, have saved me much embarrassment while still cheering my idiosyncratic Finnish-Canadian voice and deserve more than I can pay them. The paintings, photographs and outstanding errors are all my own. Most importantly, I thank my daughters, Claire and Caitlin, without whom not one word would have been written. They are the reason I write.

Made in the USA
Charleston, SC
08 April 2014